God, Purpose, and Reality

God, Purpose, and Reality

A Euteleological Understanding of Theism

JOHN BISHOP
KEN PERSZYK

UNIVERSITY PRESS

Great Clarendon Street, Oxford, OX2 6DP,
United Kingdom

Oxford University Press is a department of the University of Oxford.
It furthers the University's objective of excellence in research, scholarship,
and education by publishing worldwide. Oxford is a registered trade mark of
Oxford University Press in the UK and in certain other countries

© John Bishop and Ken Perszyk 2023

The moral rights of the authors have been asserted

First Edition published in 2023

Impression: 1

All rights reserved. No part of this publication may be reproduced, stored in
a retrieval system, or transmitted, in any form or by any means, without the
prior permission in writing of Oxford University Press, or as expressly permitted
by law, by licence or under terms agreed with the appropriate reprographics
rights organization. Enquiries concerning reproduction outside the scope of the
above should be sent to the Rights Department, Oxford University Press, at the
address above

You must not circulate this work in any other form
and you must impose this same condition on any acquirer

Published in the United States of America by Oxford University Press
198 Madison Avenue, New York, NY 10016, United States of America

British Library Cataloguing in Publication Data

Data available

Library of Congress Control Number: 2022944325

ISBN 978–0–19–286411–6

DOI: 10.1093/oso/9780192864116.001.0001

Printed and bound in the UK by
TJ Books Limited

Links to third party websites are provided by Oxford in good faith and
for information only. Oxford disclaims any responsibility for the materials
contained in any third party website referenced in this work.

Contents

Preface	ix
Introduction	1
1. Beyond the Personal OmniGod	8
1.1 A Presupposed Conception of Personhood	9
1.2 Alternatives to the Personal OmniGod?	11
1.3 Doubts about the Coherence of Personal-OmniGod Theism	12
1.4 Focusing on the Religious Adequacy of Personal-OmniGod Theism	14
1.5 Indirect Doubts about Religious Adequacy: Doctrinal and Historical Authenticity	17
1.6 Direct Doubts about Religious Adequacy: Divine Transcendence and Immanence	20
1.7 Divine Goodness	26
1.8 God and Evil	29
1.9 Theism without the Personal OmniGod?	35
2. Personalist and Non-Personalist Understandings of Theism	37
2.1 Retaining Theological Realism	37
2.2 Need God Be Understood as Omnipotent?	39
2.3 Omnipotence and Its Constraints	40
2.4 Rejecting Omnipotence—Minor Departures	43
2.5 Rejecting Omnipotence—Major Departures (e.g., Process Theism)	44
2.6 Non-Personalist, 'Naturalist', Alternatives	47
2.7 'Classical' Theism as Non-Personalist	50
2.8 Divine 'Incomprehensibility' and Its Implications	52
2.9 Setting Aside the Debate about 'Classical' Theism	53
2.10 'God Is Love': An Emergentist View	55
2.11 Love as the Overall Purpose of the Creation: Towards Euteleology	56
3. Euteleological Metaphysics	59
3.1 A 'Whole of Reality' Perspective	60
3.2 Ultimate Teleology	61
3.3 Ultimate Teleology and the Supreme Good	62

3.4	Realizing the Universe's Ultimate Purpose	65
3.5	Purpose without a 'Purposing' Agent?	67
3.6	Explaining the Universe's Existence?	69
3.7	'It Is because It Does What It's For'	69
3.8	Uniqueness of Ultimate Theological Explanation	71
3.9	'It Is because It Is Good that It Is'	72
3.10	'The Universe Exists because It Realizes Its Purpose': Cosmic Boot-Strapping?	75
3.11	The Essence of Reality and a Higher, Transmundane, Causal Order	77
3.12	No Mystery about Mystery at the Limit of Human Understanding	80
3.13	Theological Metaphysics as Ethical Posits	82
3.14	Euteleological Metaphysics and Euteleological Theism: Does God Have a Place?	84

4. **God, the Divine, and the Divine Attributes** — 87

4.1	'It's God-ing All Over': A Pantheist Identification?	90
4.2	God as Ultimate *Telos*, the Supreme Good?	92
4.3	God as Realization of the Supreme Good?	94
4.4	A Theist Ontology without a Specific Referent for 'God'?	95
4.5	A Euteleological Account of Creation *Ex Nihilo* and God's Distinctness from Creation	97
4.6	Talk about God and God's Action as Analogical	100
4.7	Euteleological Theism, Robustly Realist!	106
4.8	Truth-Making for God-Claims When God Is Not 'a' Being	110
4.9	Divine Will, Freedom, and Action (When God Is Not 'a' Being)	112
4.10	A Euteleological Account of the Divine Attributes—The 'Omni-Properties'	115
4.11	God's Existence, and the Classical, 'Metaphysical' Attributes	119
4.12	Euteleology—A Panentheism?	124

5. **The Religious Adequacy of a Euteleological Theism: The Problem of Evil** — 128

5.1	Transcendence, Immanence, and Evil	130
5.2	Theism's 'Privationist' Notion of Evil	131
5.3	Soteriology: Responding to an Existential Problem of Evil	132
5.4	Can Euteleological Metaphysics Cohere with a Viable Soteriology?	134
5.5	Soteriology for Non-Personalist Theists	137
5.6	The Power of Love	138
5.7	Intellectual Problems of Evil	143

	5.8 A Euteleological 'Theodicy'	146
	5.9 Evil and Analogizing	152
	5.10 Maintaining Faith in the Face of Evil, and Bringing Good 'from' Evil	154
6.	The Religious Adequacy of a Euteleological Theism: Worship and Prayer	158
	6.1 May Worship Risk Idolatry if Addressed to a Person?	159
	6.2 An Argument that Worship Must Have a Person as Object	161
	6.3 Worship in a Broader Sense	162
	6.4 Ritual Worship: Needed for Authentic Theist Commitment?	164
	6.5 'God Hears Our Prayer'	166
	6.6 A Euteleological Theist Account of Worship and Prayer	170
	6.7 The Object of Worship	174
	Conclusion	179
Bibliography		185
Index		199

Preface

Our collaboration on this project promoting what we call a 'euteleological' metaphysics as a preferable alternative to the 'personal-omniGod' understanding of theism began over a decade ago, when Joseph Keim Campbell invited us to participate in a symposium at the 2008 American Philosophical Association, Pacific Division Meeting, in Pasadena. The initial proposal was that we would revisit an earlier debate we had had over whether a compatibilist could run a version of the Free Will Defence. However, we quickly came to the realization that we would find it more interesting to work on a co-authored paper defending the claim that a version of the so-called 'Logical' Argument from Evil against the existence of an all-powerful and morally perfect God is still very much in play, despite a near-consensus amongst contemporary analytic philosophers that this Argument is bankrupt. Thankfully, Joe agreed to our suggestion, and our paper was included in a symposium on the problem of evil (alongside papers by Michael Tooley and Hugh McCann). A revised version was eventually published as our (2011).

We called our argument (a version of) 'the Normatively Relativised Logical Argument from Evil'. John Bishop had in effect been promoting this argument, though not under that name, for some time. Ken Perszyk had been thinking along similar lines but was too caught up in the personal-omniGod paradigm, thinking (as we now believe, quite mistakenly) that any (philosophically viable) alternative would amount to outright atheism. There were other reasons that further contributed to our dissatisfaction with personal-omniGod theism: in particular, problems with omnipotence and, more generally, with the notion of an infinite person. These reasons are related to the idea, which we develop in Chapter 1, that the personal omniGod is at once insufficiently transcendent and insufficiently immanent.

Of course, it is one thing to run a negative thesis, and another (harder) thing to develop a positive account. John Bishop in his (1998) had argued for the possibility of adequate alternatives to the standard personal-omniGod account of theism, and had sketched a potential Christian alternative based on taking metaphysically seriously the scriptural claim that God is love. Bishop developed this proposal further in his (2007b) and

(2009), presenting it as an alternative to 'classical' theism, which he at that stage, like many others, simply equated with personal-omniGod theism. Around the time that we began our collaboration, Bishop started shifting his proposed alternative in the direction of a classical theism distinct from the personal-omniGod account. Awakened by Thomas Harvey (then Bishop's student) to the significance of the doctrine of divine simplicity, Bishop no longer construed the classical theism of the medievals as committed to a fundamentally personalist metaphysics. That shift resulted in our developing the position we call 'euteleology', which we have explored in a series of co-authored papers (Bishop and Perszyk 2014, 2016a, 2016b, 2016c, 2017, and 2022). The account we develop in this book traverses some topics we've discussed before, but we are not simply reusing previously published material. This is a wholly new presentation and defence of a particular insider-perspective understanding of what it is for theism to be true (for 'reality to be the God-way', as we often say), in which we have tried to take into account some responses to our previously published work, and to bring to the fore questions of the religious adequacy of both the 'standard' personal-omniGod view and our alternative euteleological view.

Our work for this book has benefitted from several invitations to present at recent conferences and workshops, from questions and comments from participants on these occasions, and from a number of individuals who have read and commented on work we've done in undertaking this book project.

We're grateful to Thomas Schärtl-Trendel for an invitation to present our work on euteleology to a summer school on 'Affirming and Challenging Classical Theism' held at Weltenburg Abbey in 2017, and to Godehard Brüntrup for inviting us to give addresses at an associated conference in Munich on 'Analytic Theology and the Nature of God'. We thank Andrei Buckareff and Yujin Nagasawa for inviting us to present a paper on euteleology and panentheism at the 2019 Pantheism and Panentheism Project Workshop in Birmingham (a paper which was also presented at the Philosophy Research Seminar, School of Humanities, University of Auckland). For comments on particular passages from drafts of this book, we are grateful to Imran Aijaz, Matheson Russell, Robert Wicks, John Leslie, and, most especially, to Thomas Harvey, some of whose views on understanding classical theism have significantly influenced the development of our euteleological proposal. We have benefitted from the extensive comments of four anonymous readers for OUP whom we thank for enabling us to make significant improvements to earlier drafts. We are especially grateful to the late Marilyn McCord Adams for the critical attention she paid to our work. As a 'personal-omniGod devotee' Marilyn made no secret of her continuing puzzlement at our views about 'odd-God'. Yet she clearly acknowledged the importance of our concerns about the 'relational' implications of evil for personal-omniGod theism (see Chapter 1, pp. 32–3). This book is an attempt to make our alternative account of the metaphysics of theism as clear as we can, and to defend its coherence and religious adequacy. We've tried to keep Marilyn's own rigorous standards of clarity and integrity in argumentation in mind in what we have written, but must leave it to others to judge whether we have come anywhere near meeting them.

John Bishop

University of Auckland

Ken Perszyk

University of Waikato—Tauranga
February 2022

Introduction

How could the worldview of Abrahamic theism reasonably be understood if *not* in terms of the existence of a supremely powerful and good personal Creator? That's our leading question in this book.

The idea that the theist God, if such a God exists, is to be understood as an immaterial personal agent, all-powerful, all-knowing, and all-good, is well entrenched amongst Anglophone 'analytic' philosophers, and also in the wider culture deriving from the Abrahamic theist religious traditions.[1] Importantly, this is the God in whom many of our contemporaries *don't* believe—for a range of reasons, not the least being the difficulty of reconciling the existence of such a God with the horrendous evils that blight human existence and history. Non-belief in this 'personal omniGod' often results in rejection of theist religion altogether and thus, for many, alienation from inherited cultural resources for coping with life's changes and chances—though non-believers often continue to adhere to key elements of theist ethics.

Belief in God may not need to be understood, however, as 'literal' belief in an anthropomorphic personal Creator—as a good many theologians and philosophers, mostly outside the analytic tradition, will readily agree. But what alternatives are there? What positive account may be given of the metaphysics and fundamental ontology of a theist worldview if it is *not* the metaphysics of the personal omniGod? In this book, we aim to set out a particular alternative way of understanding theist metaphysics. We aim to provide, in other words, an alternative way of understanding what it is for reality to be 'the God-way'—that is, the way that theism claims it to be.

---

[1] We follow a common contemporary usage amongst philosophers which refers to belief in the revealed God of the Abrahamic traditions (principally Judaism, Christianity, and Islam) as *theism*, and that God as the *theist* God. 'Theism' has a broader sense which refers generally to belief in a god or gods. Polytheism and pantheism count as theism in that broader sense, but are contrasted with theism in the narrower sense we're using. Theism in that narrower sense holds that there is one (capital-G) God (not many gods, as in polytheism) and that, as Creator, God is distinct from all creatures and not to be identified with all that exists (as in pantheism).

We'll defend this alternative both as a coherent metaphysics of ultimate reality and as fit for understanding the theist stance on ultimate reality.

Our alternative account begins from the observation that theism holds that the created world exists to fulfil an *overall* purpose—and that this purpose is specially revealed to humanity, at least so far as human minds can grasp what it is and what its implications are for the way human life should be lived. We argue that it makes sense to hold that reality has an overall purpose *without* attributing that purpose or its realization to a supreme personal agent who produces the created world for that purpose. And we claim that theism's ultimate explanation of 'why there is something rather than nothing' may be understood as appealing, not to a necessarily existing supreme agent beyond the created order, but to the fact that contingent reality contains instantiations of the supreme good which is the ultimate *telos* at which all that exists inherently aims. In short, the idea is that the world exists because, so to say, 'it does what it's for'. We call this metaphysics 'euteleology'—a term which connotes reality's existing to fulfil a supremely good overall purpose (*eu*, well, good; *telos*, end: 'teleology' connotes functioning to fulfil a thing's proper end or good; '*eu*teleology', functioning to fulfil the good *for reality as such and as a whole*).

Our approach to developing and defending euteleology as an account of ultimate reality suitable for a theist metaphysics has been to draw on our own understanding of theism from the 'insider' perspective of *fides quaerens intellectum* ('faith seeking understanding'). Given our particular cultural and religious situatedness, this has meant that we usually have the Christian tradition specifically in mind—though, as it happens, only one of us is a 'believing' Christian, while the other is not (being well acquainted with an insider perspective on a faith tradition need not require personal faith-commitment). We see no reason, however, why philosophers whose insider faith-perspective is Jewish or Islamic might not find in euteleology good prospects for an alternative to the personal-omniGod account if that is what they seek. Indeed, discussing euteleology might potentially make for progress in inter-faith dialogue amongst the Abrahamic traditions (as might be suggested—to take one example—by our remarks in what follows about euteleology's making available a broader notion of 'incarnation'—see Chapter 3, pp. 66–7).

There are, of course, a good number of existing alternatives to the analytic philosopher's 'personal-omniGod paradigm'—such as, to mention just a few alternatives (or families of alternatives), Whitehead's process metaphysics and the process theologies that have developed from it, Tillich-style ground-of-being theologies, and Hegelian-inspired theologies. Though we refer to some of these alternatives in what follows, we haven't here attempted the (anyway, over-ambitious) task of a comprehensive critical survey of all the extant alternative options for a metaphysics of theism. Instead, what we've done in this book is, first, to reflect on the adequacy, especially the *religious* adequacy, of the personal-omniGod account. Then, on the basis of our own diagnosis of its shortcomings, we've argued that a 'non-personalist' alternative should be preferred—a metaphysics, that is, that does not feature God as a person or personal being in its fundamental ontology. Our main task has then been to develop and defend euteleology as a coherent account of ultimate reality which is suitable as a non-personalist metaphysics for theism. We will argue, in what follows, that euteleology provides a philosophically coherent and robust positive account of ultimate reality, and one which is religiously adequate for the Abrahamic traditions.

It will reinforce this account of our project to say something about our intended audience: for whom are we writing, and of what are we trying to persuade them?

First and foremost, we are addressing our fellow analytic philosophers of religion. We aim to persuade them that it should not be taken as obvious or even beyond question that the metaphysics of the Abrahamic theist worldview has to be (near enough) the metaphysics of the personal omniGod. We agree that it is incontrovertible that engaging with God in personal terms is a signal feature of the Abrahamic traditions, and any viable understanding of the ontology of theism will have to cohere with the aptness of personal talk about God. But—we aim to show—it does not follow that God has to be understood as the personal omniGod, or, indeed, as a being belonging to the general kind 'person', nor even, at the level of fundamental ontology, as 'a' being of any kind at all. Instead, we'll argue that euteleology, though a non-personalist account of ultimate reality, comports with theist themes, including the key theme that the Universe is a creation fulfilling the divine purposes. We'll also argue that coherent sense may be made of prayer and worship on a positive euteleological account of the metaphysics of theism by recognizing personal talk about God as involving a radically analogical extension of talk about human persons that conveys what are, from the theist perspective, otherwise inaccessible truths—but truths whose ultimate truth-makers are *not* to be comprehended as the possession of personal properties by a supreme immaterial and supernatural person or personal being.

Many theologians and philosophers outside the analytic tradition will, as we've noted, find unremarkable our claim that personal talk about God is not transparent to fundamental theist ontology. Many of them deny that God is a being amongst beings, and so deny that God is literally a person or personal being. For them, analytic philosophy of religion with its reigning paradigm of God as the personal omniGod, seems narrow, often ahistorical, and generally of marginal relevance for 'faith seeking understanding'. Do we have anything to say that may be of interest to these theologians and philosophers? Theologians who dismiss the analytic philosopher's personal-omniGod paradigm should, we think, be concerned by the reciprocal dismissal they themselves receive from many analytic philosophers who regard much contemporary theology as out of touch with the living theist traditions and the scripture-based faith of 'ordinary believers'. Indeed, this feeling that such theologians have 'let the side down' may have been part of the motivation for a recent movement for *analytic* theology, aiming to bring the virtues of clarity and argumentative rigour to bear anew on the task of articulating theological doctrine.[2] Perhaps, too, there is some substance to the accusation that theologians who dismiss personal-omniGod metaphysics haven't been sufficiently concerned to provide their own *positive* accounts of the metaphysics of theism—certainly not the kind of accounts that analytic philosophers of religion would find satisfying. Our account of euteleology as a fit metaphysics for theism is intended to provide just that kind of clear and rigorous positive account. Though euteleological notions are to be found in the work of philosophical theologians—medieval, modern, and contemporary—analytic philosophers have not previously made the kind of attempt we are making here to articulate the metaphysics of euteleology and defend it as meeting the demands of theist 'faith seeking understanding'.

We do see our work in this book, then, as usefully challenging a certain 'silo' mentality of outright mutual dismissal between (many) analytic philosophers of religion and many contemporary theologians. Such a challenge does, of course, risk not being heard at all if the 'silos' are too entrenched: we remain hopeful, though, of a fair hearing from within the analytic camp to which, by credentials and experience, we ourselves belong. We are hopeful, too, that theologians will appreciate the importance of our project, even if personal-omniGod metaphysics strikes many of them professionally as hardly worth serious critique. Amongst the wider public of those who

---

[2] The term 'analytic theology' appears to be due to Oliver Crisp and Mike Rea (2009). They also co-edit *The Journal of Analytic Theology*, founded in 2013.

reflect, theist faith seems commonly enough both adhered to and rejected on the assumption that, at root, it requires belief in a really existent supreme supernatural person or personal being. Theologians who regard that assumption as mistaken will surely care about how better to understand the claims theist religion makes about ultimate reality—so, our attempt at just such a positive account should be of interest to them.

Comparisons may, of course, be made between our euteleological account and the many and various understandings of theism that have been proposed by theologians and philosophers who share with us the rejection of the personal-omniGod paradigm. It is not within our scope in this book to pursue detailed comparisons with, for example, Whiteheadians and 'process' theologians, Hegelians, or, indeed, with the metaphysics of the classical medieval theologians who also, we firmly believe, reject personal-omniGod metaphysics (though we are well aware that this last claim is strongly contested by some prominent personal-omniGod theorists who are also medieval scholars). In this book, our project is just to provide as clear an account of euteleology and its motivations as we can manage, and to defend it as worth taking seriously as an account of the metaphysics of theism. Exploring questions about how close it may or may not be to classical theism, to Hegelianism, or to process views, we leave for another occasion. Nevertheless, those who do espouse a non-personalist understanding of classical medieval theism, or, indeed, any more recent metaphysics, personalist or not, that competes with the reigning analytic paradigm, may find material of interest in our elaboration of euteleology.

A final class of readers who may find euteleology interesting are those concerned with competing accounts of ultimate reality generally, independently of any special interest in Abrahamic theism. Calls to widen the scope of Philosophy of Religion beyond its historically understandable focus on the Abrahamic traditions have led to research on models of 'God or ultimate reality' generally. A euteleological account of ultimate reality may count as one such model. Though we have no quarrel with 'renewing' Philosophy of Religion to make it more inclusive of religious traditions, our development and defence of euteleology in this book is not simply a contribution to a *general* debate about alternative models of ultimate reality. Our present project is firmly focused on defending euteleology as a metaphysics *suitable for theism*: the debate we are entering, then, is a more specific one about alternative models for *an Abrahamic theist* understanding of ultimate reality. That said, however, we nevertheless do not exclude the possibility that euteleology might prove acceptable as a metaphysics suitable for understanding some non-theist religious worldviews, or even as a model of ultimate reality that counts as 'interesting atheism'.

A distinction needs to be made, then, between euteleology as a metaphysical theory of ultimate reality, and a *euteleological theism* which uses euteleological metaphysics to make intelligible the fundamental ontology of a world revealed to be God's creation in the Abrahamic traditions. Our aim in this book is definitely to defend euteleology as an apt metaphysics *for theism*. Accordingly, we will need to consider euteleology's compatibility with a coherent understanding of theist religious practices such as worship and prayer—an issue which need not arise if euteleology were deployed in some significantly different religious context, or treated purely as a potentially attractive model of ultimate reality independently of any specific religious tradition.

So far as the truth of a euteleological metaphysics is concerned, however, we are not attempting to argue in this book that euteleology *is true*, only that it *could be true*, and that it deserves serious consideration as a metaphysics suitable for making intelligible the worldview of religions in the Abrahamic theist traditions. It is, of course, an important question in epistemology whether, and, if so, under what conditions, it may be justifiable to hold a belief (such as theist belief) on the basis of a claim to special revelation. But that is not a question for our present project, which is wholly concerned with understanding the *content* of theist belief (and, in particular its metaphysical commitments). Evidently, an interest in understanding the theist worldview depends on finding it to be a 'live option', not merely logically possibly true but a serious candidate for a worldview to be believed and acted upon. Our motivation for defending a euteleological understanding of theism, then, assumes that commitment to the truth of a theistic worldview so understood could be made with epistemic integrity. Accordingly, we take it that there *is* an acceptable epistemology of religious belief which would endorse commitment to theism on a euteleological understanding. It is beyond our scope here, however, to defend any such general epistemology of religious belief—though, at certain points in our discussion, indications of what we think an epistemology for religious belief needs to include will emerge.[3]

---

[3] Bishop (2007a) provides an articulation and defence of an epistemology which understands commitment to the truth of theism as requiring a faith-venture under conditions of the essential 'evidential ambiguity' of theism in relation to other religious and secular worldviews.

We will proceed as follows. In Chapter 1, we will outline the 'personal-omniGod' understanding of theism that is widely accepted amongst 'analytic' philosophers. We will consider reasons for doubting the adequacy (especially the religious adequacy) of this understanding. We will argue that there is good reason to take seriously a search for a more adequate alternative. In particular, we think that a version of the 'Logical' Argument from Evil is still very much in play. In Chapter 2, we will consider what kind of alternative account may prove more adequate, and we provide our reasons for favouring a non-personalist understanding of theism over alternatives that retain a fundamental metaphysics of the divine as a supernatural personal being. Having thus motivated our project, we will articulate and defend (in Chapters 3 to 6) our specific proposal for a euteleological understanding of theism.

1
Beyond the Personal OmniGod

What must reality be like if the God of Abrahamic theism exists?

The worldview of Abrahamic theism takes God to be the creator of all (else) that exists, and therefore radically distinct from the world which is God's creation. God thus transcends the created world, though theism also holds that God is immanent within it. According to a standard account of theism in analytic philosophy, God's distinctness from the creation is a matter of God's existence as *a being* distinct from any and every created being. On this understanding, God is an *uncreated*, *super*natural, being—since the world of created beings is identified as the *natural* world. Standardly, too, God is understood as Creator *ex nihilo*—in the sense that God does not give the Universe existence by producing it from any prior existing condition; rather, nothing, save God's own being, exists prior to God's creative act. God must therefore have an ontological status uniquely different from that of created entities; thus, given that on this account God is *a* being (albeit uniquely great and supreme), God's being must belong to a distinct ontological category from the 'natural' realm in which created beings exist.[1]

The uncreated, supernatural, being that is God is also understood on this standard view to be essentially a person: God is a person, of the same general kind as human persons, yet a quite singular, unsurpassably exalted, instance of this general kind. Indeed, on this view—as Alvin Plantinga

---

[1] This standard account thus draws a sharp distinction between theism and 'naturalism'. For example, Alvin Plantinga (2011, ix) says,

> I take naturalism to be the thought that there is no such person as God, or anything like God. Naturalism is stronger than atheism: you can be an atheist without rising to the heights (sinking to the lowest depths?) of naturalism; but you cannot be a naturalist without being an atheist.

Amongst those whose more nuanced understanding of naturalism admits the possibility that naturalism can have religious forms, there is still a tendency to draw a sharp contrast between religious naturalism and theism: see, e.g., Mikael Stenmark (2013, 531). For the view that the terms 'supernatural' and 'natural' are not opposed for some important construals of what those terms mean, and that there is a viable form of 'theistic naturalism', see Fiona Ellis (2014). We will later return to consider whether, and in what sense or senses, our alternative euteleological account may count as a 'naturalist' understanding of theism (see Chapter 2, pp. 47–9, and Chapter 5, p. 142).

claims—God may be the paradigmatic person: '*God* is the premier person, the first and chief exemplar of personhood.... [W]e men and women are image bearers of God, and the properties most important for an understanding of our personhood are properties we share with him' (1984, 265).

As creator, the theist God is supremely powerful, but also supremely wise and supremely good. God creates to achieve God's purposes, and those purposes are great and good purposes which, through God's exercise of wisdom and power, achieve fulfilment in the creation. The standard view understands God's supreme power, wisdom, and goodness by taking the traditional divine attributes of omnipotence, omniscience, and omnibenevolence to be properties of God as a personal being. Thus, on this standard view, omnipotence ascribes to God, but to an unsurpassable degree, *the same general kind* of agential power that belongs to finite persons; omniscience, *the same general kind* of personal knowing; and omnibenevolence, *the same general kind* of personal goodness and virtue.

We refer to God under this standard conception as 'the personal omniGod', and to theists who accept this understanding of God as 'personal-omniGod theists'.[2] We will also speak of 'personal-omniGod theism' to mean theism understood as claiming the real existence of the personal omniGod. We use 'personal-omniGod theorists' as an inclusive description for philosophers who regard the idea of the personal omniGod as the right (or best available) conception of the theist God. (Evidently, a philosopher may be a personal-omniGod *theorist* without being a personal-omniGod *theist*.)

1.1 A Presupposed Conception of Personhood

Any 'personalist' account of God—such as the standard personal-omniGod account just outlined—employs some presupposed conception of what it is to be a person. Even if God's personhood is the paradigm of personhood, our grasp of what personhood is must arise from understanding what it means for humans to be persons. Yet some variation or attenuation of the

---

[2] A long list may be compiled of theist philosophers who, though they may vary significantly in the way they fill out the 'personal-omniGod' conception here outlined, undoubtedly do endorse it, including, e.g., William Alston (1989, 198); Richard Swinburne (1993 [1977], 1 and 101); and Alvin Plantinga (2000, vii, Plantinga here characterizes belief in the personal omniGod as the specifically theistic component of Christian belief). The actual term 'personal-omniGod theist' isn't often self-ascribed, however: Marilyn Adams is an exception counting herself, in an essay responding to our (2016a), explicitly amongst the 'personal omni-God devotees' (2016, 138).

concept of a person as applicable to humans is to be expected in relation to God: if God is a person, God must be a quite singular instance of personhood since God is Creator and all other persons are creatures dependent on God for their very existence. Thus, for example, personalist theists typically accept that the personal God is unlike human persons in not having a gender (though the entrenched use of the masculine pronoun to refer to 'him' has been challenged only in recent decades).[3] Personalist theists usually agree, furthermore, that God is a person *without a body*, and therefore lacks everything that goes along with embodiment including sensory modes of phenomenal consciousness.[4]

What, then, are personalists committed to when they say that God is a person (or, more cautiously, given the centrality of embodiment to personhood in the human case, a personal being)? We take them to be claiming, first, that God is an intentional agent who has the power of acting for a reason, the power of *agent-causing* outcomes in the service of an intended end or purpose. (This seems to imply that God is (self-)conscious and rational, having intellect and will.) Moreover, as a personal intentional agent, God is related to other, created, persons in *inter-personal* relationships; this implies, at least *prima facie*, that reciprocal *morally significant* relationships obtain between God and creaturely persons. Personalist theists may fill out this characterization of divine personhood beyond these features (for example, by allowing that God has emotions), but what seems essential on their view is that God is an intentional agent, with personal attributes, who is related inter-personally to other personal intentional agents.

To support these claims, consider the following three representative passages where God's personhood is further described. First, Plantinga says:

God is a *person*: that is, a being with intellect and will. A person has (or can have) knowledge and beliefs, but also affections, loves, and hates; a person, furthermore, also has or can have intentions, and can act so as to fulfill them. (2000, vii)

---

[3] Michael Rea (2016 and 2020) argues that masculine characterizations of God are no more or less metaphysically accurate than feminine ones, and that given this thesis, we ought to accept the view that feminine characterizations of God are just as legitimate as masculine ones. For a further recent discussion of divine gender, see Kathryn Pogin (2020).

[4] Plantinga includes lack of embodiment in his description of God as 'an all-powerful, all-knowing, wholly good person (a person without a body) who has created us and our world' (2000, 3). And, according to Swinburne, 'that God is a person, yet one without a body, seems the most elementary claim of theism' (1993 [1977], 101).

Second, T. J. Mawson writes:

[A]ll theists see God as a person... A person is a person... who is rational; who has beliefs; who is to be treated as the object of moral respect; and who reciprocates that attitude in actions that he or she performs. (2005, 14)

Third, Michael Peterson, William Hasker, Bruce Reichenbach, and David Basinger write as follows:

To say that God is *personal* is to say at least the following things: God has *knowledge and awareness*; God *performs actions*; God is *free* in the actions he performs; and God can *enter into relationships* with persons other than himself. (2009, 77)[5]

1.2 Alternatives to the Personal OmniGod?

Is it correct to think of God as the unique, unsurpassably great, all-powerful, all-knowing, and perfectly good personal agent that the standard analytic philosopher's account of theism takes God to be? Is it correct to understand the theist worldview as founded on the claimed existence of a supernatural being, the personal omniGod? This is a question, not directly about whether God exists, but about the prior issue of *the adequacy of* a presupposed understanding of what God is—namely, the personal-omniGod understanding. Analytic philosophers *on either side* of the debate about God's existence usually share this standard understanding of what the debate is about. Atheist philosophers are often just as confident as their opponents in assuming that the concept of God *just is* the concept of the personal omniGod: indeed, committed atheists typically jealously guard the God in whom they don't believe.

We'll now consider various grounds for doubting the adequacy of the analytic philosopher's standard personal-omniGod account, some purely or largely philosophical, and others—we think, more significant—which are concerned with the account's religious adequacy. Those philosophers and theologians who think it a commonplace to reject the 'anthropomorphic'

---

[5] Peterson et al. here say that God is 'personal' rather than 'a person' for the reason that they want to make room for both Trinitarian and non-Trinitarian versions of theism; in effect, their account of God's personhood is that God is either one or at least one person.

notion of God as a supreme personal being will probably find that we are rehearsing—at unnecessary length, perhaps—familiar inadequacies in the personal-omniGod account. Our aim, however, is to convince our fellow analytic philosophers that the possibility of understanding theism without recourse to a personal-omniGod (or similar) metaphysics may not reasonably be dismissed out of hand, given the doubts which we are about to canvass. We may not 'convert' committed personal-omniGod theists—but we do aim to show, at least, that serious debate on alternative ways of understanding (Abrahamic) theism deserves a central place on the agenda of the philosophy of religion.[6] By the end of this book, we hope, we will have made the case for including in that debate, as a serious candidate for an account of fundamental theist metaphysics, the euteleological account we will propose and defend from Chapter 3 onwards.

1.3 Doubts about the Coherence of Personal-OmniGod Theism

Some doubts about the adequacy of the personal-omniGod account of theism concern its overall logical coherence. For example, doubts may be raised about the coherence of the idea of an immaterial, non-embodied person, with agent-causal powers whose exercise necessarily has no physical realization since those powers are deployed in giving the physical world its existence.[7] In addition, questions may be raised about the coherence of one or more of God's personal omni-attributes taken individually (for example, is the notion of an omnipotent being coherent?), or about their mutual

---

[6] As noted in the Introduction, there is a new, growing literature by analytic philosophers on different models or concepts of God. See, e.g., Jeanine Diller and Asa Kasher (2013), Andrei Buckareff and Yujin Nagasawa (2016), and Simon Kittle and Georg Gasser (2022). Yet it continues to be widely assumed that alternatives to the personal-omniGod conception must *thereby* be alternatives to a theistic conception of God. While our proposed euteleological metaphysics makes, on one level, a contribution to the wider discussion of alternative concepts of God, we have the further (and primary) intention to defend euteleological metaphysics as an apt way to understand the fundamental ontology of the worldviews of Abrahamic theist religions.

[7] Swinburne (1993 [1977]: 102–7) offers a coherence proof for the concept of a non-embodied person. But his proof may be contested: for a recent critique, see Herman Philipse (2012, §7.5, 109–13). (There is an extensive literature on the problems facing inter-actionist dualist theories of mind—for an introduction to this and other central topics in the Philosophy of Mind see, e.g., John Heil 2019.) For a defence of the claim that there is a tension, if not inconsistency, in the notion of an 'infinite' or 'unlimited' person, see Perszyk (2018a and 2018b).

consistency when taken in combination (for example, is omnipotence compatible with perfect moral goodness?).[8] More significantly perhaps, even if the conception of God as personal omniGod is coherent in itself, understanding how other features of an overall theist worldview can be compatible with the existence of such a God may yet be problematic. A familiar case in point is the question of the consistency of God's omniscience (foreknowledge) with human free will. Another important example is the 'problem of evil': if the existence of evil is accepted, does it not follow that God either lacks the understanding or the capacity to avoid evil or else has no desire to do so, and cannot therefore have all the personal omni-properties at once? There has been a vast amount of debate over whether doubts such as these (and more) about the coherence of personal-omniGod theism are, or are not, well-founded.[9]

These philosophical debates seem not, however, to have generated much motivational pressure for questioning the adequacy of a personal-omniGod conception of God. There has been a high level of confidence that doubts about this conception's coherence can be resolved, though many points of dispute and divergence emerge when philosophers offer detailed articulations of the theist worldview with the aim of vindicating its coherence. Personal-omniGod theism is thus not a single, unified position, but rather a somewhat unruly family of views whose boundaries are not precise (so that discussion at a high level of generality, such as our own, sometimes needs to include reference to views 'near enough' to the personal-omniGod account). This diversity arises from disputes about a range of questions, such as how to understand omnipotence and the constraints that may legitimately be placed on it, whether the personal omniGod is or is not 'within' time, the sense in which God is a necessary being, and the scope of God's omniscience especially in relation to human free action—for example, can God know future free choices, or have 'middle' knowledge of what any agent

---

[8] Proponents of the claim that the personal-omniGod conception is internally incoherent include Anthony Kenny (1979), Michael Martin (1990, especially ch. 12), Edwin Curley (2003), and Nicholas Everitt (2004, chs. 13–15). See also the papers in parts 4 and 5 of Michael Martin and Ricki Monnier (2003).

[9] Providing full references for these debates is impractical given the voluminous literature. For a sample of useful introductions, of varying degrees of difficulty, to the main debates referred to in this and the following paragraph, see Edward Wierenga (1989); Richard Gale (1991, especially chs. 1–4); Joshua Hoffman and Gary Rosenkrantz (2002); Michael Murray and Michael Rea (2008, especially chs. 1 and 2); and J. P. Moreland, Chad Meister, and Khaldoun A. Sweis (2013).

God could create *would* (freely) do in any set of circumstances in which that agent might be created?[10]

The extent of internecine disagreement amongst personal-omniGod theists and their near neighbours might well strike an outside observer as fragmentation symptomatic of a 'paradigm' under stress and ripe for conceptual revolution.[11] Yet, from within that paradigm, the fact that there are conflicting accounts of the theist worldview interpreted as positing a supernatural personal Creator can seem unsurprising: divergent views and lively disputes, it may be said, are only to be expected in the historical trajectory of 'faith seeking understanding', given the sublime greatness of theist faith's object and the limits on human comprehensibility of the divine.

1.4 Focusing on the Religious Adequacy of Personal-OmniGod Theism

So long as doubts such as those just rehearsed are presented as purely philosophical, they are not likely, we think, to prompt personal-omniGod theists to take seriously inquiries into alternative ways of understanding theism.[12] We think that personal-omniGod theists will feel confident that philosophical doubts can be laid to rest for as long as they retain confidence that one could not reasonably doubt the *religious adequacy* of the personal-omniGod understanding of theism. That confidence might be shaken, however, since (as we will shortly argue) reasonable doubts may arise about whether the personal-omniGod account is religiously adequate to the theist traditions, their practices, values, and overall orientation to reality.

---

[10] For an introduction to these and other debates within the personal-omniGod 'paradigm', see the references just cited in note 9.

[11] The idea that theism is a 'degenerating research programme' in Imre Lakatos's sense has been canvassed often enough by critics—recently, e.g., by Gregory Dawes (2009, 164) and Herman Philipse (2017). This allegation, we think, wrongly assimilates theological explanation to the same explanatory dimension as natural scientific explanation: for discussion, see Bishop (2018a).

[12] And, of course, *atheists* whose atheism rests on their being personal-omniGod theorists will have no motive to encourage consideration of alternative construals of theism. Indeed, they may have the contrary motive, since an atheism that depends on reasons for not believing in the existence *specifically* of the personal omniGod, or for believing, *specifically* that the personal omniGod does not exist, is an atheism that will be undermined if its target conception of God as the personal omniGod is called into question.

But what do we mean by 'religious adequacy'? Religious adequacy is adequacy *to* the theist religious tradition as lived out. A particular understanding of the theist worldview, with its specific conception of God, will thus be religiously adequate when and only when it makes a coherent fit with the way belief in God actually functions for believers in their communal life within one of the Abrahamic faiths. The concept of God may thus be understood as *a 'role' concept*—it is the concept of *something belief in which functions in particular ways in religious life*. What are these 'particular functions' of belief in God, and, accordingly, of the object of such belief? To answer this question we need to specify what these 'God-roles' are— and that may be done in summary by observing that whatever God is, God must be *uniquely worthy of worship* (that, if you like, is *the* God-role). If belief in God functions in the community of believers as belief in that which is the sole proper object of worship, then understanding the concept of God requires an account of what worship is and when it has its proper object.

Theist worship does not consist merely in special ritual and liturgical practices of adoration, thanksgiving, and praise (these practices are important, but they constitute worship only in a narrow sense). Worship (in its full sense as understood in the Abrahamic traditions) is a matter of practical commitment to a whole ethos and way of life rooted in a cognitive and affective orientation to reality which places God at the centre.[13] That overall orientation has rich content, which would need for its full articulation both a systematic theology and a systematic theist ethics. But some indication of the God-roles may yet be given by saying that the One to whom the highest possible worth ('worth-ship') is to be afforded is the One in whom unconditional trust is placed as the source and goal of all existence, the One who is both source and revealer of the good purposes for which the creation exists, and the One in whom our human hope for fulfilment (or 'salvation') may be placed, despite our limitations, sinfulness, and mortality.

The concept of the theist God is thus the concept of that which successfully fills the God-roles—that is, the concept of that which is the sole proper object of worship. Accordingly, there is (at least) logical space for different

---

[13] We will discuss theist worship, and the importance of worship in its 'full sense', in more detail in Chapter 6, when we consider doubts about the religious adequacy of the non-personalist interpretation of the metaphysics of theism we'll be proposing in Chapters 3 and 4.

conceptions of what it is that fills the God-roles.[14] It is therefore possible to *interrogate* any particular conception of God (along with its associated overall theist worldview) in order to judge whether God-according-to-that-conception is fit to fill the God-roles as the unique proper object of worship.[15] Indeed, the stronger claim may be made that believers (or some believers) need to make such a judgement about their own reflective understanding of the object of their faith, in order to avoid idolatrous attachment to what Paul Tillich aptly calls a 'false ultimate'.[16] These judgements of a given conception's fitness as the sole proper object of worship may properly be made only from the 'insider' perspective of reflective faith-commitment to the living-out of a particular theist faith-tradition (though non-believers are not altogether excluded, provided they achieve sufficient empathy with the insider perspective to appreciate how belief in God actually functions in the relevant faith community). The activity of *fides quaerens intellectum*, then, opens up space for criticizing inherited ways of interpreting the tradition's worldview and values in the light of that tradition's *continuing* faith-experience. This faith-based scrutiny allows for some reassessment of received understandings of revealed truth from the sources acknowledged by the tradition as authoritative: inherited teachings may thus sometimes be judged to have distorted the roots of the faith-tradition. It would be a major (and probably ill-advised) task to try to chart in advance the boundaries for such reassessments by providing criteria for justifiably amending or replacing received conceptions of God or (for that matter) received reflective understandings of the specifics of the God-role. We make no such attempt, appealing only to the claim that this kind of critical activity does properly belong to 'faith seeking understanding'. In the rest of this chapter we'll raise particular doubts about the adequacy of the standard personal-omniGod conception of the God of Abrahamic theism, hoping to persuade the reader that some of them, at least, may reasonably be thought weighty enough to prompt a lively interest in possible alternatives.

---

[14] We are thus distinguishing between the *concept* of God, which is a role-concept, and particular *conceptions* of that which fills the God-roles. This use of the concept/conception distinction is similar to its use by John Rawls (himself following W. B. Gallie 1956) in relation to the notion of justice (see Rawls 1999, 9).

[15] It follows that, despite surface appearances, 'God' is *not* a proper name, but rather primarily the name of a role—a name which may then be derivatively conferred on whatever it is that *successfully* fills the God-role. See Mark Johnston (2009, 6), who suggests that 'God' functions as an honorific 'compressed title', though evidently not the kind of title that could ever be lost by that which merits it. The view that 'God' is a title, not a proper name, has a strong pedigree in contemporary analytic philosophy of religion: see, e.g., Nelson Pike (1969).

[16] See Tillich's account of faith as 'ultimate concern' (2001 [1957], 1 and 21).

1.5 Indirect Doubts about Religious Adequacy: Doctrinal and Historical Authenticity

We are claiming, then, that the personal-omniGod conception of what it is that fills the God-roles is open to scrutiny as to its religious adequacy. Why might it reasonably be thought lacking?

One type of concern may be that understanding God as the personal omniGod is doubtfully consistent with certain doctrines specific to a particular theist tradition. A key case in point is presented by the Christian doctrines of Incarnation and Trinity.[17] We will not press this kind of concern, however: doctrinal waters such as these are challenging, and we won't try to argue here that they cannot be navigated safely by personal-omniGod theorists.[18] It might perhaps be true that personal-omniGod metaphysics and the doctrine of the Trinity cannot ultimately be reconciled. But lengthy theological debate would be needed to sustain that conclusion, and, besides, such a debate would be tangential to our present purposes, since the doubts we wish to claim may reasonably be held about the religious adequacy of personal-omniGod theism apply across the different Abrahamic traditions and do not depend on specific doctrines from any one of them.

Another potential source of concern about the religious adequacy of personal-omniGod theism is that it may not be authentic in the sense of being faithful to the inherited understanding of theist traditions that our

---

[17] To elaborate briefly: if Jesus the Christ, a historical person, is also taken to be God incarnate, it seems to follow that he cannot be *the very same person* as God (God unbegotten, that is) if God is understood to be a person in the same general sense. The doctrine of the Trinity might appear to endorse that claim, proposing a conception of God as one God in three persons (the Father, the Son, and the Holy Spirit). Do personal-omniGod theorists of Christian theism then have to postulate that God is one person who somehow consists in three persons? Or is the personal omniGod to be identified with God the Father only, rendering it puzzling how the Son and the Spirit can also be God (just as the Father is)?

[18] The use of the Latin term *persona* in Trinitarian formulations—corresponding with the notion of *hypostasis* in Greek formulations—is often said to differ significantly from our contemporary concept of a person. But there is controversy amongst analytic philosophers on this point. For example, William Hasker argues that the Church Fathers had the concept of personal agency and spoke in ways that imply straightforward attribution of personal agency to Trinitarian 'persons' (2010, 422–3). Simon Hewitt observes, however, that

> in *Summa Theologiae* 1a, q29, a3...Aquinas defends the applicability of *persona* to each of the trinitarian hypostases, but does so having explicitly rejected the suggestion that God is a *persona*, in the same sense as us (which, for Aquinas following Boethius, is that of an individual substance of a rational nature).   (2020, 4, note 7)

For further discussion of how Christian doctrines of Incarnation and Trinity relate to our understanding of God as a person, see, e.g., Thomas Morris (1986) and Thomas McCall and Michael Rea (2009).

forebears' reflective faith found adequate and handed down to us. And, indeed, there's a case to be made for the claim that personal-omniGod theism differs significantly from the 'classical' philosophical understanding of theism that was dominant in medieval times and until the Enlightenment.[19] Under this classical account philosophical theologians attributed to God properties in tension with a metaphysics of God as a personal agent, properties such as *atemporality*, *immutability*, *impassibility* (that is, the 'inability' to undergo or suffer anything), and *simplicity* (the property of lacking all 'composition'). While no one ever denied that God was person*al* in the sense that God could rightly be described by humans in personal terms—as knowing, willing, and acting—these descriptions were typically treated cautiously, as (following Aquinas, for example) *analogous extensions* of language about finite human persons to something belonging to a different category or, indeed, transcending categories altogether. Accordingly, classical theism did not assume that personal talk about God was *immediately transparent* to an underlying, comprehensible, metaphysics of the divine as a supernatural person or personal being. So, from the fact that the medievals used personal language about God—and affirmed that God has beliefs and emotions (for example, undisturbed happiness or bliss) and performs intentional actions—it doesn't follow that they understood God to be a person at the level of their fundamental metaphysics.

Personal-omniGod theorists have differed over the extent to which they think they need to 'save' or accommodate the classical divine attributes. They have usually thought that at least some of these attributes need judicious modification or even outright rejection for a coherent understanding of the theist worldview according to the conception of God as personal omniGod.[20] They have also differed over whether to regard the classical

---

[19] For three prominent examples of philosophers who consider understanding God to be a supernatural person as inauthentic to classical understandings of theism, see David Burrell (1987), Herbert McCabe (1987), and Brian Davies (2006, especially 61–2, and 2004, ch. 1, where Davies distinguishes 'classical theism' from 'theistic personalism'). More recent examples include Edward Feser (2013), David Bentley Hart (2013), who affirms that '[God] is not a "being" at least in the way that a tree, a shoemaker, or a god is a being; he is not one more object in the inventory of things that are, or any sort of discrete object at all', and Roger Pouivet (2018, 8) who writes, 'The claim that God is a person is...not at all a simple way of formulating classical theism, as Swinburne suggests. It is instead a whole other form of modern theism.' This claim that classical theists would deny that God is a person is controversial, however. See notes 21 and 25 below for more details.

[20] Robert Coburn (1963), Nelson Pike (1970, 121–9), Anthony Kenny (1979), and Richard Gale (1991, 52 and 92–3) reject the coherence of the notion of an atemporal person. The question of the compatibility of God's omniscience with his immutability is discussed (for instance) by Norman Kretzmann (1966), and, with his atemporality, by A. N. Prior (1962), Stephen

theism of the medievals as clearly distinct from the personal-omniGod paradigm. Indeed, some contemporary personal-omniGod theists construe Aquinas and other medievals as *accepting* a personalist divine metaphysics and, therefore, as being themselves personal-omniGod theists, or near enough.[21]

Even if personal-omniGod theism is clearly *not* the classical philosophical theism of (for example) Maimonides, Ibn Sina, and Aquinas, it would not follow *just on that account* that personal-omniGod theism is less religiously adequate. That an understanding of God and the theist worldview is a received understanding provides *indirect* evidence that it is a religiously adequate understanding, since its status as an established understanding may be presumed to depend on its *having been* judged religiously adequate. The religious adequacy of a way of understanding the divine must ultimately be judged, however, by reflecting *directly* on faith as it is now being lived out in the relevant tradition—whether or not that understanding is wholly

---

Davis (1983, 29), and Nicholas Wolterstorff (2010). Many reject God's being (strongly) immutable and impassible on the ground that these properties are incompatible with omniscience or with perfect goodness or with being a person. As to the question of simplicity, Brian Leftow (personal correspondence) expresses doubts about whether there could be a simple person ('simple' in the sense of lacking composition of any kind) that acts through will and intellect. It's unlikely, he thinks, that a simple being could have freedom involving the ability to do otherwise, and it couldn't have a mind in the sense of a system of many distinct causally involved mental states within itself. But perhaps, he conjectures, its one mental state could be what makes it true that it thinks and wills various things. Plantinga (1980, 47 and 52–3), on the other hand, is in no doubt that divine simplicity is incompatible with personhood.

[21] Philosophers quite often treat classical theism and personal-omniGod theism as equivalent, sometimes without recognizing any issue here—for a recent example, see Tim Mawson (2013, 26). Katherin Rogers (2000, 65) says explicitly that 'for classical theism, God is indeed a person'. William Vallicella (2016, 381), amongst others, would agree: 'Classical theism is a personalism: God is a person and we, as made in the image and likeness of God, are also persons.' Marilyn Adams's (2013, 22) view is more cautiously nuanced:

> [M]y favorite five scholastics—Anselm, Bonaventure, Aquinas, Scotus, and Ockham—appreciate what I call 'the Metaphysical Size Gap': God as immeasurably excellent is in a different ontological category from creatures, and yet is still a 'personal' agent who acts by thought and will to do one thing rather than another in the created order.

Philosophers such as these, then, evidently believe that even if (as classical theism emphasizes) we cannot simply 'read off' a divine metaphysics from our analogizing personal talk about God, nevertheless there are good reasons for accepting a metaphysical understanding of God as a person or personal being. But, as indicated in note 19, it is controversial whether medieval, classical theists such as Aquinas in fact held (or would have held) that God is a person. Brian Davies (2011, 125–6) is adamant that Aquinas 'would positively disparage' the suggestion that God is a person. Ben Page (2019, 299, 304, 312), however, thinks Davies might be mistaken. Sam Lebens (2021) says '[t]he God of Maimonides is not a person' (p. 7), though he himself proposes 'a seemingly paradoxical claim, drawn from the Jewish tradition, according to which God is both fully, and not at all, a person' (p. 1).

'received' or contains 'reformed' or 'revisionary' aspects. In the end, then, competing contemporary understandings of the metaphysics of theism need to be assessed for their religious adequacy in relation to contemporary perspectives on the living faith itself. And there are, of course, many such perspectives, some starkly opposed to others, even (indeed, perhaps especially!) *within* each strand of Abrahamic monotheism. Judgements of the religious adequacy or inadequacy of a given proposal for the metaphysics of theism will thus always be relative to *some* particular views of living theist faith—and they will carry weight when those views are sufficiently widely shared.

1.6 Direct Doubts about Religious Adequacy: Divine Transcendence and Immanence

We set aside, then, putative *indirect* grounds for holding that personal-omniGod theism is not religiously adequate and consider what reasons may be given for drawing this conclusion by *directly* considering whether the idea of God as an omnipotent and omniscient supernatural person fits with faith as lived out in the theist revelatory traditions—at least according to sufficiently widely, if not universally, shared perspectives on that faith.

We will argue, in this section, that one might reasonably hold that the personal omniGod lacks both the right kind of transcendence and the right kind of immanence needed for an adequate filler of the God-roles. Then, in the next two sections, we'll advance what we think is the most serious concern that may be held about the personal omniGod's religious adequacy—namely, the concern that an omnipotent, omniscient, supernatural person cannot be a perfectly good person and so cannot properly fill the theist God-roles.

Consider first, then, God's transcendence. Anselm famously characterized God as *that than which nothing greater can be thought*.[22] This is not a characterization of what God is, so to say, 'in Godself'. Rather, it expresses the requirement—implicit in the absolute supremacy of the proper object of worship—that, whatever God may be, God's reality is such that the idea of something with greater reality is simply unthinkable. Anselm's formula thus implies that (as already noted) the concept of God is a role-concept, and the

---

[22] Anselm, *Proslogion*, ch. 2. For more discussion, see, for example, Morris (1987a and 1987b).

formula provides a criterion for being an adequate 'filler' of that role. No conception of God can be adequate unless what is thereby thought about is such that nothing greater than it is even conceivable.

Philosophers have often supposed that accepting Anselm's formula leads straightforwardly to the conclusion that God is the personal omniGod. They have reasoned along the following lines. That-than-which-a-greater-cannot-be-thought must possess *ontological* supremacy; so, God must be *a being* such that none greater can even be thought. God must therefore be a unique unsurpassably great *instance* of the highest possible *kind* of being. If rational persons are then assumed to be that highest kind of being, Anselm's formula yields the conception of God as a personal agent whose power, knowledge, and goodness are so great that no agent with greater power, knowledge, or goodness can be conceived—that is, a personal agent who is omnipotent, omniscient, and perfectly good.

It is not obvious, however, that ontological supremacy must belong to 'a' being. Some may suggest, plausibly enough—many defenders of the 'social' doctrine of the Trinity, for example—that the *relational* being of a just society of persons is greater *qua* being than the greatness of any individual, however powerful, wise, and good.[23] Furthermore, and more radically, it may be argued that the being of that-than-which-a-greater-cannot-be-thought must transcend the being of an entity of any kind.[24] In that case, God cannot be 'a' person, nor a society of persons, no matter how great, unique, or paradigmatic. On this view, Anselm's formula may be held to exclude the personal-omniGod conception, on the grounds that this conception of God makes God 'too small' through limiting the absolute transcendence of inconceivably unsurpassable greatness of being.

The contention that God cannot be 'a' person or personal being may be bolstered by appeal to the doctrine of divine simplicity, commonly affirmed by medieval theologians, including Anselm.[25] The claim that God is

---

[23] Analytic social trinitarians, however, reject characterizing God as a society of persons. See, e.g., William Hasker (2013).

[24] Though 'being' as applied to God must have something in common with 'being' as applied to us, too naïve or straightforward a doctrine of the 'univocity of being' may lead us astray. For further discussion, see, e.g., Brad Gregory (2008, especially §2). For an extended argument against the claim that Anselm's formula entails personal-omniGod theism, see Jeff Speaks (2018).

[25] See, e.g., *Monologion*, chs. 16 and 17, and *Proslogion*, ch. 18. This is not, of course, to say that there was just one medieval doctrine of simplicity. Nor is it to suggest that there were no metaphysical differences between the main proponents of 'the traditional doctrine of simplicity' (Augustine, Anselm, and Aquinas). For discussion, see Katherin Rogers (1996). Rogers (2020) considers more closely the differences between Anselmian and Thomist approaches to

simple—in the apophatic sense of lacking all 'composition'—seems to function to safeguard reflective faith's respect for the transcendence of God's reality over that of all created things. God's lack of composition implies that God does not 'consist' of a substance that 'has' or possesses a collection of attributes—so that God is not 'separate from' God's goodness (for example), as with a finite being for whom its goodness is *an aspect* from which, with its other attributes, it is 'comprised'. Furthermore, God lacks the 'composition' of essence and existence—from which it follows that God's supreme reality does not consist in being an item of *any* general kind, since (on the Aristotelian metaphysics assumed under at least the Thomist approach to simplicity) any particular instance of a kind requires the 'composition' resulting from 'adding' existence to the essence that distinguishes that kind. *A fortiori*, then, God is not a person or personal being. Thus, on this understanding, God's being simple ('non-composite') does not convey positive insight into what God is, but, rather, secures God's radical 'otherness' from every existent thing of any kind—an 'otherness' which is not to be thought of as the mundane distinctness of a particular being from other particular beings.[26]

By contrast, on the personal-omniGod account of theism, God's transcendence in relation to the created world amounts to God's being a supernatural *entity* uniquely distinct from all created entities, as the supreme entity on which all other entities depend for their existence. Construing God's otherness as God's otherness *as a supernatural being* may, however, be

---

simplicity. Rogers herself takes the view that classical theists *did* take God to be a person, whereas here we are construing divine simplicity as grounds for the contrary view. For another example of a philosopher who endorses the positive notion of a 'simple' (and immutable) person, see William Mann (1983). Eleonore Stump (2016) offers an interpretation of Aquinas as coherently affirming the classical attributes of atemporality, immutability, and simplicity while also understanding God to be a personal being.

[26] For further elucidation along these lines of the idea of divine simplicity and its implications, see Brian Davies (1987, 2000, 2004, and 2010), Herbert McCabe (1987, Part I), and David Burrell (1987). Burrell's view is that *simpleness* (and *eternity*) are 'formal features' of divinity, as distinct from properties or attributes. He takes formal features to be prior to a consideration of attributes, and these formal features, he contends, secure the proper distinction of God from the world (see, e.g., Burrell 1987, 77). While it is common for simplicity to be referred to as a divine attribute, the thesis of divine simplicity is *not* really a thesis about a particular attribute God possesses, but rather a thesis concerning the way God's attributes are related to each other and to God or God's essence. It may accordingly be helpful to understand the thesis of divine simplicity more as an account of the logic or grammar of our talk about God, which then excludes as 'ungrammatical' metaphysical theories of God as 'a being amongst beings' yet without itself constituting a positive metaphysical theory about the nature of God. In this connexion, see Simon Hewitt's defence of a 'Grammatical Thomism' (2021). Ben Page (2019) argues that the key debate between those who think and those who deny that God is a person ultimately comes down to how one understands divine simplicity (see also note 29).

thought to 'reduce' and compromise divine transcendence. That is certainly how proponents of divine simplicity will see it, on the apophatic construal of simplicity that we have outlined. On that account, as just argued, divine simplicity rules out God's being a person. And, in any case, taking God to be, literally and metaphysically, a person may seem suspiciously like an idolatrously anthropomorphic construction of the divine in our own human image.[27] It's also worth noting that the theist theme of humanity created in the image of God does not—as seems commonly enough assumed—entail that, since (mature) humans are persons, God must be a person also. The properties of images do not necessarily belong also to those things of which they are images; for example, an image of a mountain may be two-dimensional, but the mountain clearly is not.

Personal-omniGod theism may also be found wanting in its account of divine immanence—the presence of God *within* creation. The personal omniGod is the ultimate sustaining agent-cause of all that exists, and, accordingly, God has complete knowledge of all that exists. God's supernatural presence and awareness is thus all-pervasive in creation. There seems no scope for any further immanence, however: with God as a personal being, God's distinctness as creator necessarily makes God's relation to creatures a relation of one being to all other beings, with God's being, as the being of the Creator, in a distinct ontological category from that of all other beings. But any such 'being-to-beings' account of divine immanence may be thought unsatisfactorily weak: a religiously adequate view, it may be claimed, sees God as far closer to creatures than producers are to their products, and closer to created persons than any other person can be, even in the closest of inter-personal relationships. As Brian Davies puts it, using a spatial metaphor, 'God does not stand outside creation as an entity over and against his creatures. He is not other to creatures as they are to each other' (1987, 70). Of course, God *is* 'other' to creatures. Davies's point, however, is that this otherness is not the *kind* of otherness that amounts to the distinctness

---

[27] The idea that a god who is 'a person' is improperly anthropomorphic is as old as philosophy in the West (see Xenophanes, Fragment 15). Theist religion may be regarded as more developed than 'primitive' religions just because its understanding of God as transcendent and absolute avoids this idolatrous trap. Robert Sokolowski, e.g., in contrasting the character and novelty of the Christian conception of God with ancient, pagan conceptions, remarks that 'the Christian God is not a part of the world and is not a "kind" of being at all' (1982, 36). And Gary Legenhausen (1986, 317) says that, within Islam, 'because of God's transcendence, [God] cannot be called a person, not even analogically', adding that '[i]n brief, the Muslim argument against the personality of God is that personality is a limiting factor and is therefore incompatible with the infinite nature of God'.

of persons from each other. When God's reality is understood as properly transcendent—that is, without construing it as the reality of 'a' being, however exalted, in relation to other beings—a more profound immanence of the divine in all creation becomes possible than could ever be accommodated so long as the God on whom everything depends is understood as a particular personal being.[28]

Proponents of personal-omniGod theism may, of course, reject divine simplicity—at least as carrying the implications we have drawn from it.[29] Personal-omniGod theorists will insist that God's uniqueness as the supernatural and immaterial personal Creator provides all the transcendence and immanence that a religiously adequate conception requires.[30] They are

---

[28] Brad Gregory makes a similar point (2008, 502–3):

> [P]erhaps God is not a 'highest being' or a 'supernatural entity' that can in any sense be properly conceived within or as a component of a more comprehensive reality. In other words, perhaps God is real and is radically distinct from the universe; perhaps God is metaphysically *transcendent*.... A radically transcendent God would be neither outside nor inside his creation.... Rather, if real, such a God could be wholly present to everything in the natural world precisely and only *because* he would be altogether *inconceivable* in spatial categories. Divine transcendence would thus be not the opposite but the *correlate* of divine immanence.

Compare also Kathryn Tanner (2013, 147–9) who provides a cogent defence of the claim that divine immanence and divine transcendence should be understood as coinciding.

[29] The majority of analytic philosophers of religion in recent times have rejected divine simplicity. As Mike Rea (2016, 99) admits, '[a] suitably strong theology of transcendence will imply that relatively few (if any) [positive] characterizations of God are strictly metaphysically accurate.... As is well known, analytic theologians tend to have very little sympathy...for strong theologies of divine transcendence.' If construed as a positive attribute implying God's identity with his attributes, divine simplicity does indeed seem open to the charge that it entails that God is a property or universal (Plantinga 1980). God might, perhaps, be understood as having his attributes all made true by the one thing, namely God's own uniquely simple undifferentiated being (so that, e.g., God's mercy and his justice are not really distinct)—as implied by recent proposals for a 'truth-maker' construal of divine simplicity. For more on the truth-maker account of simplicity, see, e.g., Jeffrey Brower (2008) and Alexander Pruss (2008). Ben Page (2019, 311) says that 'the truth-maker account seems to have been formulated partly in order to claim that God is a person'. On the interpretation we are favouring here, however, divine simplicity is construed apophatically, not as a positive feature, as both Plantinga's objection and a 'truth-maker' account seem to assume. On an apophatic account, the whole point of divine simplicity is that God is simply(!) not the kind of thing to which the ordinary substance-attribute scheme of description can apply.

[30] The medieval view of God's omnipresence (as found in Anselm and Aquinas in particular) is commonly interpreted by personal-omniGod theorists as taking God's presence everywhere to be reducible to God's omniscience and/or omnipotence. See, e.g., Edward Wierenga (1997); Brian Leftow (1998); and William Wainwright (2010). The majority of contemporary models of divine omnipresence are variants of such 'derivative' accounts—God's presence or location is understood non-literally/non-spatially, and God is present everywhere in virtue of standing in some epistemic or causal relation to other things that are themselves (directly) located. However, on some recent accounts, omnipresence is not reducible to other divine attributes and is understood literally/spatially. See, e.g., Hud Hudson (2009, 2014) and

likely to scoff at appeals to divine simplicity made in mounting a case for the superior religious adequacy of a non-personalist view. Perhaps they will see the doctrine of divine simplicity as a prime example of speculation about 'the God of the philosophers'. Very likely, they will insist that it is surely obvious that, to be religiously adequate, a conception of God must be of God as a personal being, given the pervasiveness of personal language about God in liturgy and scripture, and the presupposition of prayer that God is a person who can hear and respond.

But this reaction is not altogether fair. The medieval theologians who affirmed an apophatic doctrine of divine simplicity were responding to lived religious experience and the testimony of canonical scriptures. They were entirely at home with personal talk about God, and steeped in the practice of prayer. The apophatic thesis of divine simplicity was not, then, a case of Athens imposing on Jerusalem, though it did deploy conceptual resources from Greek philosophy, and it did pose for reflective faith the question how a God who was not a personal being, nor 'a' being of any kind, could meaningfully be said to know, to will, and to act. Any non-personalist understanding of theism will, of course, face that same question, and we'll return to it in relation to our own euteleological metaphysics in Chapter 4. For now, we are just making the point that the classical *via negativa* theological tradition, with its doctrine of divine simplicity, was a response to a profound feature of theist religious sensibility, namely the sense of God's absolute transcendence as conveyed within the Abrahamic scriptural traditions. Consider, for example, the idea found in the Jewish tradition that God's name is so holy that it requires a safer surrogate—an idea plausibly interpretable as rejecting the possibility of fitting the divine into any human category. Consider, too, whether understanding God as a person amongst persons fits with God's refusal to be named when God speaks from the burning bush, urging Moses to say to those who ask that it is 'I am' who sent him. Or ask yourself whether thinking of God as an omnipresent supernatural person can adequately capture the closeness of the presence of a God who says in the Qur'an 'We have already created man and know what his soul whispers to him, and We are closer to him than [his] jugular vein' (Surah Qaf 50:16).[31] Consider, too, the immanence of the God 'in whom we

---

Alexander Pruss (2013). For a critical discussion of their accounts, and a general taxonomy of models of divine omnipresence, see Ross Inman (2017).

[31] Cf. Augustine, who says, addressing God (*Confessions*, 3, 6, 11) 'You were more intimately present to me than my innermost being, and higher than the highest peak of my spirit' (2014, 83).

live, and move, and have our being', to quote Peter's sermon to the council of the Areopagus (Acts 17:28): how could creaturely persons live 'in' a being who is itself another individual person, relating to creatures as one being to another?[32]

We are not suggesting, of course, that these doubts about the adequacy of a personalist account of divine transcendence and immanence suffice by themselves to defeat personal-omniGod theism. Despite these doubts, there may yet be good reason to understand theism as personal-omniGod theism—or as something near enough to it which preserves the idea of God as a supernatural personal being. We will be returning (in Chapter 6) to discuss an objection of the kind already mentioned—namely, that key religious practices such as worship and prayer presuppose that God is a personal being. For now, however, we are seeking only to show that there can be *reasonable motivation* for a serious consideration of alternatives to the prevailing personal-omniGod account of theism. And we think that philosophers of theism ought to appreciate that considerations such as those raised in this section concerning divine transcendence and immanence may reasonably lead some reflective theists to doubt the religious adequacy of the personal-omniGod conception of the object of theist worship—and, accordingly, reasonably motivate an interest in alternative ways of conceiving of the theist God.

1.7 Divine Goodness

Sincere doubts about the personal omniGod's religious adequacy may also arise for some reflective theists from the concern that an omnipotent, omniscient, supernatural person cannot be a perfectly good person and so cannot properly fill the theist God-roles. We think that personal-omniGod theists should acknowledge that, even if they believe they have reasonable ways of settling these doubts, others may reasonably find them persistent enough to be motivated to seek an alternative understanding of theism.

---

[32] For many medieval mystics (Christian and Islamic), it's fine to depict God as a person for pedagogical reasons so long as one also realizes that ultimately God is beyond being, i.e., absolutely transcendent. See, e.g., Amber Griffioen and Mohammad Sadegh Zahedi (2019, 284–9). But even those who are dubious about taking mystics as a guide to an adequate understanding of the divine need to ponder the significance of the scriptural witness to God's transcendence to which we are here drawing attention.

Anselm's formula implies that God must be unsurpassably great *in goodness* as well as in being: the filler of the God-roles must be, we might say, *onto-ethically* unsurpassably great. Accordingly, if God is a person, God's unsurpassably great goodness is the perfect goodness of a person. Being good *as a person* requires being *morally* good, and moral goodness includes goodness in relation to, and relationship with, other persons. If God is a person, then, God's perfect goodness must imply perfect moral goodness in relation to, and relationship with, other persons. But, now, if God is a person, God is someone on whose exercise of personal agency all finite, creaturely, persons depend for their very existence. Can such an absolutely all-powerful person be also perfectly morally good in relation to those dependent persons? If not, to worship such a person commits the idolatry of worshipping ultimate power independently of ultimate worth.

Supreme power and supreme goodness do seem in some tension when combined as attributes of an individual personal being. Lord Acton's (1907 [1887], 504) dictum—'Power tends to corrupt, and absolute power corrupts absolutely'—might perhaps be a basic metaphysical insight, rather than simply a general observation about human behaviour in the political sphere. In any case, a person with unlimited agential power looks like an apotheosis of the 'controlling ego' from which, as theist ethics proclaim, finite persons need to be transformed if they are to be saved. How could it be right, then, to worship infinite controlling personal power if salvation depends on overcoming our sinful self-centred urges to exercise that very kind of power? Would that not be to affirm as unsurpassably good the very same thing that must be judged essentially flawed in finite persons?

Any attempt to build these suspicions into an argument for the conclusion that a person of unlimited agential power could not be wholly good is likely to be resisted by personal-omniGod theorists as resting on assumptions that are improperly anthropomorphic—assumptions, that is, which fail to respect the ontological gap between finite persons and the person who is Creator of all.[33] Possessing extensive controlling power over others may invariably generate *in a finite person* the tyrannous vices of 'playing God', but, it will be said, it cannot be a meaningful accusation *against God* that God 'plays God'! Nevertheless, the challenge remains to provide the assurance that God, understood as a person with an unlimited power of

---

[33] Alternatively, personal-omniGod theorists might say that these suspicions rest on a simplistic understanding of power. We will consider more nuanced views of power and divine omnipotence in Chapter 2 (especially Sections 2.3–2.5).

agency, can also be a perfectly good person—and perfectly good *in relationship with* finite creaturely persons, in all God does that affects the nature and quality of those relationships.

When the creaturely dependence of finite persons on God is understood as a matter of God's personal agency, the personal relationship between God and finite persons has to reach across a radical ontological gulf. As we have remarked before, if God is a person, God has to be a *supernatural* person, in the sense that God's being is distinct from the being of anything in the created, natural, order. But then it is hard to see how the mutuality generally considered essential to fulfilling personal relationships could exist across that natural/supernatural divide. God looks to be too dominating a person for freely chosen loving relationship with him to be possible within the natural historical order—and, since God cannot avoid being the ultimate 'matchmaker', God's dominance might also undercut the worth of 'horizontal' historical relationships amongst finite persons. Some philosophers have argued, similarly, that if God the creator is a supreme personal agent, finite agents will lack the full realization of values such as privacy and independence.[34] And others have made the radical claim that the very idea of God as a supernatural being is idolatrous.[35]

These are purported reasons, then, for judging it to be an idolatrous mistake to ascribe the perfect goodness essential for worship-worthiness to a personal being with omnipotent, and ultimately all-controlling, agential power as creator of all that exists. But personal-omniGod theorists may—once again—feel confident that satisfactory replies may be found to these kinds of reservations about how an omnipotent and omniscient personal agent could stand in right relationship to finite persons. Concerns about the obtrusiveness of such an agent might, for example, be resolved by arguing that God may somehow hide or suspend his underlying omnipotent presence, reducing his dominance from the perspective of finite creatures and so providing space for human freedom and authentic faith-ventures. Indeed, the task of giving a coherent account of human freedom in a world with an omnipotent and omniscient personal Creator will be a key element in any proposed metaphysics of personal-omniGod theism.

---

[34] Guy Kahane (2011) argues on grounds such as these that it would be worse in certain respects if such a dominating personal God exists than if he doesn't.

[35] Mark Johnston claims that 'the very ideas of religion as essentially supernaturalist, and of God as essentially a supernatural being, are idolatrous conceptions' (2009, 39). Johnston locates the core of this idolatry in belief in a personal after-life 'in which the large-scale defects of this life are not just redeemed but *removed*' (p. 124).

That task is not straightforward, however: with an all-powerful, all-knowing person in ultimate control, it seems that human freedom cannot enjoy real autonomy; yet, if God surrenders omnipotence to make room for the free exercise of creaturely agency, God's trustworthiness for salvation may be compromised by a subsequent lack of full control. As already noted, though, there are internal differences and disputes within the personal-omniGod camp on this key issue, and personal-omniGod theists may regard it as reasonable to hope that, somewhere in this mix, at least the seeds of a coherent and religiously satisfying view of the perfectly good personal Creator freely relating to significantly morally free created persons may be found.[36]

1.8 God and Evil

The question whether the personal Creator could have perfect goodness as a person, and act with perfect goodness in relation to finite persons, becomes most pressing, however, when it is raised in the context of the problem of evil. The 'logical' Argument from Evil—alleging that the personal God cannot be both all-powerful and all-good given the existence of evil—is widely regarded as decisively refuted. For all we know, God could have a morally adequate reason for permitting (and, ultimately, causing) all the evil that exists. And, in case it may seem that no such 'excuses' could arise for a genuinely all-powerful agent, we may speculate about how even omnipotence may face logical limitations which generate the need to trade off evil against outweighing good. For example, we may suggest that God's morally adequate reasons for permitting evil could arise from restrictions on God's options logically consequent on God's decision to create a world where some creatures exercise morally significant free will.[37]

---

[36] For example, perhaps the 'open theist' claim that God neither has nor could have foreknowledge of free creaturely actions needs to be incorporated (for an account of 'open theism' see, e.g., Charles Pinnock et al. 1994). For further suggestions about how the personal omni-God's dominance might be softened in relation with created persons, see Eleonore Stump's (1979) account of the role of petitionary prayer as a buffer to God's otherwise overwhelming us. Note also replies made by personal-omniGod theists to J. L. Schellenberg's 'argument from divine hiddenness' (1993 and 2015), which attempt to explain how the personal omniGod could exist and yet be hidden. See, e.g., Daniel Howard-Snyder and Paul Moser (2002), and Adam Green and Eleonore Stump (2015).

[37] It is widely believed that Plantinga's 'Free Will Defence' (for example, in his 1974b) has refuted the 'logical' version of the Argument from Evil as exemplified in J. L. Mackie's (1955), though a few philosophers think that some version of the 'logical' argument remains in

However, even if such a 'Free Will' response to the Argument succeeds in showing how evil can coherently exist in the personal Creator's creation (which may be contested),[38] it is important to recognize that the question may linger whether one may reasonably regard the all-powerful person who permits (and, ultimately, causes) evil as having the perfect goodness required to be the fit object of worship. This is a crucial dialectical point: the problem of defending the consistency of the omnipotent personal God's goodness with the existence of evil might seem to be resolved, yet the question may remain whether the kind of goodness that this apparent solution shows to be compatible with existing evil *is goodness enough* for the goodness of the uniquely worship-worthy God. And that question, of course, is a question about *the religious adequacy* of a conception of God and God's goodness. To be the proper object of worship a personal God must have perfect, flawless, personal goodness. But perfect personal goodness may require more than acting so as to maximize overall good outcomes (or 'global' goods).

As Marilyn Adams argues, God's perfect goodness may need to be understood as a goodness that seeks *to be good to* every created person. If that is so, then, omnipotent God would not necessarily vindicate his perfect goodness in permitting evils on the grounds that he does so for the sake of achieving otherwise logically unobtainable outweighing 'higher' goods (such as significant moral freedom and the further goods for which such freedom is necessary). In particular, God's perfect personal goodness would

---

contention, including Richard Gale (1991, ch. 4); Quentin Smith (1997); Graham Oppy (2004); and David Lewis (2007). Most philosophers agree, however, that the focus is now wholly on 'evidential' versions of the Argument as exemplified by William Rowe (1979 and numerous other papers)—i.e., versions which maintain that evil's existence (or its variety and profusion), though not logically incompatible with God's existence, nevertheless gives rational support for believing that, very probably, God does not exist. Sometimes, Rowe expresses a more qualified view, namely, as arguing that '*putting aside* whatever reasons there may be for believing that God exists, the evils that occur in our world make belief in atheism more reasonable than belief in theism' (2004, 4). It also appears to be widely believed that the success or failure of evidential versions of the Argument rests ultimately on the adequacy of some version of 'Skeptical Theism', which emphasizes that outweighing goods and their entanglement with apparently pointless evils may be beyond human knowing. (For more on Skeptical Theism, see, e.g., Trent Dougherty and Justin McBrayer (2014).) Recently, however, discussion of the 'logical' Argument from Evil has revived in response to James Sterba (2019). Sterba takes God's providence over creation to be analogous to the care an ideally just state takes of its citizens, and argues that God would therefore need to meet a set of 'evil prevention' moral requirements which seem empirically not to have been met.

[38] See, for example, Mackie's (1982, ch. 9) criticisms of Plantinga's (1974b) Free Will Defence. We discuss Plantinga's views further in Chapter 2 (Section 2.3) in considering divine omnipotence and its limitations.

not be compatible with his permitting what Adams calls 'horrendous' evils—evils which, on her definition, render it *prima facie* doubtful that the lives of those affected could be a great good to them on the whole. Even if horrendous evils *are* outweighed ('balanced off') by goods unobtainable without them, their existence seems, on the face of it, to be incompatible with God's perfect goodness as one who is good to every created person. Adams goes on to argue that God *is* able to vindicate his perfect goodness (so understood) by 'defeating' horrendous evils through bringing created persons implicated in it (perpetrators as well as sufferers) into the incommensurably great bliss of eternal, post-mortem relationship with him.[39]

It seems clear that Adams assumes that, while God would have caused injustice in his relationships with created persons if he had merely balanced off their sufferings against greater goods, God will introduce no defect in his relationships if those sufferings are defeated in the way described. But we think this assumption may be contested.[40]

If God first caused or permitted created persons to suffer horrors and then compensated them—even 'incommensurably'—God would be responsible for what might plausibly be judged a less than fully just and loving relationship with those other persons. God would have an unavoidably manipulative relationship with created persons, whilst they, for their part, could hardly give God their final trust, being naturally wary of compensations bestowed by one who once caused them such suffering.[41] If these judgements are correct, then, on Adams's 'defeat' scenario, all-powerful God turns out to be, through his own free action, in less than perfectly loving

---

[39] See Adams (1999, 31) for the claim that God must be good to each creature. For her discussion of the distinction between 'defeating' and 'balancing off' evils, see pp. 20–1. For more on this distinction, see Roderick Chisholm (1968/9). The difference between 'balancing off' and 'defeating' is found earlier, as Chisholm acknowledges. See, e.g., G. E. Moore (1959 [1903], 27–36 and ch. 6).

[40] We set aside the issue of how Adams's strategy for an account of God's defeat of horrors could be applicable to the question of why God permits ordinary human and especially intense, *non-human* animal suffering. On the problem of non-human animal pain and suffering, see Michael Murray (2008).

[41] Some might admit that if God directly caused their intense suffering and then tried to compensate them for it, God would rightly be accused of being manipulative. They might insist, however, that if God merely permitted horrors, having good reasons to take a more hands-off approach to governing the world, we should not be quick to cry manipulation. We don't think this ploy works. The personal omniGod, as creator, is the producer and sustainer of all else that exists. Some of what God produces and sustains is directly produced by producers other than God, but they are producers that God ultimately produces and sustains as producers. God is thus ultimately, if indirectly, causally responsible for all horrors. If God does (as Adams insists) eventually bring participants in those evils into the joy of eternal relationship with him, he will be coping with the effects of evils he himself ultimately produced.

and just relationship with created persons who suffer horrors, and, therefore, not perfectly morally good, and, therefore, not the fit object of worship.

There is, then, a version of the Argument from Evil that highlights an inconsistency in the theist worldview on the personal-omniGod interpretation of its metaphysics—but only relative to the assumption that certain ethical judgements relating to right relationship amongst persons are endorsed from the perspective of that worldview.[42] Marilyn Adams agrees that there is, indeed, a deep issue about whether God would have perfectly loving relationships with finite persons on her scenario. She writes as follows:

> Even if God was within divine rights in permitting or producing [horrendous evils], there is the leftover question of whether and/or how God means to be good to us after the worst has already happened. John Bishop and Ken Perszyk have pressed a still deeper question: whether a God who set us up for horrors by creating us in a world like this has exhibited perfectly loving relationality toward us. Notice that the issue here is not Plantinga's pastoral question of how it is psycho-spiritually possible for participants in the worst evils to hold on to their trust in God. Instead, Bishop and Perszyk raise the morally prior question of whether a God who sets us up for horrors by creating us in a world like this, is trustworthy, whether God's track record in putting us in harm's way and not rescuing us takes God out of the category of people to whom it is reasonable to entrust oneself as to a parent or intimate friend. Such questions take us to the heart of relationship ethics, to the ethics of abandonment and betrayal, forgiveness and reconciliation. (Adams 2017, 25)

Adams here concedes the need to take seriously our claim that God's relations with creatures would fall short of the moral ideal under her 'defeat' scenario. As a personal-omniGod theist, she would nevertheless no doubt contest this claim, and perhaps might do so (as her reference to 'the ethics of abandonment and betrayal, forgiveness and reconciliation' may suggest) by holding that perfectly loving relationships with the personal God might

---

[42] We have previously drawn attention to this 'right relationship' version of the 'logical' Argument from Evil in our (2011) and (2016a). Other versions of such a norm-relative Argument from Evil are available—including the argument implicit in Dostoyevsky's character Ivan Karamazov's request to return his entrance ticket (Dostoyevsky 1958 [1880], Vol. 1, 287), which is relative to the specific ethical judgement that a supreme person who allows a child to be tortured to death when he could have prevented it cannot be perfectly good, no matter what else may be at stake.

be restored if the perpetrators and sufferers of horrors are able, post-mortem, not only to forgive each other, but also *to forgive God* for 'setting them up' for horrors.[43] Such a suggestion would need to explain, however, how it can be that if God needs forgiveness, it is not already presupposed that God is not perfectly morally good.

Alternatively, Adams might argue that God's relationality with persons is simply not subject to the moral norms that apply to finite persons and their relationships—a claim not much of a stretch beyond her avowed view that God does not have moral obligations to his creatures but is rather honour-bound in the manner of a benign patron to clients or a feudal lord to serfs.[44] That strategy, however, attenuates the notion of a person as it applies to God: being a person is conceptually a matter of being a person amongst persons, in relation with other persons, and (in certain ways, and under certain conditions) answerable to other persons. 'Putting God in the dock' may reasonably be thought blasphemous, but, arguably, if that blasphemy is to be avoided a conception of God as a person or personal agent cannot be maintained.[45]

There are, then, reasonable grounds for doubting the perfect goodness of an all-powerful personal being, and thus for rejecting such a being as the fit object of worship. A person on whose agency all else ultimately depends

---

[43] It is an important burden of Adams's 'defeat' scenario that it rests on the possibility that history continues in a post-mortem existence—i.e., on the possibility that significant inter-personal transactions and developments can take place in a life after death. Many personal-omniGod theists will not be concerned about this commitment, though some may balk at the fact that Adams's emphasis on God's unlimited resources in defeating evil leads her to universalism.

[44] Following the medieval philosophical theologians, Adams denies that God has moral obligations to his creatures—yet she still adheres to a personalist divine metaphysics. She writes as follows:

> To my mind, analytic philosophers of religion make an idol of morality, insisting that God's perfect goodness must be moral goodness, and maintaining that we have rights against God who has obligations to us. By contrast, my favorite five [Anselm, Bonaventure, Aquinas, Scotus, and Ockham] were unanimous that God is too big to be networked to us by rights and obligations. (2013, 22)

[45] According to Locke (1979 [1690], bk II, ch. 27, §26), '*Person*...is a Forensic Term appropriating Actions and their Merit; and so belongs only to intelligent Agents capable of a Law, and Happiness and Misery.' This forensic aspect seems essential to our modern sense of the term 'person'. This forensic sense did not, however, originate with Locke but goes back to the Romans: slaves, who had no legal rights and obligations, were not 'persons' (the *Lewis and Short Latin Dictionary* includes the following definition of *persona*: '*a being having legal rights and obligations* (including the state, etc.; not including slaves...)).' The medievals, then, would have been familiar with this forensic aspect of the concept of a person, and would have understood their claim that God neither has obligations nor has to invoke his rights in dealings with his creatures as entailing that God is not a *persona* in the sense defined.

could not—it may reasonably be thought—act in such a way as to be in perfectly good personal relationship with created persons. Such a supreme person might be judged too ineluctably dominating and yet at the same time too supernaturally remote to be capable of being in perfectly loving relationships with finite persons. Once one adds in the facts about the horrors in which many created persons actually participate, it becomes even more plausible to find fault in God's personally relating to them, even if (as on Marilyn Adams's account) God deploys unimaginably impressive resources in being good to sufferers 'after the worst has happened'. Specific commitments in relationship ethics are, of course, required to support these judgements—but the specific commitments needed, though not beyond debate, are hardly unreasonable.

Our 'normatively relativized' logical Argument from Evil is not a knock-down proof of the irrationality of personal-omniGod theism: rather, what it shows is that, for those who endorse certain reasonable judgements about what amounts to perfectly good personal action in relation to other persons, taking an omnipotent, ultimately all-controlling, personal agent as fitting the God-role would be idolatrous since, in the light of those normative judgements, such a being cannot—given the facts about horrendous evils—be judged to have the perfect worth required for the true object of worship. Personal-omniGod theorists may, of course, sincerely avow that they do not share the normative assumptions that generate this conclusion—assumptions about what God's personal goodness would have to be if God is to be worship-worthy. But they ought not to deny that those normative assumptions may be held reasonably, nor that, when they are held, they give rise to serious—and, for some, decisive—doubts about the worship-worthiness of the personal omniGod. On questions such as those here at issue, we think one may find oneself obliged to recognize that a position contrary to one's own may be supported by reasonable grounds, without thereby needing to accept, on pain of irrationality, an obligation to give up or modify one's own view. That's the situation in which, we think, personal-omniGod theorists ought to find themselves, if they consider fairly the doubts we've raised about the personal omniGod's transcendence and immanence (in Section 1.6) and relational goodness to sufferers of horrendous evils (in the present section). To grant sufficient motivation for considering alternative understandings of theism, personal-omniGod theists need only accept, as we have argued they should, that others may reasonably find unsatisfying replies which may, for them, dispel the doubts raised.

1.9 Theism without the Personal OmniGod?

The doubts we have canvassed in the preceding sections relating to divine transcendence and immanence and the perfect goodness of God in the light of horrors would, of course, if they could not be answered satisfactorily, serve as grounds for atheism. Or, at least, they would support atheism *if* the theist God has to be understood as the personal omniGod. We have, however, presented these doubts as doubts which some may reasonably hold about *the religious adequacy* of the personal-omniGod conception of the theist God. And doubts about religious adequacy are, necessarily, doubts *from the perspective of a religiously committed theist*. If these doubts could not be put to rest, *personal-omniGod atheism* would follow, but *outright atheism* need not. People for whom these doubts persist may be and may remain wholeheartedly committed to theist faith. For them, reflective faith, seeking understanding, rejects as religiously flawed the personal-omniGod understanding of theism, yet proceeds in the expectation that a different understanding may be found which may be endorsed as religiously adequate. Personal-omniGod atheism is thus for them only a rejection of an inadequate understanding of theism, motivated by continued theist faith-commitment and a determination to gain a better understanding of its object.

Doubts about the religious adequacy of the conception of God as personal omniGod may motivate, then, a search for an alternative, and preferable, understanding of theism. But what possible alternative accounts are there? We'll consider this question in the next chapter. We will explain why we think that a preference for a non-personalist understanding of the theist worldview is reasonable for those who retain theist commitment (or, at least, wish to keep it open as a reasonable stance) but who, like ourselves, persist in the kinds of doubts we have canvassed about the adequacy of personal-omniGod theism. This discussion in Chapter 2 will serve as a preliminary to our exposition and defence of a euteleological metaphysics in Chapters 3 and 4, given the potential we believe euteleology has as a metaphysics for theism alternative to the metaphysics of God as a person or personal being. We will not be claiming to provide a *complete* defence of euteleology as a fit metaphysics for theism. We will, however, (in Chapters 5 and 6) deal with two components which are vital for such a defence. These are, first, the question whether a euteleological theism may be vulnerable to a form of the Argument from Evil; and, second, the question how any non-personalist account can be adequate given what seems to be presupposed by the practices of worship and prayer. With these key components of a defence of its religious adequacy in place, we will be concluding that a euteleological theism deserves further consideration as a serious contender, both philosophically and religiously, for an understanding of theism without the supposedly perfectly good, all-powerful, and all-knowing personal supernatural agent on whom all else depends.

2
Personalist and Non-Personalist Understandings of Theism

How may the content of theist belief be understood other than as having, at its core, belief in a supernatural all-powerful, all-knowing, and perfectly good personal being—the personal omniGod? There are a good many other ways of thinking about gods or divinities, but can any of these provide viable ways of understanding *theism itself*, where theism is belief in the God of the Abrahamic religious traditions? Do those who, like ourselves, believe they have good reason to reject the personal-omniGod understanding of theism have recourse to any adequate alternative?

In this chapter, we will explain our reasons for favouring a *non-personalist* understanding of theism over *personalist* alternatives to personal-omniGod theism which retain a fundamental ontology of the divine as a supernatural personal being. Then, we will explain what motivates the specific, euteleological, non-personalist account whose main commitments we'll sketch at the end of this chapter, and then develop and defend in Chapters 3 and 4. Thus, we'll be situating euteleological theism in relation to other options for alternatives to the analytic philosopher's standard personal-omniGod understanding of theism—though we won't try to chart the full conceptual space of options here. We hope, however, that our account of what has motivated our development and defence of euteleology may help advance understanding of what the range of viable options are for a fundamental ontology of theism, and how they relate to other options for theories of ultimate reality (such as pantheist theories, for example) which do not count as theistic.

2.1 Retaining Theological Realism

One possibility that may tempt some philosophers who seek an understanding of theism without the personal omniGod is to adopt a non-realist interpretation of theism of the kind that logical positivism encouraged.[1] According to this view, theological claims are not 'factually meaningful', but have some other function—for example, as referring to a *fiction* constructed through unconscious collective processes to express and reinforce adherence to the religious community's core values. Theological non-realism captured the imagination of a generation of believers—or should we say ex-believers?—who found themselves no longer able to credit God as a real being, but continued to feel that the role played by belief in God remained culturally, morally, and spiritually important.[2]

Non-realist interpretations of theism do not, however, satisfy the criterion implied by Anselm's formula: only what is 'most truly' real can be unsurpassably great so far as greatness *in respect of being* is concerned.[3] Theological non-realists might well, of course, reject Anselm's formula, and the conception of worship on which it is implicitly based. Such a strategy seems, however, to be a *revisionary* one: arguably, theological non-realists more clearly identify their own view if they characterize it (as some do) as a 'religious atheism' or 'post-theism'.

In any case, we want to emphasize that the alternative to personal-omniGod theism we develop and defend in this book is not intended as a 'post-theist' revision, but as an understanding of the fundamental real ontology *of Abrahamic theism itself*. We accept theological *realism*. That is, we hold that any adequate understanding must construe theism as making distinctive claims about how things really are—*in reality*, and not, for example, purely within a fictional realm that plays a worthy mythical role in securing commitment to high ideals. We understand theist commitment as essentially involving a specific practical stance about the nature of ultimate reality as being, so to say, 'the God-way', quite independently of any

---

[1] For the famous 'falsification' debate over Antony Flew's presentation of the logical positivist view of theological utterances, see Flew and MacIntyre (1955).

[2] For defences of theological non-realism by theologians, see, e.g., Rudolf Bultmann (1961); Don Cupitt (1980); and Lloyd Geering (1994). Recent defences (especially of theological fictionalism) by philosophers include Robin Le Poidevin (1996, especially ch. 8, and 2016); Andrew Eshleman (2005); Peter Lipton (2007); and Natalja Deng (2015). For an overview of varieties of theological fictionalism, see Michael Scott and Finlay Malcolm (2018).

[3] This conditional claim is a conclusion which Anselm's Ontological Argument *does* support, we think, rather than the categorical claim that God exists and does so necessarily. Aquinas rejects Anselm's argument, without naming him, in *Summa Theologiae*, I, Q2, a.1, ad.2. Aquinas agrees, it seems, that if you really understand God as 'that than which nothing greater can be thought', you cannot help but understand that God exists (i.e., cannot help but think of God as existing), but he holds that it doesn't follow from this that God actually exists (i.e., exists extra-mentally).

human belief, theory, or fictional mythic construction. Personal-omniGod theism adheres to a metaphysics of theism—an account of the way reality fundamentally is if theism is true (if reality is 'the God-way')—according to which reality is the God-way only if there really exists a supernatural being which is the personal omniGod. Our alternative rejects that account, but it still purports to specify the way reality has to be for it to be the God-way.

It will emerge that our euteleological alternative understands what it is for reality to be the God-way in a manner that resists identifying God with any individual entity or particular feature of reality (or even with reality as a whole). For a euteleological theism, divine attributes are not to be understood as properties of a supreme individual entity. Nor is the address to God involved in worship and prayer to be understood as essentially directed to such an entity. It may therefore seem that euteleological theism *is* anti-realist at least with respect to God's existence as a personal being or individual entity and with respect to key religious practices. We will therefore return to the realism/anti-realism issue in later discussion. We will be maintaining our firm view that an adequate understanding of theism must be a realist one, and that our euteleological account is indeed a realist one, even if it has a feature which it shares with theological fictionalism (see Chapter 4, especially Section 4.7).

2.2 Need God Be Understood as Omnipotent?

Excluding non-realist options, then, what kinds of options may there be for differing understandings of how reality may be the God-way—that is, the way it is if theism holds true? There's an important difference between *personalist* options which retain the idea that God is a person or personal being, and *non-personalist* options which reject that idea, at least at the level of theism's fundamental ontology.

We'll consider, first, personalist alternatives which depart from the personal-omniGod account by holding that God's personal agency, though very powerful, is not fully *omnipotent* agency. A natural response to concerns about whether an omnipotent personal agent could also be perfectly good is to reject God's agential omnipotence, whilst retaining the conception of God as a perfectly good personal being. The problem of evil, in particular, seems more tractable if God doesn't have to be conceived as an *all*-powerful agent.

As remarked in Chapter 1, there are disagreements within the personal-omniGod 'family' over how to understand omnipotence. It may therefore be contentious whether a particular personalist account of theism does or does not retain omnipotence. Nevertheless, there are some conceptions of the theist God that *are* clearly outside the personal-omniGod mainstream because, though they retain a personal and supernatural Creator, they explicitly reject God's omnipotence. In our view, however, alternatives which remain committed to an ontology where God is a personal being do not succeed in dispelling the doubts raised in Chapter 1—namely, doubts about whether religiously adequate accounts may be provided of divine transcendence and immanence and of God's goodness as perfect personal goodness given the existence of horrendous evils. So long as God continues to be understood as a supernatural personal being these doubts about religious adequacy may remain sufficiently persistent to motivate interest in the possibility of a non-personalist account of theist metaphysics. To support this claim, we will now briefly review ways of understanding theism that adjust or reject agential omnipotence while (typically) retaining the idea of God as a supernatural personal being.

2.3 Omnipotence and Its Constraints

How, then, is God's omnipotence usually understood? It is rarely regarded as absolutely unlimited. Personal-omniGod theorists generally agree that God's unsurpassably great agential power is subject, like all agential power, to logical restrictions: God cannot create a round square, for example. Many hold, perhaps more controversially, that God's essential nature—in particular, God's goodness—may also limit God's power, so that, for example (as Hebrews 6:18 affirms), God is not able to lie. If God lacks the very power to do wrong, though, it seems that God has omnipotent agency only in a somewhat stretched sense.[4]

---

[4] For a defence of the claim that God's goodness limits God's power see, e.g., Wierenga (1989, 17). Personal-omniGod theorists have often been willing to allow that an omnipotent being may be unable to do many things that we who are clearly non-omnipotent may easily do. Those who aim to stick to the view that agential omnipotence has only logical limitations then have to work the trick of arguing that what appear to be non-logical limitations (such as God's not being able to lie) are really logical limitations, and hence not genuine limits on the power of divine agency at all. Understanding or defining omnipotence relative to what's logically possible to do given one's nature or essential properties is problematic, however: e.g., it seems that 'Mr McEar', a man who is so essentially limited that he can only scratch his left ear (and do

More controversially still, some philosophers claim to retain God's agential omnipotence despite its being subject to *non-logical* limitations. In particular, Alvin Plantinga's (1974b) 'Molinist' Free Will Defence ('FWD') against the 'logical' Argument from Evil relies crucially on the possibility that there are logically *contingent* truths over which God has no control and which therefore constrain God 'prior to' creation. Plantinga's FWD aims to show the consistency of the existence of the personal omniGod with the existence of (moral) evil by relying on the possible truth of the hypothesis of 'transworld depravity'. This hypothesis amounts to the claim that the essences of all possible free creaturely agents are such that, in whatever world God were to create (instantiate) them, they would freely choose to do wrong with respect to at least one moral choice. Thus, if the condition of transworld depravity obtains, though there are possible worlds in which all free creatures always freely do what is right, God cannot actualize any of these worlds.[5]

The possibility that (what came to be called) 'counterfactuals of creaturely freedom' might constrain God's options for creation depends on attributing *libertarian* freedom to finite free agents—more specifically, the 'agent-causal' freedom to resolve a free choice situation one way or another independently of all prior causal conditions including the actions of other agents, both creaturely and divine. Even if the notion of libertarian freedom is coherent (which is open to dispute[6]), a divine omnipotence constrained by what free creatures would freely choose to do in given situations in which they might be actualized seems to be a notion of agential omnipotence stretched to breaking-point. God's creating finite agents with libertarian

---

what little else may be entailed by ear-scratching) turns out to be omnipotent. The example was introduced in recent times by Plantinga (1967, 170) and baptized 'Mr McEar' by Richard La Croix (1977, 189, note 5); Thomas Flint and Alfred Freddoso (1983, note 4) tell us that the identification of this problem goes back to (at least) the late middle ages.

[5] Plantinga's FWD is Molinist because it presupposes that God can have 'middle' knowledge of what would occur if certain conditions were to be actualized. The claim that this kind of knowledge is available to God was made by Luis de Molina (1535–1600), after whom 'Molinism' is named: middle knowledge is somehow intermediate between God's knowledge of all possibilities and God's knowledge, consequent on God's creative act, of what is actual. It is contested whether there is any such thing as middle knowledge. For an introduction to the main contemporary debates, see Perszyk (2013). Plantinga (1985a and elsewhere) suggests that the assumption of Molinism in his FWD was a mere concession to atheologians such as Mackie. For a detailed evaluation of this claim, see Perszyk (1998).

[6] The coherence of a libertarian account of finite free action (widely assumed by personal-omniGod theorists) is contested by compatibilists, both within a theological context and outside it. For an excellent critical discussion of the main types of libertarianism, see Randolph Clarke (2003). Robert Kane (2005) is an accessible introduction to some of the main problems with libertarianism.

freedom must surely limit God's effective omnipotence, making finite agents tantamount to 'mini-co-creators' with God. If that is correct, then Plantinga's defence *rejects* God's omnipotence and, accordingly, implies a revised alternative to the conception of God as personal omniGod.[7]

Plantinga's Free Will Defence, then, arguably gives up on the omnipotence of the personal God. That is not, of course, how Plantinga himself sees it; but there certainly are a good many philosophers who explicitly propose 'personalist' alternatives to the personal-omniGod conception which reject omnipotence, and in the next two sections we will review some of these in order to explain why our own preference is for a non-personalist alternative. While we have Plantinga's FWD in mind, however, we'll detour briefly to revisit and reinforce a major plank in our argument in Chapter 1— namely our appeal (in Section 1.8) to a 'normatively relativized' 'logical' argument from evil as a key motivating factor for seeking an alternative to the personal-omniGod account of theist metaphysics.

As well as (arguably) giving up on omnipotence, it's also arguable that in any case Plantinga's FWD fails to vindicate the personal God's perfect goodness. Doubts may remain about whether God, when understood as creating a world containing evil under the constraints envisaged in Plantinga's FWD scenario, could possibly have the perfect personal goodness needed to be worthy of worship. Mackie would not be alone in thinking that the God of Plantinga's FWD would be guilty of 'malice aforethought' (1982, 176). For example, could God be a supremely perfect person worthy of worship if God knew Hitler's counterfactuals of freedom, went ahead and created him, and placed him in precisely those circumstances that God knew would result in the Holocaust? Plantinga's FWD may thus seem to leave wide open the vital issue of *the religious adequacy* of a personal God who allows evil for freedom's sake.[8] Plantinga evidently thinks God *will* have personal

---

[7] As noted earlier (Chapter 1, p.30) the coherence of Plantinga's FWD is disputed, with Mackie (1982, ch. 9) rejecting it primarily on the grounds that it admits non-logical limitations on omnipotence. What Mackie found particularly incoherent was the idea that 'prior' to creation an omnipotent God would simply have to put up with certain contingent truths (it is important to emphasize that transworld depravity, which supervenes on contingently true counterfactuals of freedom, would be merely an accidental property of those creaturely essences that it afflicts). Others also hold the view that Plantinga has in fact abandoned omnipotence. See, e.g., Wes Morriston (1984).

[8] As Nelson Pike points out, it is not clear that a perfectly good God who found himself unable to create a world with free creatures who never went wrong, would go ahead and create them nevertheless, rather than creating a world without morally significant freedom or even no world at all (see Pike 1979, 454f). (Furthermore, a religiously adequate resolution of the problem posed by a 'logical' Argument from Evil seems to require understanding what, for all

goodness sufficient for worship-worthiness, provided that the world God creates—despite the misfortune of transworld depravity—exhibits an overall net surplus of goodness over evil.[9] Yet, as we have argued in Chapter 1 (Section 1.8), it may reasonably be held that God's perfect personal goodness must include always acting perfectly well in relation to other persons, and, furthermore, that it is reasonable (though not rationally obligatory) to hold an ethics of inter-personal relationship from which it follows that the personal Creator could not have acted perfectly well in relationship with the created persons implicated in horrendous evils. Reasonable assumptions about what's needed for *worship-worthy* personal goodness may, then, support the view that, given horrendous evils, a personal agent, whether strictly omnipotent or not, who exercised world-actualizing power in creating this world *logically could not* have *that kind* of perfect goodness. A norm-relative version of a 'logical' argument from horrendous evils may thus remain intact, even if (as is anyway contestable) Plantinga's FWD is conceded to be successful in its own terms. Contrary to what many seem to have thought, Plantinga's Free Will Defence does not close the door on 'logical' arguments from evil against the reasonableness of belief in the existence of the personal omniGod.

2.4 Rejecting Omnipotence—Minor Departures

Some philosophers make omnipotence-related adjustments to the standard personalist account of theism, but not particularly with a view to resolving the specific doubts about the religious adequacy of personal-omniGod theism we raised in Chapter 1 (Sections 1.4–1.8). For example, Peter Geach rejects omnipotence understood as power to *do* all things, in favour of

---

we know, could possibly give a perfectly good and all-powerful God morally sufficient reason for permitting evil. But an appeal merely to the logical possibility of transworld depravity may not be enough for that, especially given Plantinga's own emphasis on the point that, for the purpose of 'defence', the hypothesized third proposition (consistent with omniGod's existence and entailing moral evil) 'need not be true, or probable, or plausible...or anything of the sort....it can do its job perfectly well even if it is extraordinarily improbable or known to be false' (1985b, 43; see also Plantinga 1974b, 165).)

[9] Plantinga's FWD relies in part on the possible truth of the following value-judgement: 'a world containing creatures who are sometimes significantly free (and freely perform more good than evil actions) is more valuable, all else being equal, than a world containing no free creatures at all' (1974b, 166). The idea that a favourable balance of (moral) good over evil is enough for consistency with God's perfect goodness is also found in Plantinga (1967, 132) and (1974a, part I, §A, subsections 4, 9, and 10).

'almightiness', understood as power *over* all things—and Geach does so because he thinks that a coherent account of agential omnipotence is simply not to be had.[10] But doubts about the perfect goodness of the personal Creator given the existence of horrendous evils, or about God as 'a person amongst persons' lacking the necessary divine transcendence, evidently won't be dispelled by moving from omnipotence to almightiness in Geach's sense.

A similar point applies to Yujin Nagasawa's (2008) proposal that 'Anselmian' theists need be committed only to the 'maximal God thesis', not the 'omniGod thesis'. Nagasawa's suggestion is that the idea of God's 'omniperfection' (understood as possessing maximal power, plus maximal knowledge, plus maximal goodness) be replaced by the idea of God's having *the maximal consistent set* of power, knowledge, and benevolence.[11] But, as Nagasawa himself notes, 'even if it is left open that God is not omniperfect, one might still wonder why there is evil in the actual world' (2008, 596): indeed, in accordance with our line of argument in Chapter 1 (Section 1.8), it may reasonably be argued that—relative to accepting certain norms about goodness in personal relationship—whatever a 'maximal God' may be able to do to defeat horrendous evils after they have happened, that being cannot be worthy of worship if it could have, but did not, prevent those evils from occurring in the first place.

2.5 Rejecting Omnipotence—Major Departures (e.g., Process Theism)

But perhaps God really *could not* have prevented horrors from happening? Perhaps the 'maximal consistent set of power, knowledge, and benevolence' in virtue of which the Creator is *overall* the greatest possible being matches

---

[10] Geach agrees that God may be said to be omnipotent where the term is used, as Thomas Hobbes put it, as 'an attribute of honour', but continues as follows:

> When people have tried to read into 'God can do everything' a signification not of Pious Intention but of Philosophical Truth, they have only landed themselves in intractable problems and hopeless confusions; no graspable sense has ever been given to this sentence that did not lead to self-contradiction or at least to conclusions manifestly untenable from a Christian point of view. (1977, 4)

[11] A similar proposal to Nagasawa's was made by George Schlesinger (1988), who suggested that it need not be impossible for there to be a being with more power (or knowledge, etc.) than God; what is impossible is for there to be a being who is *overall* greater than God by virtue of having this added power (or knowledge, etc.).

loving goodness and vast wisdom with a power in relation to the created world which is significantly constrained and even weak—or, at least, has become so, through the *kenosis* (self-emptying) of the divine creative act. That is the view of some philosophers who retain a personalist account but depart from omnipotence boldly and decisively, and who believe that so doing may facilitate our reconciling the existence of evil with our understanding of divine power and goodness in relation to creatures.

Process theology provides a prime example of just such a bold rejection of omnipotence (understood as unilateral agential power).[12] Process views typically hold that God co-evolves with the world in a give-and-take relationship with creatures, and God's saving power is a persuasive 'lure', the power of love, a matter of empowerment rather than dominating control, so that God doesn't—and, indeed, *cannot*—unilaterally have the agential power to control all things. Views like this, though they usually retain an understanding of God as a personal being,[13] are clearly outside standard personal-omniGod theism, since they reject the idea that God is omnipotent on any of the standard accounts of omnipotence given by personal-omniGod theists.

Another view which rejects God's agential omnipotence is Peter Forrest's (2007) speculative 'developmental theism'. On Forrest's account, God is *primordially* an omnipotent agent who brings into existence a universe which achieves great good at the cost of great suffering, and God then *develops into* a morally perfect personal being seeking to be good to each creature but—through the kenosis of creation—no longer all-powerful.[14]

How much can these kinds of revisions to the standard understanding of divine power achieve in countering the doubts about religious adequacy we raised in relation to the personal omniGod in Chapter 1? In so far as these departures from omnipotence still retain God as a personal agent, they are committed to understanding God's goodness as personal goodness, and hence, at least *prima facie*, amounting to (or including) moral goodness. And God's moral goodness does seem more open to defence as consistent

---

[12] Process theism is based on or derived from the work of A. N. Whitehead, with subsequent developments by Charles Hartshorne: there is a wide variety of process views. For a useful introduction, see John Cobb and David Ray Griffin (1976), or, more recently, Robert Mesle (1993).

[13] Most process theologians appear to belong within the personalist camp (see, e.g., Griffin (2000, 13)), though this may not be true of Whitehead himself. See Cobb (2003, 12–14) and Viney (2014, 11–12) for further discussion.

[14] Forrest's developmental theism clearly retains divine personhood: he defends what he calls 'properly anthropocentric metaphysics' (2007, ch. 2, §2).

with the facts about evil when God's power is understood as the power of love—a power to influence and even at times to goad, but never to exercise dominating control over creaturely persons. Such a God may even be, as some theologians have maintained, a 'co-sufferer' with us.[15]

Still, concerns about God's moral goodness in relationship with creatures may remain on any view in which God continues to be understood as the personal agent whose free action brings into existence *ex nihilo* a world in which horrendous evil occurs. On such a view, even if God is not omnipotent, God's *ultimate* responsibility for horrors cannot be denied, assuming, of course, that God knew at the outset that a decision to create (when God could have refrained) would have, or would be likely to have, the existence of horrendous evil as a consequence.[16] One might, however, *reject* creation *ex nihilo*—as process theists standardly do. And, indeed, creation stories in the Hebrew scriptures (see Genesis 1 in particular) do portray the Creator as bringing order to or from a primordial chaos rather than as creating *ex nihilo*.[17] So, there seems room for the kind of alternative process theologians favour, namely, a metaphysics that holds that God and the world are co-primordial and that God's creative project is essentially a process in which God and the natural order co-evolve, with God being affected by, and having to respond to, what occurs in the natural world, in order to continue to make it, truly, God's creation.

Such an account has the difficulty that it apparently posits something co-eternal with God which may constrain God's power—which is inconsistent with the absolute ontological primacy and independence that must be attributed to God, if God is to fit Anselm's description as 'that than which a greater cannot be thought'. This difficulty might be overcome under a 'panentheism' in which the world is, in some sense, 'in' God, though God is 'more than' the world (unlike in pantheism, which identifies God with the world taken as an overall unity).[18] Alternatively, it may be possible to retain

---

[15] On the notion of a co-suffering God, see, e.g., Jürgen Moltmann (1974); Nicholas Wolterstorff (1987, 1988); and Paul Fiddes (1992).

[16] The idea that the existence of evil is inconsistent with the doctrine of creation when creation is understood as *ex nihilo* goes back at least as far as Hermogenes, as reported by Tertullian in his *Treatise against Hermogenes*, c. 203 CE.

[17] The doctrine of creation *ex nihilo* didn't become standard teaching until around the last quarter of the 2nd century CE. Gerhard May (1994) provides the classic discussion of this doctrine's emergence.

[18] A panentheist view of this kind is found in Hartshorne: 'The world consists of individuals, but the totality of individuals as a physical or spatial whole *is God's body*, the Soul of which is God. So there is no eternal, worldly, individual to rival God' (1984, 94; emphasis ours). According to Cross and Livingstone (2005, 1221), the standard generic definition of 'panentheism' ('all-in-God-ism') is 'the belief that the Being of God includes and penetrates the

creation *ex nihilo*, yet argue (with the 'open theists') that God's maximal knowledge cannot include any advance recognition that horrendous evil will certainly result from giving effect to Love's desire to share its life with finite creatures.[19]

Some may think, then, that there are personalist accounts of theism which offer good prospects for dispelling doubts about the Creator's goodness arising from the existence of horrendous evils. It may seem that a personal God's goodness may be preserved by revising the standard account of God's omnipotence and/or omniscience. But, even if there are such prospects, a new kind of doubt about the religious adequacy of the resulting conception of God may then emerge which did not affect the personal omniGod: can a less-than-omnipotent God still have *enough* power to be trustworthy in the role of ultimate saviour, something which is an essential component of God's role as theism conceives it? Can a co-suffering God, for example, or a God who has to take risks and 'wait and see' how to respond to the free actions of his creatures, also be trustworthy as saviour and fulfiller of the purposes of creation? In any case, however, adjustments to God's omnipotent power which still retain God's status as a supreme personal being will continue to situate God as Creator in a separate 'uncreated' ontological category; so, those doubts will remain which we outlined in Chapter 1 (Section 1.6) about whether adequate transcendence over, or immanence in, the creation could belong to a God who is an individual supernatural personal being.

2.6 Non-Personalist, 'Naturalist', Alternatives

We think there is reasonable motivation, then, for those who reject personal-omniGod theism for the kinds of reasons we have canvassed to

---

whole universe, so that every part of it exists in Him, but (as against pantheism) that His Being is more than, and is not exhausted by, the universe.' 'Pantheism' is there defined as 'the belief or thought that God and the universe are identical' (p. 1223). We'll say more later about what the world's being 'in' God may mean in considering whether our euteleological theism may be classified as a version of panentheism (see Chapter 4, Section 4.12).

[19] See, e.g., Philip Clayton (2008), who draws on process thought and tries to synthesize it with key insights from open theism. Arguably, however, the open theist ploy of denying foreknowledge (or middle knowledge) doesn't get God off the hook for horrors, for it turns out that (if God is not to succumb to the charge of reckless risk-taking) God has nearly perfect 20-20 vision before horrors occur and retains (under open theism) the power to intervene unilaterally to prevent them. On a straight process view, it seems that God simply cannot unilaterally prevent evil given the constraints on his power, though God might have gotten (far) less evil if he hadn't encouraged the evolution of free beings such as ourselves.

reject *altogether* personalist accounts committed to a fundamental ontology of God as a personal being. That motivation favours, not only a *non-personalist*, but also what may be described as a *naturalist* metaphysics for theism—although caution is needed in the use of this term if the intended notion of a 'naturalist theism' is to be properly grasped.[20]

Theism's affirmation of God's distinctness as Creator from, and transcendence over, all created beings that make up the natural Universe clearly signals that God's existence is, in a certain obvious sense, a *super*natural matter. No viable account of theism can be 'naturalist' if—as is common in contemporary philosophical usage—'naturalism' names the thesis that concrete reality consists ultimately of nothing more nor less than the natural Universe *as known or potentially knowable through empirical scientific inquiry*.[21]

As already noted, however, when God's existence is understood as the existence of a personal being who creates the natural Universe *ex nihilo* by way of his own free intentional action, the essential distinctness of God from creation requires that God exists as a being belonging to a separate ontological category from that of created beings. A 'supernatural/natural' dualism of concrete beings then results, as between uncreated beings (necessarily with just one member) and created beings (all others). As we argued in the previous chapter (Chapter 1, Section 1.6), this dualism may be religiously problematic because both God's transcendence over and God's immanence in the creation may be thought to be unsatisfactorily limited if God relates to creatures as one individual being to other individual beings. To avoid this problem, then, we need to favour a non-personalist metaphysics for theism for which God is, not only not a person, but also not 'a' being at all. Such a metaphysics might then reasonably be described as 'naturalist', in so far as its ontology of concrete beings places all such beings in a single ontological category (in other words, for such a metaphysics, to be 'a' concrete being is to be a creaturely, natural, one). That sort of naturalism,

---

[20] One of us—Bishop (2018b)—has previously defended a non-personalist understanding of theism under the banner of 'naturalist theism'. In earlier joint work, too, we've used the term 'naturalism' to describe our proposed theist metaphysics, but we've been careful to distinguish the sense intended from other senses of the term, as we are about to explain here (see our 2016a, 116).

[21] This kind of naturalism may be called 'scient*istic* naturalism'. We think that this term is preferable to the more common 'scient*ific* naturalism', since the latter term may refer just to the methodological principle that bars the positing of non-empirically testable entities, rather than to the 'scientistic' metaphysical claim that nothing can be concretely real unless the question of its existence is able to be settled in principle by empirical tests.

however, is consistent with affirming God's absolute transcendence over all beings, and is distinct from the kind of naturalism that holds nothing to be concretely real unless it features in the ontology of the natural sciences. We seek a non-personalist theist metaphysics, then, that affirms God's transcendence yet rejects an understanding of that transcendence as a matter of God's reality consisting in God as a transcendent *being*.[22]

There are many who will urge, however, that any such non-personalist understanding of theism must fail to be religiously adequate in ways a good deal more concerning than those which we have suggested may be thought to impair the religious adequacy of personalist accounts which imply a dualism of supernatural (uncreated) and created beings. We have already acknowledged (Chapter 1, Section 1.6) what lies behind this allegation— namely, the claim, not only that the sacred scriptures of the theist traditions use personal language in reference to God, but also that the very concepts of key theist religious practices such as worship and prayer render it essential that the one who is worshipped, and to whom intercession is made, is a personal being who can hear and respond. It might be conceded, then, that the doubts we have so far raised about the religious adequacy of conceptions of God as a personal being have *some* weight—and yet it still be contended that much weightier doubts attach to the religious adequacy of any non-personalist account.

We acknowledge that point of view, we know it is widely held—and we take it seriously.[23] We maintain, however, that a fair assessment of the

---

[22] An adequate account of theism that avoids the kind of ontological dualism associated with God as an individual personal being, which we have described here as a certain kind of naturalism, might equally reasonably be described as a non-dualist supernaturalism, since, to be adequate, it must somehow accommodate God's absolute transcendence over, and therefore distinctness from, the natural created order. As remarked in Chapter 1 (note 1), Fiona Ellis argues that there are senses of 'naturalism' and 'the supernatural' which need not be opposed. An 'expansive naturalism' (Ellis 2014, 2) can accommodate elements that would count as non-natural or supernatural from a natural scientistic perspective. As we'll explain in the following two chapters, the alternative euteleological metaphysics we propose posits, beyond anything science could contemplate, a transcendent overall purpose for the creation, yet without commitment to a dualism *of beings* (uncreated and created). In Ellis's terms, then, our proposal counts as a form of 'expansive naturalism'.

[23] Here is a small sample of philosophers who claim that it is essential to theism to believe that God is a person or personal being. Richard Swinburne (1996, 3): 'Theism claims that God is a personal being—that is, in some sense a *person*'; William Wainwright (2017): 'theists believe that a maximally great reality must be a maximally great *person* or God'; William Alston (1981, 151): 'The conception of God as a personal agent is deeply imbedded in Christianity and in other theistic religions'; H. P. Owen (1967, 97): 'THEISM signifies belief in one God (*theos*) who is (a) personal, (b) worthy of adoration, and (c) separate from the world but (d) continuously active in it'; and John Hick (1973, 4–5): '*Theism*...is strictly belief in a deity, but is generally used to mean belief in a personal deity.'

relative alleged religious inadequacies of personalist versus non-personalist accounts can be made *only after* the elaboration of a non-personalist interpretation of theism has been attempted. We've already argued (Chapter 1, Section 1.6) that the idea that God transcends personhood even though God is properly addressable by humans in personal ways is clearly to be found in the scriptures of the theist traditions, and that, therefore, no swift, open and shut, dismissal of non-personalism as religiously inadequate can be justified. We think that it's only fair, then, to allow that, given the doubts raised about personalist understandings of theism, it's worth persisting with the project of trying to articulate as best we may a plausible candidate for a non-personalist account. The hope will then be that an understanding of theism without a supernatural personal being will not only provide more religiously adequate notions of divine transcendence, immanence, and goodness (given the facts about evil), but also make available reasonable accounts of both prayer and worship. Whether that hope can be fulfilled is a question we will consider in Chapters 5 and 6, once we have explained and defended euteleology as our best candidate for a non-personalist understanding of the metaphysics of theism (in Chapters 3 and 4). In the remainder of the present chapter we'll explain what led us to favour a specifically euteleological metaphysics for a non-personalist account of theism's stance on the nature of ultimate reality.

2.7 'Classical' Theism as Non-Personalist

It might well be suggested that the best candidate for a non-personalist understanding of theism will be (some version of) the classical theism of the medieval philosophers which (as observed in Chapter 1, Section 1.5) seems in tension with personal-omniGod theism. Though analytic philosophers do, as we have noted, have a tendency to treat personal-omniGod theism as 'classical' theism, the medieval philosophical understanding of theism is open to an interpretation that neither takes God to be a personal being nor treats God's distinctness from creation as a separation of God *as a being* from the world of creatures. Why not argue, then, that the way forward is to champion this traditional non-personalist account of theist metaphysics as the authentically classical theism?[24] Such an approach would

---

[24] This approach would thus endorse Brian Davies's distinguishing authentically classical theism from 'theistic personalism' (2004, 8) (already noted, Chapter 1, pp. 17–18). It may,

focus on defending divine simplicity under an interpretation which (as noted in Chapter 1, pp. 21-2) entails that, since God lacks the 'composition' of essence and existence, God is not an individual entity of any kind, and therefore not a supernatural person producing and operating upon the created world from outside it.

But how may such a classical theism provide us with an understanding of what God *positively is*? Its emphasis seems to be on *negative, apophatic,* theology: God is *im*mutable, *a*temporal, *im*passible. God's simplicity is also apophatic: as already noted, God's simplicity is God's *non*-compositeness. And God's necessity, too, may just be God's *non*-contingency.

Positive descriptions for the divine are not hard to find, however. Theist faith-commitment has rich positive content. By faith, believers accept as revealed truth a 'salvation-historical' narrative of divine action, and God may thus be positively described with reference to this narrative—as, for example, the God of Abraham, Isaac, and Jacob, the One who brought Israel out of Egypt, etc.[25] Specific doctrines, too, may be accepted as divinely revealed, and these also give rise to positive descriptions—for example (so far as Christianity is concerned), descriptions of God as Tri-une, as incarnate in the Christ, 'reconciling the world to himself' (2 Corinthians 5:19). Evidently, then, classical theism affirms of God positive *faith-tradition-mediated* descriptions of these kinds.

Reflective theist faith does, however, seek understanding beyond what's conveyed by the faith-tradition-mediated descriptions which suffice for 'simple', accepting, faith. (Simple faith may, perhaps, be the purest and best kind of faith. We're not wishing to imply that reflective faith is superior, though we think that a faith community that lacked reflectiveness altogether would be impoverished.) Reflective faith seeks to understand *who or what it is* that is revealed as the One who brought Israel out of Egypt, who, in Christ, was reconciling the world to himself, and so on. Reflective faith seeks especially to understand *the grounds of the worship-worthiness* it

---

incidentally, be preferable to use the term 'personalist theism' to note understandings of theism for which God is a person or personal being, since, as Thomas Schärtl-Trendel has pointed out to us, 'theistic personalism' is often taken to denote a certain movement of existentialist Catholic philosophy in early 20th-century Germany. For further discussion of the question whether classical, medieval theism is, or is not, personalist, see Schärtl-Trendel's 'Introduction' to Schärtl et al. (2016).

[25] The One who speaks from the burning bush, though, as noted before (Chapter 1, pp. 25-6), refusing to be named, does describe himself to Moses, saying, 'I am the God of your ancestors, . . . the God of Abraham, the God of Isaac, and the God of Jacob' (Exodus 3:6).

affords to this Revealed One, lest it risk being drawn into idolatry through attachment to philosophical theorizing that over-reaches itself.

2.8 Divine 'Incomprehensibility' and Its Implications

But may reflective faith reasonably expect anything more than a negative, apophatic, *understanding* of the God about whom it accepts as revealed many positive truths? Confining oneself to the apophatic might seem just what's required when the quest for understanding is undertaken with a humility that accepts *divine incomprehensibility* (itself, of course, a higher order apophatic attribute). To contemporary ears, 'God is incomprehensible' may be heard as the assertion that God is wholly unintelligible—in other words, as the assertion that we have no idea what we are talking about when we talk about God. But divine incomprehensibility doesn't have this implication: it implies that God can't be 'comprehended' only in the sense that finite minds cannot gain the kind of controlling intellectual mastery over what God is as they can over a theorem of Euclid, for example, and not in the sense that God's nature cannot be understood at all.[26]

The question thus arises *how much* intelligibility reflective theist faith may be able to attain. The suggestion that such understanding can only be apophatic may be one possible view. But, in fact, there is wide acceptance of the idea that reflective faith may proceed beyond comprehending what God is not. A *purely* apophatic theology seems empty and perhaps not even coherently stateable. Philosophers of theism have offered positive, *cataphatic*, accounts of God's being and nature, and have thought that doing so does not commit the hubris of trespassing beyond the limits of human understanding. They have thought, in other words, that some positive understanding of the revealed divine can be achieved while recognizing its limitations and remaining humbly respectful of God's incomprehensibility.

Apparently positive understandings of God are to be found, too, in the works of the medieval philosophers themselves. Their account of theism holds that God is *a se* (literally, 'from oneself'). Although aseity is an absolute *lack* of ontological dependence, God's existing without any dependence on any other being is surely a supremely *positive* attribute (indeed, arguably, it is from God's positive aseity that all the apophatic attributes are derived).

---

[26] Stephen T. Davis (2017) argues that, contrary to much of the tradition, God as revealed to us does *in part* accurately reflect God's essence. God's essence is not totally hidden from us.

We may also find in the work of the medieval theist thinkers characterizations that make intelligible (though not fully comprehensible) the divine aseity. Aquinas, for example, says that God is 'pure act'[27]—though maybe this is an apophatic description in disguise (if it means just that there is no 'potency', or unrealized potential, in God). But Aquinas also says that God is *ipsum esse subsistens*, which is surely an indisputably positive description, and the source of a contemporary view which takes Aquinas's positive conception of God to be of 'Being itself'.[28]

In any case, it is beyond dispute that some positive account is needed of the essential elements in the theist worldview—of what it is, fundamentally, for reality to be 'the God-way'. Without some positive account, there's no way of understanding what's at issue when we ask important questions about the justification of theist faith-commitment, such as whether it contributes to, or may even be necessary for, a life well lived, or whether it is or is not to be preferred to alternative religious or non-religious overall orientations to the world. Given the centrality to the theist worldview of the idea of God as Creator of all (else) that exists, *on the face of it* a positive understanding of the theist worldview will include (indeed, will turn on) a positive account of what God is. However, although the two seem closely linked, understanding what it is, positively, for reality to be the God-way is *not* just the very same thing as providing a positive account of who or what God is. (The importance of this point will be apparent in Chapter 4 when it emerges that, on our euteleological proposal, although a positive description may be given of what it is for reality to be as theism claims it to be, God is not to be identified *as a particular entity* amongst other entities at the level of euteleology's fundamental ontology.)

2.9 Setting Aside the Debate about 'Classical' Theism

How appealing would it be, then, for those seeking a non-personalist interpretation of theism to try to defend (some version of) the classical theism found in the medieval philosophical theologians? Affirming divine simplicity interpreted as an essentially apophatic claim provides an understanding

---

[27] See, for example, *Summa Theologiae*, I, Q9.
[28] God is described as *ipsum esse subsistens* at *Summa Theologiae*, I, Q3, a.4 and *Summa Contra Gentiles*, I, 22. According to Mark Johnston, 'on Thomas's view, in the disclosure [to Moses] of the tetragrammaton [Exodus 3: 13–14], the Highest One reveals himself as "Ipsum Esse," that is, Being, or Existence Itself' (2009, 97).

of theism for which God is *not* a supernatural personal being producing and operating upon the world from 'outside' it. But what more would need to be added to offer enough *positive* understanding to secure religiously adequate accounts of God's transcendence, immanence, and goodness in the face of horrors? And are there positive accounts of these attributes which fit with a non-personalist metaphysics and overcome the kind of doubts that arise when these attributes are interpreted as belonging to a personal being?

For example, could Aquinas's *ipsum esse subsistens* succeed in exhibiting God as, at once, absolutely transcendent over creation yet also fully immanent within it? Aquinas's account certainly portrays concrete reality as profoundly integrated—as the sheer actuality ('pure act') in which each particular thing participates and on which it is wholly dependent.[29] But how does *ipsum esse subsistens* fare when it comes to God's goodness—goodness which, to recall the implications of divine simplicity, Aquinas does not think God 'possesses' in the way that a personal being does? Horrors, in all their concreteness, must on this view be sustained by, and somehow participate in, Being Itself, a view which, on the face of it, is at odds with God's goodness—although, arguably, this difficulty might be removed by appeal to the classical doctrine that evil is *privation of the good*—the lack of the good *that is due*, the good *that there ought to be*.[30]

But we will not ourselves proceed under the banner of defending classical theism as a non-personalist understanding of theism. We sympathize with such a project, and we will deploy resources from the medieval philosophical theologians in presenting our own non-personalist alternative, including the just mentioned 'privationist' account of evil to which we will return in Chapter 5 (see Section 5.7). But we are neither envisaging nor advertising the proposal we are about to elaborate as a revival of a classical theist view—even if, in fact, it might be reasonable to view it in that way. This is for the following reason.

In so far as positive understanding of God is offered in medieval classical theist metaphysics, it is often (rightly or wrongly) regarded as 'too

---

[29] As W. Chalmers Smith's 19th-century hymn, 'Immortal, invisible, God only wise', has it:
> To all life thou givest—to both great and small;
> In all life thou livest, the true life of all…

In fact, the suggested idea of God's immanence is more radical still: 'in all *existents* thou *exists*, the true *existence* of all'.

[30] For a defence of 'evil as privation of the good' in dealing with the problem of evil, see, e.g., Brian Davies (2006).

'philosophical' and religiously remote if not wholly inept. For example, if Aquinas's positive account of God is taken to be that God is 'Being itself', it may seem either that God is being identified with an abstract or Platonic universal, or else, in pantheist style, with concrete existence as a whole. Neither identification could be adequate for the fit object of theist worship. This reaction may be unfair. But we won't attempt the task of vindicating an anyway (amongst analytic philosophers) controversial non-personalist account of classical theism against the general charge that such an account is, at the very least, too religiously austere. Rather, while acknowledging the influence on our thinking of a non-personalist way of reading classical theism, we'll try to consider *directly* how a non-personalist understanding of theism might be drawn from the 'insider' perspective of faith-commitment in a theist religious tradition. We'll do this, in particular, from the perspective of Christianity, the only tradition in which we are well-enough versed to have reasonable prospects of articulating an insider's view. A similar project might, of course, be conducted by those well versed in the 'insider' perspective of Jewish or Islamic faith, and—it may perhaps be—the results would converge.

2.10 'God Is Love': An Emergentist View

We'll continue, then, to trace the path that led us to our euteleological proposal, now that we have explained our preference for a certain kind of non-personalist understanding of what it is for reality to be as theism claims it to be ('the God-way'). Those in search of a non-personalist account who reflect on Christian sources specifically may be struck by the ethically potent scriptural identification of God with love: 'God is love, and those who abide in love abide in God, and God abides in them' (1 John 4:16b). Christianity teaches that God abides where there is love, in the sense of *agapē*, signifying right, just, and harmonious relationship.[31] The character of agapeistic

---

[31] This identification of God with love is ethically significant because of its obvious connexion with the 'new commandment' Jesus gave his disciples at the last supper: 'I give you a new commandment, that you love one another. Just as I have loved you, you also should love one another' (John 13:34). Christian theologians have, of course, explored the idea that God is love—for recent examples, see Thomas Jay Oord (2010 and 2015) and Paul Fiddes (2017). (Fiddes is notable for arguing that identifying God with love need not imply any reduction of God to something created; Fiddes also resists a common view that *agapē* needs to be sharply distinguished from other forms of love, especially from *eros*.) The idea that God's power is the power of love is an important theme in process theology (a point to which we return below).

relationship is aptly described using a term applicable in Christian theology to the love that unites the Persons of the Trinity, namely, *perichoresis*, which literally means that each 'gives way, or makes space, for the other'. Agapeistic relationship is thus born from and sustained by love of another as oneself, a deep welcoming and appreciation of the other's worth. The bold scriptural claim that God *is* love might suggest a metaphysics for (Christian) theism which takes God's being to be essentially relational and to consist in perichoretic, agapeistic, relationship amongst persons. This suggested account, though highly person*al*, is non-personalist in its metaphysics, since it understands God not as 'a' person, but, rather, as the highest form of actual, concrete, relationship amongst persons. According to this proposal, God 'resides' nowhere else but where concrete loving relationships flourish.[32]

How adequate would such a proposal be—namely, that God is the (highest form of) love that *emerges* in the Universe in relationships amongst persons? It seems clear that a purely *emergentist* conception of the divine, such as this, lacks certain essentials for an adequate understanding of theism: as Thomas Schärtl-Trendel observes, it 'turns theism's understanding of the God-world relationship on its head' (Schärtl et al. 2016, 16). Rather than God's being the creator on which all else depends, a God who literally is love (= concrete loving relationships) would be contingently dependent on the long history of the evolving Universe. Christian theology says that 'God is love', but it does not follow that God's being may be reduced to identity with the concrete loving relationships that occur within the Universe. Such an identification seems clearly incompatible with God's transcendence, as Creator, over all that is created, loving relationships included.

2.11 Love as the Overall Purpose of the Creation: Towards Euteleology

Nevertheless, though God may not be reduced to loving relationality amongst creatures, 'God is love' may relate to an important aspect of reality's being the God-way, namely that, as God's creation, reality *has an overall purpose*, or ultimate *telos*. 'God is love' may be interpreted as conveying a

---

Our interest at the present stage of our discussion is just in considering whether the 'God is love' idea could provide an adequate non-personalist fundamental ontology for a (Christian) theist worldview.

[32] One of us tentatively proposed an account of this kind in previous work. See Bishop (2007b) and (2009).

Christian understanding of *what that overall purpose is*—namely, the concrete existence of loving, agapeistic, relationships.[33] It is this idea, in any case, which prompts the suggestion that what we are calling a *euteleological* metaphysics may provide a suitable non-personalist account of the fundamental ontological commitments of theism. The key features of *euteleology* are (in brief outline) as follows.

First, euteleology brings to the foreground the notion of an overall *final* cause of the Universe's existence: it claims that the Universe has an ultimate end or *telos*, and that it possesses this *telos* inherently—that is, in the absence of any agent who *produces* the Universe *for* that purpose. Reality's inherent ultimate *telos* is the good for reality as a whole, and hence it may be identified with the supreme good.

Second, euteleology accepts that the Universe has an ultimate efficient cause; but it holds that there can be such a cause *without any supernatural personal agent*. According to euteleology, the Universe is actual *just because it fulfils its supremely good inherent purpose*. This may seem a startling proposal, apparently envisaging a Universe raising itself into existence by its own bootstraps. But we'll explain and defend this ultimate explanation of the Universe's existence as coherent on the assumption that a higher causal order is applicable to reality as a whole in virtue of its inherent directedness upon the supreme good—a higher causal order distinct from the mundane causal order of productive efficient causes. (In admitting such a transcendent causal order we are admitting something supernatural in the sense of something beyond the ontology that is scientifically admissible, but we are avoiding a dualism of supernatural (uncreated) versus natural *beings*.)

We will elaborate these features and defend the coherence of euteleology as a metaphysics of ultimate reality in the next chapter, Chapter 3. Our aim in so doing is to develop an account of what the metaphysical commitments of theism may reasonably be thought to be if they are *not* commitments to the fundamental ontology of a supreme supernatural personal being. Thus, we are developing and defending euteleology in order to show, not that it is true, but rather that it's possibly true and that it's what reflective theist faith 'seeking understanding' may reasonably be regarded as taking to be true.

---

[33] A full theory of *agapē* would be no small task. As indicated in the previous section, we take it that the key idea in *agapē* is the idea of 'right relationship'. This provides a broad account that needn't exclude from *agapē* other forms of love such as *philia* or *eros*. Philia is agapeistic, then, when friends are 'rightly related' to each other. Erotic relationships can also be, or fail to be, agapeistic.

Accordingly, we aim to show that euteleology is an apt metaphysics for theism. In Chapter 4, we will consider whether and how God could feature in a euteleological metaphysics. We will argue that a euteleological theism will not identify God with *any* 'grand item' in its fundamental ontology, yet may nevertheless preserve talk about God as conveying truths accepted by faith by appeal to the idea that God-talk involves a radically analogous extension of our mundane practice of attributing properties and actions to persons. Finally, in Chapters 5 and 6, we'll consider further questions pertaining to the religious adequacy of a non-personalist euteleological theism.

3
Euteleological Metaphysics

Our agenda for this chapter is to give an exposition of a *euteleological* metaphysics of ultimate reality and defend its coherence. We won't be arguing for its truth; we will be arguing that it could possibly be true, and we'll be envisaging it as a viable non-personalist metaphysics for theism. As we've argued in the previous two chapters, the search for a non-personalist understanding of theism is well motivated—a search, that is, for an understanding that does *not* feature God as a supreme person or personal being, belonging to an ontological category distinct from that of created beings. As explained at the end of Chapter 2, we think that the idea, essential to theism, that creation has an overall unifying purpose which it exists to fulfil can provide the basis for a non-personalist metaphysics which proves viable as an account of the metaphysical commitments and fundamental ontology of theist faith 'seeking understanding'. This non-personalist metaphysics is the metaphysics we call *euteleology*.

In this chapter we'll develop a euteleological understanding of theism as an account of what theists may *positively* be committed to holding if personalist accounts are rejected. Non-personalist theorists who reject the metaphysics of the personal omniGod (and, more widely, of God as any kind of supreme personal being) will do well, we think, not to be satisfied with a purely negative account of what it is, at the level of fundamental ontology, for reality to be 'the God-way'. By the end of this book, we aim to have shown that euteleology deserves to be taken seriously as an option for a non-personalist positive account of theist metaphysics. Our exposition of euteleology, then, is as a potentially viable metaphysics for theism. In this chapter, however, our focus will be on explaining exactly what a euteleological metaphysics is and defending its coherence. Whether euteleology *adequately* captures the commitments of theist faith at the level of fundamental ontology may be doubted: indeed, it may seem to some that euteleology is (obviously) atheistic. We will seek to resolve such doubts in the remaining chapters: but, first, we need to set out carefully just what a euteleological metaphysics is and how it may be envisaged as a non-personalist account of theism's underlying metaphysics.

3.1 A 'Whole of Reality' Perspective

How may theists who reject personalist accounts try to articulate positively what they think reality must be like for it to be 'the God-way'? Theists are often said to have more in their ontology than atheists because theists augment the total inventory of 'natural' beings with an additional being, namely, God. Yet a theist ontology may instead amount to an account *of reality as a unified whole* that is 'richer' than anything atheism would accept. That kind of alternative will appeal to theists who reject the metaphysics of God as a supreme person—assuming that an ontology fit for theism can indeed be sufficiently 'rich' without including a uniquely exalted supernatural being amongst the beings it admits. It is just such an ontology that a euteleological metaphysics purports to provide.

We'll now explain how a euteleological theism may articulate a suitably rich account of reality when reality is 'the God-way'. As made clear at the outset, we are not here trying to *justify* theist belief that reality *actually is* the God-way; we are attempting only to specify a euteleological way of understanding *what it is* for reality to be the God-way. Nevertheless, it is pertinent to consider whether it could be reasonable to believe or accept (in the sense of practical commitment, with or without actual belief) that reality is the God-way as the euteleological account understands it. Euteleological metaphysics must at least be coherent, then, and a theist faith that understands itself as committed to a euteleological metaphysics must also satisfy whatever further constraints apply to reasonable faith-commitment. There's no requirement, however, that an acceptable metaphysics for theism should be rationally compelling given our total publicly shared evidence. Indeed, we're taking it that, whatever one's preferred account of theist metaphysics, full religious commitment in the Abrahamic traditions must be acknowledged as involving a faith-venture beyond what counts as reasonable on the basis of publicly shared evidence, even if (as is, of course, itself controversial) the basic tenets of theism may be shown true, or more likely true than not, by certain natural theological arguments.[1]

---

[1] A full defence of this claim would require support from an acceptable epistemology of religious (and similar 'whole worldview') beliefs. As noted in our Introduction, the task of

We will also need to defend the religious adequacy of theism on a euteleological understanding of it, using the same criteria we deployed earlier (see Chapter 1, Section 1.4) in expressing our doubts about the standard personal-omniGod account. On the face of it, a euteleological theism is in trouble since its rejection of the metaphysics of God as 'a' supreme supernatural being may seem too much of a divergence from any religiously adequate account of theism. As already noted, we're reserving for later chapters consideration of key questions about the religious adequacy of a euteleological theism. Our concern in this chapter is articulating a euteleological metaphysics so that it is as clear as we can make it what a euteleological theism would be.

3.2 Ultimate Teleology

The starting point for developing a euteleological metaphysics is a claim which is widely agreed to be central to Abrahamic theism, namely that reality has an overall unifying purpose. Theism affirms that the world is God's creation. Hearing this, what usually first comes to mind is the idea that God, the Creator, is the ultimate source ('First Cause') of all concrete contingent existence. A euteleological account, however, interprets theism by starting from *another* implication of the world as God's creation. This is the implication that the world has, and exists for the sake of achieving, some ultimate overall purpose or unified set of purposes. Theism takes the world of concrete existence to be meaningful and purposive, not merely through having parts or aspects which have purposes (such as biological organs and organisms, and persons and their artefacts and machines), but in so far as reality has an overall, integrating, ultimate purpose.

Euteleology begins, then, from an idea central to theism (though not necessarily exclusive to it), namely, that the Universe is 'purposive': the Universe exhibits an all-encompassing and unifying ultimate teleology. We're using 'the Universe' (with a capital 'U') here to refer to all that concretely and contingently exists, ever has existed, or ever will exist. Thus, if, as envisaged on some cosmologies, there are multiple, small 'u', spatio-temporal universes of which our own is but one, then 'the Universe' refers to that multiplicity as a whole. If the capital-U Universe is a 'multiverse', then a euteleological

---

defending such an epistemology is beyond our present scope. Bishop (2007a) attempts that task, providing an extended discussion of the conditions for justifiable faith-ventures.

metaphysics holds that the entire multiverse exists to fulfil an overall ultimate and unifying purpose.

3.3 Ultimate Teleology and the Supreme Good

Euteleology's next affirmation is that the ultimate unifying *telos* for the sake of whose realization the Universe and everything in it exists is *the supreme good*. To explain what this claim means, we begin by noting that anything that has, or exists for, a purpose (*telos*), has the realization of that *telos* as a good—the good *for it*, the good which constitutes its flourishing as the kind of thing it is, or its successfully fulfilling the purpose for which it was designed. The *attributive* use of 'good' is thus intrinsic to teleology—that is, the use of 'good' as qualifying some specific kind of thing, K, as in 'a good K'. Where something has a purpose, that *telos* is the good *for* a thing of that kind, and it is good for that thing to fulfil (or realize) the *telos* proper to its kind. But this notion of goodness is a *relative* one; it is the notion of goodness *as* a given kind of thing, fulfilling the purpose proper to that kind. (Hitting its target, for example, may be the good for a missile; but this good is merely relative—its fulfilment when a missile succeeds in hitting human targets may be a moral evil.)

Euteleology's posit of an ultimate unifying purpose introduces the notion of a good which is not relative to a specific kind of thing, but is the good *for reality as such and as an integrated whole*. Accordingly, for euteleology there is an overall purpose such that to be real is essentially to be 'directed upon' that purpose and its fulfilment. This purpose is the ultimate *telos*: there can be no purpose higher than the overall purpose for the sake of which each and every existent exists. This ultimate *telos*, then, the good for reality as such and as a whole, is the supreme, highest, good. And euteleology's conception of the supreme good is *realist*—that is, the good is what it is independently of any finite mind's preferences or beliefs.[2]

---

[2] Peter Geach (1956) famously claimed that 'good' is *always* used 'attributively' and not 'predicatively', and others have taken a similar view (see, e.g., Judith Jarvis Thomson 2008). It's therefore worth remarking that it doesn't seem necessary to appeal to some different, non-attributive, concept of goodness in order to accommodate the notion of a supreme good for the sake of which the Universe and everything in it exists, since for euteleology the supreme good is still a good *for* something—namely, for reality as such and as an integrated whole. Once we admit the bold notion of such an overall good, we're talking about what's good at the highest possible level of generality—namely, the good for something just in so far as it is real. At this limit, then, the attributive notion of the good yields a notion of goodness that may reasonably

Euteleology brings to the fore, then, the theme, familiar in theism, that the Universe of contingent existents exists in order for good of the highest possible kind (the supreme good) to be concretely realized in finite particulars and their properties and relations. According to this theme, the Universe, in all its complexity, has an overall axiological unity conferred by its existing for the ultimate purpose of concretely realizing the supreme good. That ultimate purpose is a unifying purpose in the sense that every existent has, specifically to its kind, a purpose that, if fulfilled, makes some contribution towards realizing the overall *telos* which is the supreme good. (We are taking it that, according to euteleology, if there are real entities that do not belong to the contingent Universe, such as, for example, mathematical entities, and moral and other axiological facts, then directedness upon realizing the supreme good is essential to their reality also.[3]) Thus, the assertion that reality inherently has an ultimate *telos*, which, as the good *for* reality, is the highest good, applies not just to the totality of what is real (concrete and abstract), but to each and everything that is real.

Euteleology may accordingly be described as affirming 'purposivism' in so far as it holds that reality has an overall, unifying, ultimate purpose for its existence. Abrahamic theism is committed to a purposivist metaphysics. Other kinds of worldview might also have that same commitment: consider, for example, *an*anthropocentric purposivism, as defined by Tim Mulgan as holding that 'there is a cosmic purpose but human beings are irrelevant to it' (2015, 1).[4] A purposivism of that kind would not be consistent with theism, however, since the Abrahamic traditions hold that God's purposes can be, and are, fulfilled in human existence. It is important to recognize, though, that the Abrahamic traditions *also* accept that divine purposes are fulfilled throughout the creation, in ways beyond both human existence and human knowledge or even conceiving.

To affirm that reality has an overall unifying and ultimate purpose is, of course, to invite the question what may be known about that purpose.

---

be described as absolute. Richard Kraut has recently made a sustained critique of the notion of absolute goodness, but apparently doesn't envisage the idea of absolute goodness as the good for reality as such and as an integrated whole, though he does devote a chapter to discussing the 'attributivist' view (2011, ch. 30).

[3] There is long-standing controversy over how 'abstract', 'necessary', existents or subsistents are related to God. If their existence is to be consistent with God's sovereignty and aseity, do they have somehow to count as created by God or else belong intrinsically to God's own nature? For discussion, see, e.g., William Lane Craig (2017).

[4] Our use of the term 'purposivism' is drawn from Mulgan's use of it in his term 'ananthropocentric purposivism'.

Theism links a purposivist metaphysics with the epistemological claim that the nature of the supreme good for the sake of which the Universe exists is specially revealed to humanity through certain specific historical events and writings (the details of which vary, of course, depending on the particular Abrahamic tradition). According to theism, although quite a lot about the good for humans and other creatures may be knowable 'naturally', the ultimate and supreme good for which humanity and all else exists under divine purposes can be known (or, at least, accepted) by human beings only as specially divinely revealed.[5] The content of that special revelation is limited, disclosing only what humans need to accept in practice about the nature of the supreme good in order to play their part in fulfilling the Universe's *telos*. And humanity's part in fulfilling that *telos* is a significant one: according to the theist traditions, humans not only share with creatures generally in having capacities that can contribute to realizing the ultimate *telos*, they may also participate in states of affairs which constitute that realization.

Theism holds that human morality is grounded in God's purposes in creation: that is to say, virtuous character, and just and right action and relationship are what they are in so far as they promote and/or accord with the fulfilment of those divine purposes. For euteleology, human morality is governed by the nature of the supreme good, which is reality's ultimate

---

[5] This characteristic claim of Abrahamic theism—that the ultimate good for the sake of which the Universe exists cannot be known purely 'naturally'—might be defended along the following lines. A natural understanding of the ultimate good would require treating the capital-U Universe as *an instance of a kind* relevantly analogous to a natural kind. But there is necessarily only one Universe, so the Universe is not anything like an instance of a natural kind. It might be replied that, since Leibniz, we have become familiar with treating the necessarily unique 'actual world' as an instance of the 'kind' constituted by indefinitely many 'possible worlds' (ways concrete existence as a whole could be, or could have been). It seems feasible, then, to understand the realization of the supreme good (on some substantive account of it) as the proper end for the 'kind' of thing that a *possible* Universe is. Perhaps so—but how could there be *natural* knowledge of what that ultimate end is, even if, as proponents of the teleological argument maintain, it may be naturally known that the Universe shows the activity of intelligence and hence has *some* overall purpose or unified set of purposes? Substantive claims about the 'natural' end of things of kind K are justifiable only when kind K has enough empirically available instances for the Aristotelian categorical notion of 'the (typical) K' to get a grip—and that is necessarily not the case when it comes to possible Universes. The attributive good for possible Universes, then, could only come to be accepted 'non-naturally'—on the basis of (purported) special revelation, as in the Abrahamic theist traditions. (This argument implies that any *non-theist* purposivist metaphysics will have to appeal to its own sources of 'non-natural' revelation, unless, of course only negative, apophatic, claims are made about what reality's overall unifying purpose is.)

Claims about special divine revelation imply divine revelatory actions: we'll consider how God's actions may be understood under a non-personalist interpretation of theism such as a euteleological one in the next chapter (see Chapter 4, Sections 4.6 and 4.9).

unifying purpose—and, evidently, that purpose may be identified as the divine purpose in creation if euteleological metaphysics may indeed, as we shall argue, be defended as apt for theism.[6] It is beyond our present scope to attempt any general account of what the revealed supreme good is believed to be in the theist religious traditions. A non-personalist euteleological understanding of theism will, however, need to assume that we can give a religiously and morally adequate account of the supreme good as revealed which does not logically imply the existence of a supreme personal being. In seeking to secure that assumption we'll continue to make use of a particular Christian understanding of the supreme good discussed in Chapter 2 (Section 2.10), namely, as known to humanity in the *agapē*-love revealed in Christ and enjoined upon his followers. On that Christian understanding, wherever fully loving and just, agapeistic, relationships obtain the ultimate purpose for which the Universe exists is fulfilled.

3.4 Realizing the Universe's Ultimate Purpose

As well as viewing the Universe as directed upon the supreme good as its *telos*, theism also proclaims *that the Universe's ultimate purpose is achieved*: the supreme kind of good actually is concretely realized. In general, things may exist for a purpose which they never actually succeed in realizing. (For example, the New Zealand farmer Richard Pearse built an engine-powered plane using bamboo, canvas, and metal in 1902. Though he became airborne in it for short distances, he probably didn't achieve the *telos* of controlled flight, but his machine clearly had that *telos*.[7]) It seems doubtful that *the entire Universe* could exist to realize the supreme good and yet that end never be achieved—yet there seems no obvious logical inconsistency in such a scenario, so we might tentatively infer that a Universe whose purpose remains unfulfilled is at least a logical possibility.

---

[6] Aristotle argues (*Nicomachean Ethics*, Book I) that *to teliotaton* (the most final end for human action, for whose sake other ends may be sought but which could not itself conceivably be sought for the sake of anything else) must be the supreme good (see Bernard Williams (1962) for discussion). For Aristotle, *eudaimonia* (usually, but perhaps not entirely felicitously translated as 'happiness') is the highest human good and the most final human end. For a euteleological theism, the most final end for human beings is to contribute to and participate in the realization of the divine purposes, reality's ultimate *telos*.

[7] It is generally agreed that the Wright brothers made the first controlled flight near Kitty Hawk in North Carolina in 1903.

An 'unfulfilled purposivist' metaphysics, might, then, be barely possible. Theism clearly proclaims, however, that there is no such failure of the divine purpose. Furthermore, theism holds that a concrete Universe wouldn't exist at all unless its purpose was fulfilled, since God wouldn't create without fulfilling God's purposes in creation, though the way those purposes are achieved in the existing Universe is contingent and expresses God's freedom in creation.[8] According to theism, the supreme good *is* actually achieved: concrete realization of the supreme good does come to exist. Personalist accounts of theism ground this guarantee in the power and goodness of God as a supernatural agent. Euteleology, as a non-personalist metaphysics, obviously could not ground the affirmation in that way. Nevertheless, euteleology does make that same basic affirmation, claiming not just that the Universe exists for the purpose of realizing the supreme good, but also that *this purpose is achieved within the Universe*—euteleology affirms, we may say, that the Universe 'does what it's for'.[9]

Euteleology claims that the Universe realizes its *telos* just in the sense that the Universe *contains within it actual instantiations or manifestations* of the supreme good. Euteleology, then, need not construe the 'realization' of the Universe's *telos* in the way that personalist accounts of theism often understand it. For euteleology, the realized ultimate purpose need not imply any literal ultimate consummation of concrete reality in which good has defeated evil and justice and peace prevail everlastingly—although the victory of good over evil is an essential theist soteriological theme which a euteleological theism must accommodate. We'll reserve for later discussion (in Chapter 5) the question of how that theme may be treated on a non-personalist interpretation of theism where the defeat of evil cannot be understood as secured by the ultimate all-controlling power of a perfectly good personal agent. What's important here, while the initial exposition of euteleology is our chief concern, is to emphasize that the euteleological affirmation that the Universe realizes the supreme good is *not as such* the claim that there is an *eschaton* in which concrete reality exists and persists

---

[8] We'll say more about these modal issues below (Section 3.11) when we come to consider euteleology's account of the ultimate explanation for the existence of a contingent concrete Universe.

[9] The 'eu-' prefix in the name 'eu-teleology' may thus be taken to connote both that the Universe has an overall unifying *telos* which is the supreme good for reality as such and as a whole, and the fact that the Universe does indeed achieve this *telos*. Evidently, one may agree that the world exhibits real teleology, without accepting that this empirically accessible teleology belongs within a wider *eu*teleology of a Universe unified by its directedness upon an ultimate purpose, reality's supreme good, which gets fulfilled within it.

for ever in a state of perfect overall goodness. It is the (it may seem, more modest) claim that concrete reality contains within it that which is supremely good and which, as such, 'finalizes' or fulfils the Universe.

Euteleology takes it to be essential, then, that the concrete instantiations or manifestations of the supreme good that the Universe contains are not merely partial approximations to an unrealizable ideal, but, rather, *full* instantiations or manifestations of the highest kind of goodness. That claim fits with the Christian 'incarnational' theme that the highest kind of goodness may be, and is, realized *in its full character* within our changing world. That makes it apt to describe instances of the supreme good which manifest its full character as *incarnations* of supreme goodness—in a sense of 'incarnation' wider, of course, than used in the Christian doctrine of 'the Incarnation'. (We think that Christians may quite legitimately use 'incarnation' in this more general sense, since, according to Christian teaching, *agapē*-love is instantiated in the world in its full character, paradigmatically through the person of Jesus the Christ, but also in all who love neighbour as self.[10])

3.5 Purpose without a 'Purposing' Agent?

A euteleological metaphysics—as so far explained—affirms that the Universe exists for an overall unifying purpose, namely, the realization of the supreme good, and, furthermore, that this purpose is actually achieved. These claims would surely feature in anybody's understanding of the metaphysical commitments of theism, whether personalist or non-personalist. What makes euteleology a *non-personalist* metaphysics is that it takes reality's having its overall ultimate *telos* to be *inherent* in the nature of the real. Euteleology does *not* attribute the purposiveness of the Universe to its production by a supremely powerful agent who intended to achieve those purposes and designed and constructed the Universe in order to fulfil that intention. Euteleology holds that the Universe is 'directed upon' an end, but for euteleology there is no Direct*or*. According to euteleology, the essence, or 'what-it-is', of 'being real' is existing for the sake of making the supreme good concretely real.

---

[10] Recall the traditional antiphon sung at the washing of feet on Maundy Thursday: *ubi caritas et amor, Deus ibi est* ('where there is charity and love, there is God').

Now, it might be objected that purposes cannot simply be inherent in the reality of a thing: a thing can have a purpose, it may be said, only if *some intentional agent* uses, or makes, that thing for purposes intended by that agent. Notoriously, however, this claim, thus universally stated, leads to an infinite regress, since, if the claim is true, *an agent's* having a purpose will have to be attributed to the activity of some *further* intentional agent. The regress may be blocked only by accepting that certain kinds of things *do* have purposes inherently. But, it will be said, it is *minds*, and only minds, that have purposes inherently: a mind may direct itself upon fulfilling a telic end, but matter can exhibit teleology only derivatively from the activity of mind.

It does not seem to be obvious, however, that inherent purposiveness is somehow more intelligible as intrinsic in minds than in matter—though this has certainly been an entrenched modernist assumption. In any case, on the face of it, the claim that teleological order cannot inhere in matter is empirically false: biological teleology is a real and pervasive phenomenon, yet explicable through evolutionary theory without appeal to the activity of mind. And it begs the question to argue that 'natural' evolutionary explanations don't go far enough just because teleological phenomena have to originate in the activity of mind. Accordingly, it seems quite coherent to hold that the Universe is inherently directed upon an ultimate *telos*. If, finally, it is held that whatever is inherently purposive must itself be 'a mind' or 'minded', then euteleology may be given a 'panpsychic' construal by taking its claimed inherent directedness upon its overall telic good as implying that the Universe is inherently 'minded'.[11] So long as the dualism of 'purposing' Mind and 'purposed' Universe is avoided, proponents of euteleology may be indifferent as to whether the Universe's inherent directedness upon its ultimate *telos* is a case of purposiveness being inherent in 'matter' or in 'mind'. They may even regard that question as largely a verbal dispute, since they neither could nor need make any claim to understand *how* telic directedness resides essentially in reality as such and as a whole: their claim is only that this is a coherent possibility, and an important one to consider as apt for the metaphysics of theism.[12]

---

[11] There has been a revival of interest in panpsychism amongst analytically minded philosophers in recent years. See, e.g., Godehard Brüntrup and Ludwig Jaskolla (2017). We are here remaining neutral on the question whether it is or is not defensible to understand inherent purposiveness as sufficient for 'mindedness': our point is only that, if this claim is defensible, then euteleology may be understood as committed to panpsychism (relative to that conception of 'psyche').

[12] Our defence here of the coherence of inherent purposiveness in the Universe and our criticisms of the assumption that it must be attributed to the activity of a supernatural mind

3.6 Explaining the Universe's Existence?

Here's a deeper objection, though: if the Universe's 'directedness' upon an ultimate unifying *telos* is inherent, then, whether or not we say that it is thereby 'a mind' or 'minded', it might be argued that we still lack any explanation of the Universe's actual existence. Why should anything concrete happen to exist at all, let alone something with the (as we are supposing) unified complexity of a Universe existing to realize the supreme good? Theism offers an answer to this question—and it seems an essential feature of theism that it does so. Theism provides, that is, an *ultimate theological explanation* for existence as a whole. Personalist accounts of theism achieve this by claiming that the Universe is created by God and that God's own existence as a supreme personal being is necessary, and so not in need of explanation in terms of anything else. Reality-as-a-whole is thus *partitioned* on personalist accounts: the divine part, God, necessarily exists and the Universe, the created part, exists contingently because produced and sustained through God's freely exercised intentional agency. This explanation connects the Universe's existence with its having, and realizing, its overall purpose: God caused the Universe to exist in order to achieve God's purpose of realizing within it the supreme good.

Can a non-personalist euteleological metaphysics provide an ultimate explanation for the Universe's existence? How may such an explanation proceed other than by appeal to a first cause who is a supreme immaterial personal agent who creates to fulfil creation's ultimate purpose?

3.7 'It Is because It Does What It's For'

We summed up euteleology on our account so far as affirming that the Universe 'does what it's for'. Now, we'll suggest that euteleology can indeed

---

redeploy key points from Hume's famous criticisms of the teleological argument in the version proposed by the character Cleanthes in Hume's *Dialogues Concerning Natural Religion* (1993 [1779], see especially parts II, IV, and XII). We think that teleological arguments for the existence of an intelligent designer like ourselves only vastly wiser and more powerful invariably beg the question whether teleofunctional complexity can be inherent in the natural world. Accordingly, they are best seen, not so much as arguments, but as *articulations* of an anthropocentric dualist stance which takes 'order' to be inherent in mind and able to be taken on by matter only through the activity of a mind or minds of the same general kind as human minds. For an excellent discussion of Hume's critical focus on anthropomorphic conceptions of God in the *Dialogues*, see David Holley (2002).

provide an ultimate explanation for the actuality of the Universe by claiming that the Universe exists *because* it does what it's for. We are proposing, in other words, that once we affirm the basic euteleological claims—that the Universe inherently has the supreme good as its *telos*, and that it 'does what it's for' in so far as goodness of the highest kind is concretely manifested within the Universe—we *already* have enough to explain why the Universe exists.

It may immediately be objected that, though we may have given (in Aristotelian terms) a *final* cause—and, indeed, a *formal* cause—of the Universe's existence, we haven't given an *efficient* cause. Euteleology specifies the Universe's telic end (its final cause), and it specifies the 'what-it-is' of the Universe as concrete existence inherently directed upon fulfilling that end (its formal cause). But there seems to be no explanation of the Universe's *actual existence* (no efficient cause)—and, it might be claimed, since euteleological metaphysics lacks a personal creator, it *cannot* proceed beyond ultimate final and formal causation to ultimate efficient causation.

It can be fair to make the objection that euteleology can offer no ultimate efficient causal explanation of contingent concrete existence, however, only if *the only possible* efficient causal explanation of the Universe's actuality is that it is due to the intentional agency of a supernatural being whose own existence needs no explanation in terms of anything else. But, in fact, there *are* other kinds of efficient cause apart from agent-causes in which an agent brings something about or produces something: in particular, there are (Humean) event-causes which don't produce their effects but, rather, necessitate (or probabilify) them as a matter of logical subsumption under natural laws. But Humean event-causation, with its implicit appeal to regularities or laws within the Universe, is patently in the wrong league for explaining the existence of the natural Universe itself. When it comes to the Universe as a whole, then, might it be true, as some have argued, that the only possible explanation for its existence is as resulting from personal intentional agency?[13]

Other possibilities cannot be ruled out. An efficient cause is, at root, just the kind of cause that explains *the actuality of* its effect. On that definition, there's conceptual space for the ultimate efficient cause of the Universe's existence to be something other than a productive agent-cause—and our

---

[13] See, for example, William Lane Craig (2000 [1979]): given that the Universe's coming into existence cannot be subsumed under natural laws (which, of course, presuppose that the Universe already exists), Craig argues that it must have a 'personal explanation'.

proposal, we submit, is an option in that conceptual space. The Universe's fulfilling the supreme good which is its *telos* may indeed be the explanation for the Universe's very existence.

3.8 Uniqueness of Ultimate Theological Explanation

It may be objected that there is no precedent for the idea that something's doing what it's supposed to do could *by itself* explain why that something exists. One may, however, question whether it's fair to expect explanations of phenomena within the Universe to provide a precedent for an ultimate explanation of the existence of the Universe as a whole. The actuality of the entire Universe is a unique kind of *explanandum*, so a unique kind of *explanans* must surely be in order. The standard personalist explanation for the Universe's existence also has unique features: there's no precedent within the Universe's natural causal order for agent-causation *ex nihilo* by an immaterial personal being. Our proposal for the way in which euteleology may provide an ultimate theological explanation may not fairly be dismissed, then, just on account of its lack of precise precedent in natural efficient causation—not, anyway, by those whose own version of an ultimate theological explanation must be open to the very same objection.[14]

Nevertheless, one might reasonably hope for more insight into the supposed explanatory force of euteleology's claim that the Universe exists because 'it does what it's for' before accepting it as a coherent candidate for ultimate theological explanation. Maybe, as a matter of logic, we can't expect an *exact* precedent for what explains the actuality of the whole Universe, but any such proposed ultimate explanation must bear *enough* likeness to familiar forms of explanation for its explanatory force to be intelligible, even if the way such an explanation 'works' cannot be expected to be fully comprehensible. Proponents of personalist accounts typically argue that this requirement *is* met on those accounts: agent-causation *ex nihilo* by an immaterial being—though, necessarily, unprecedented *within* the Universe—gains explanatory

---

[14] Some atheists might try arguing that the idea of an ultimate explanation of existence as such makes no sense, precisely on the grounds here noted—namely, that there can be no precise precedent within our ordinary explanatory practices for such a unique kind of explanation. We think that such an argument fails to appreciate the potential for *analogous extension* of explanatory precedents, but we will not pause here to elaborate that response, since our focus is on what ultimate theological explanation could consist in on the assumption that such explanation is not ruled out altogether.

intelligibility, they will say, from our familiarity with our own personal embodied agent-causation. This intelligibility relation rests, of course, on contestable 'mind-body interactionist dualist' assumptions: if materialists are correct in thinking that the action of a finite mind could not involve interactions between an immaterial self and its body, then, evidently, finite action fails to throw light on the act of creation by an infinite immaterial mind. It is contestable, then, just how much understanding our familiarity with our own finite action can provide for an account of the Universe as created by a God who is a personal being. But our question now is about how to provide *any* intelligible familiarity for our proposed non-personalist, euteleological, ultimate theological explanation of the Universe's existence. How, that is, may we vindicate the intelligibility of holding that the Universe's realizing its *telos* has explanatory force in answering the question why the contingent Universe exists at all?

3.9 'It Is because It Is Good that It Is'

May euteleology avail itself, perhaps, of an *extreme axiarchic* explanation of the Universe's actuality—that is to say, an explanation of something's existence purely in terms of its being good that it should exist? Or may it even be that euteleology's proposal to explain the Universe's existence in terms of its realizing the supreme good which is its *telos* is *itself just such* an extreme axiarchic explanation of the Universe's existence in terms of its goodness? If so, euteleology might do well to endorse John Leslie's sustained contemporary defence of what he calls 'the Platonic idea' that 'the good is the ethically required, and that ethical requirements, when not conflicting with other, stronger ethical requirements, can themselves be creatively powerful' (Leslie 2001, 155).[15]

---

[15] For a full appreciation of Leslie's project, see Leslie (1979, 1989, and 2016), as well as further articles listed at Leslie (2016, 62). Leslie himself deduces from extreme axiarchism—which he now prefers to call 'the Platonic theory'—a 'pantheism of infinitely many infinite minds', with 'the universe in which we find ourselves being nothing but a structure contemplated by one such mind' (Leslie 2016, 58–60). Leslie's (2001) provides a full exposition and defence of his 'infinite minds' pantheism. Leslie mentions other philosophers and theologians he regards as accepting or being sympathetic to versions of extreme axiarchism, including A. C. Ewing, John Polkinghorne, Hugh Rice, Nicholas Rescher, and Derek Parfit (for details, see Leslie 2001, ch. 5). Leslie has recently expanded this list to include *inter alia* our own previous exposition of euteleology (Bishop and Perszyk 2016a) as an example of 'writers in this NeoPlatonic tradition' (Leslie 2019), so it seems worthwhile paying attention to the question whether our 'it is because

It's true that Plato has Socrates (albeit with a show of reluctance) propose an extreme axiarchic idea at *Republic* 509b. But the proposal is made in the context of a comparison between the role of the Good in the intelligible world and the role of the Sun in the sensory world. The suggestion is that, just as the Sun causes not only the visibility of sensory objects but also their very existence, so the Good not only makes the Forms intelligible but is also the source of their being. Plato's extreme axiarchism, then, has to do with the ontological dependence of the eternal Forms on the supreme eternal Form of the Good, and doesn't envisage that the changing world of our experience might derive its actuality from the Good. Furthermore, Plato doesn't understand the Good as an abstract 'ethical requirement', but rather as an eternal and perfect reality that contrasts with the lesser reality of 'the world of appearance'. Leslie's theory is thus considerably bolder than Plato's own proposal, which, in any case, Plato himself evidently regarded as excitingly speculative.[16]

Leslie's bolder-than-Platonic theory—that 'ethical requiredness' can itself be creatively powerful—will not even be coherent, however, if it is true (as is surely plausible) that only what is concretely real can explain the actuality of concrete existence. Leslie tries to persuade us that this principle is false, since, he claims, there are 'senses in which abstractions are known to be able to do things' (2001, 176). But we don't find his examples fully convincing. It's true that 'the fact of being a square (an abstraction of a sort) can prevent a peg from fitting into a round hole with the same cross-sectional area' (2001, 176): but such a fact doesn't seem to support the claim that an abstraction *as such* can be causally efficacious, since the preventative causal power in this case belongs to the concrete peg which *concretely instantiates* the general, abstract, property of being a square with the relevant cross-sectional area. It is an important truth, though, that one cannot *understand* why the peg won't go in the hole without understanding what's happening—or not happening—at the level of abstract generality.

---

it does what it's for' explanation is really just a case of a 'NeoPlatonic' 'it is because it is good that it is' explanation.

[16] In the dialogue, when Socrates is finally cajoled into articulating the idea that the Good may be the source of the very being of all the Forms, Plato has Glaucon expostulate (*Republic* 509c) 'Heaven save us, hyperbole can no further go!', but we think that Leslie's proposal shows that it can. Leslie himself (in personal correspondence) doesn't think he deserves as much credit for originality as we are inclined to give him. He thinks at least something very like Leslian extreme axiarchism was developed over centuries by numerous philosophers and theologians who thought they were following Plato's lead.

We won't pause to dispute Leslie's other examples, or his critique of the kind of claim we have just made that abstractions won't have any causal power 'in themselves', since those disputes seem less pressing in the light of the challenge Leslie issues when he says that 'anything able to explain Why There Is Something Rather Than Nothing...couldn't itself be an existent' and 'would have to be an abstraction of some kind' (2001, 176). In other words, there may simply be no other option for an interpretation of ultimate theological explanation, even if (as we ourselves believe, contrary to Leslie) familiar examples of purely abstract causal efficacy are not to be found. Explaining existence as fulfilling an abstract ethical requirement might then be apt for the unique case of the existence of an entire Universe even though such a mode of explanation has no precedent in accounting for specific phenomena within the Universe. We therefore accept that an ultimate explanation of existence of this kind cannot be ruled out.[17] In which case, ultimate efficient causation does *not*, somehow obviously, have to be agent-causation by an immaterial supernatural agent—a conclusion which will be welcomed by those like ourselves who seek viable non-personalist interpretations of theism.

Nevertheless, an extreme axiarchic explanation doesn't seem to qualify as a *theological* explanation, not so much, perhaps, because 'God' doesn't explicitly feature,[18] but more importantly because theological explanation must rest on what is most fully and ultimately real, and *purely abstract* ethical requiredness (though it obtains necessarily) seems not to be that. This deficit might be repaired by holding—what may anyway seem reasonable— that the abstract ethical requiredness of concrete existence cannot itself be ontologically fundamental and must depend on the Good understood as, or as belonging to, an eternal and necessary perfect reality. Such an 'eternal and necessary perfect reality' might be understood either in a 'Platonic dualist' fashion, locating the Good in an ontological realm distinct from the world of contingent beings, or else in line with the neo-Platonist 'monist

---

[17] We agree, then, with Mackie (1982, ch. 13), who, as Leslie notes (2001, ch. 5), accepts that extreme axiarchism, though 'an implausible speculation', cannot be excluded *a priori* as a logical impossibility.

[18] Leslie allows that God *could* feature in an extreme axiarchic explanation of existence. One possibility is to identify God with the abstract ethical requiredness of existence, while another is to hold that it is a personal God's existence, as creator of the world, that is ethically required. But Leslie's own 'infinite minds pantheism', which results from his own assumptions about what constitutes the highest good (unlimited minds, and an unlimited number of them), is definitely not intended as a way of understanding the metaphysics of Abrahamic theism.

emanationist' tradition of Plotinus, which understands the Universe as emanating from 'the One'.

3.10 'The Universe Exists because It Realizes Its Purpose': Cosmic Boot-Strapping?

Our proposed euteleological ultimate explanation for the Universe's existence, however, represents what we believe to be a *further* possibility beyond both an explanation appealing to a necessarily existing concrete but supernatural or non-natural source (personal or otherwise) and an explanation appealing to purely abstract ethical requiredness. To say, as euteleology does, that the Universe exists because it does what it's for is to propose to explain concrete existence *in terms of something about concrete existence itself*, namely the fact that it fulfils its inherent purpose.

This way of explaining contingent existence by appeal to a feature of contingent existence itself may look obviously flawed, as it seems to entertain the idea that a cosmos could lift itself into existence by its own boot straps. A Universe already has to exist for realizations of its *telos* to occur within it. Is it not incoherent, then, to suggest that those realizations—or the fact of their occurrence within the Universe—could explain why the Universe itself exists?

Actually, it *does* make sense to say that hearts (for example) exist because (usually) they do what they are supposed to do, namely, pump blood. However, the evolutionary explanation for the existence of animals with hearts which backs this claim essentially makes reference to a wider mundane causal context in which such animals emerged. If we use this form of explanation to explain the existence of *the whole Universe*, there obviously cannot be any wider mundane causal context. The *entire* explanation for the Universe's actual existence must then be just that it contains states of affairs that fulfil its purpose—and that may seem to involve illegitimate boot-strapping, as if one were to say that it is our safely dwelling in our house that *by itself* explains why our house is actual. Furthermore, our proposed euteleological explanation of the Universe's existence provides an account of 'creation' *ex nihilo* in an especially strong sense: on this account, not only does the Universe not get made from anything pre-existent, but its actuality is due to nothing outside itself whatsoever. But, then, it seems baffling how such an 'explanation' could *genuinely explain*, rather than just amount to a fancy way of accepting the Universe's existence as an ultimate brute fact.

Besides, if we're canvassing this euteleological explanation as a *theological* explanation, won't it obviously prove ineligible for the reason that theism is committed to the principle that nothing comes from nothing? Perhaps cosmological arguments for a necessary First Cause may be resisted by questioning the applicability of the causal principle to the Universe as a whole, but there's surely no disputing that *theists themselves* hold it to be so applicable.[19]

We'll respond to these questions and concerns in the next section—by elaborating the point already made that, on anyone's account of its content, an explanation for the existence of the entire contingent Universe is bound to have unique features. We'll argue that a key feature of any such ultimate explanation is an appeal to a higher order of causation that transcends mundane empirical causation amongst existents within the Universe. We will be claiming that an ultimate explanation of the Universe as existing 'because it does what it is for' *is* coherent, once it is recognized that the causal priority of concrete realizations of the supreme good within the Universe is not mundane causal priority, but priority in a higher, transcendent, causal order.

But, first, it's worth observing in a brief aside that the puzzling kind of causal boot-strapping involved in this euteleological proposal for an ultimate explanation of the Universe's existence seems to have a precedent in Christian tradition. At the Council of Ephesus (431 CE) it was affirmed that Mary was not just the mother of the Messiah (the Christ), but also *theotokos* ('God-bearer'). This description seems to imply the 'boot-strapping' claim that Mary was parent to her own (ultimate) creator.[20] Such a causal anomaly might be avoided by holding that Mary gave birth only to Christ's human existence, his divine existence having been prior and eternal. But, although

---

[19] For an example of critical discussion of the question whether the principle that from nothing nothing comes applies to the Universe as a whole, see Wes Morriston (2000, especially pp. 152–4). This paper initiated a debate in subsequent issues of *Faith and Philosophy* over William Lane Craig's 'Kalām' Cosmological Argument, and in particular its key premise that whatever begins to exist has a cause of its existence.

[20] The Marian antiphon, *Alma Redemptoris Mater*, makes just this point: *tu quae genuisti, Natura mirante, tuum sanctum Genitorem* ('you who, while Nature marvelled, gave birth to your holy Creator'). The same 'boot-strapping' causality (from the natural perspective, anyway) is implied in various scriptural passages, for example in Revelation 22:16 where it is said that Jesus is both the source (root) and offspring (descendant) of David. In the Gospels, Mark 12:35-7 relates Jesus's own teaching about the Messiah: though the Messiah is David's son, David nevertheless calls him 'Lord', so how can he be his son? And the first chapter of John's Gospel identifies Jesus as the Word who 'in the beginning…was with God, and…was God', 'not one thing came into being except through him': yet, from the natural perspective, Jesus was born 'late in time', as the hymn has it, causally dependent on his ancestry.

the 'one Lord Jesus Christ' is indeed '*eternally* begotten of the Father' (as the Nicene Creed affirms), the claim that Mary gave birth only to Christ in his human nature seems inconsistent with the affirmation by the Council of Chalcedon (451 CE) of the unchanging inseparability of Christ's divine and human natures in one *hypostasis* (substance). And that Council, too, reaffirmed Mary as *theotokos*. Engaging in Christological disputes (fascinating as they are) is not our present task: rather, our present interest is just in making the point that, for the claim that Mary gave birth to her own creator to be intelligible, appeal must be made to a higher order of causation than the mundane, empirical, one: the eternal Word may be dependent on Mary and her ancestry according to mundane causality, but in the higher, transmundane, causal order the dependency is quite the reverse. We'll now indicate, then, how euteleology's ultimate explanation for the Universe's existence deploys this same idea of a transcendent causal order higher than the mundane.

3.11 The Essence of Reality and a Higher, Transmundane, Causal Order

The idea that something that comes to exist in the Universe might be, or be essential to, the ultimate efficient cause of the Universe's existence makes no sense within the mundane, empirical, order of agent- and event-causation. It can make sense, however, if a higher transcendent causal order is implicated—and, as we'll now explain, such a transmundane causal order must be implicated when the mundane causal order is placed in the context of the Universe having, and realizing, an ultimate overall inherent purpose which is the supreme good.

First, it needs to be acknowledged that explaining contingent existence in terms of a feature of itself (as our proposed euteleological explanation of the Universe implies) isn't going to work without some appeal to a *necessary* feature of reality. But euteleology *does* posit such a necessarily real feature. That feature is not the necessary existence of a supernatural personal being—nor, indeed, of any power or agency. Instead, what's ultimately necessary about reality is reality's being *inherently* 'directed upon' the realization of the supreme good. For euteleology, then, capital-R Reality (reality as a whole) is 'more than' the Universe considered just as the sum total of contingent concrete existents—yet no dualistic ontological partitioning of beings of the kind familiar on personalist accounts is thereby implied. Rather, Reality is 'more than' the Universe in so far as *what it is to be real* is to exist for the sake of making the supreme good concretely real. This inherent directedness upon the supreme good *transcends* every contingent being, and transcends also the totality of contingent beings taken together. It is (as Leslie might observe) a 'requiredness'—a requiredness that supreme goodness be concretely realized, a requiredness that belongs to the very essence of being real.[21]

On the euteleological view, the necessary directedness of what's real upon realizing the supreme good is *not as such* the ultimate explainer of contingent existence (in the direct manner in which Leslie's extreme axiarchism seems to envisage ethical requiredness giving rise to what's ethically required). Reality's *telos* is the contingent realization of the supreme good; accordingly, reality's 'eutelicity' (let us call it) entails that whatever Universe is actual exists wholly contingently. Furthermore, for euteleology, it's contingent that any concrete Universe exists at all (the 'null' Universe is logically possible). Euteleology's ultimate explanation for the existence of 'something rather than nothing' is that the contingent concrete Universe includes realizations (fulfilments, manifestations, incarnations) of the good for reality as such and as a whole, that is, of the supreme good. Those realizations are themselves contingent existents—although, if it's true that the concrete Universe exists 'because it does what it's for', it is *conditionally* necessary that if anything concrete exists at all, some concrete realization of the supreme good contingently exists. But there's no appeal to any necessary being: *at the level of beings*, euteleology's ultimate explanation for 'something rather than nothing' deploys the contingent to explain the contingent. (This sheer contingency of the existence of concrete beings seems to us to fit an important theme in Abrahamic theism—namely, the idea that the good is not a pure ideal but, as a matter of 'gift' rather than necessity, is instantiated and manifested contingently within the concrete historical world.)

---

[21] Some of our remarks in this paragraph, and in the previous section, may suggest (as has Leslie himself in personal correspondence) that our euteleology is close to, or even a 'clone' of, Leslie's extreme axiarchism. We think it an open and interesting question how exactly our euteleological account of ultimate theological explanation relates to Leslie's 'Platonic' ultimate explanation for existence—but this is a topic which requires fuller treatment than we can here undertake, and which need not be settled in the context of our present exposition and defence of a euteleological metaphysics as a viable non-personalist understanding of the basic metaphysical commitments of theism. Though we think we see significant differences between euteleology and Leslie's theory (as we indicate in what follows), we are certainly supportive of his extreme axiarchist account as a clearly coherent alternative to the standard ultimate explanatory appeal to a necessarily existing supernatural personal agent.

Nevertheless, what *is* absolutely necessary in euteleology, namely, reality's eutelicity—its inherent direction upon realizing the supreme good—provides the context in which we may make intelligible euteleology's explanation that the Universe exists 'because it does what it's for'. As well as affirming reality's necessary eutelic directedness, euteleology also affirms that reality's *telos* is in fact realized. These contingent realizations of reality's supreme good—or, perhaps more strictly, the fact that they obtain—may then be held to be the ultimate efficient cause of the Universe's existence *in a posited higher transcendent causal order* distinct from the mundane causal order.

This notion of some kind of transmundane causal order clearly belongs to the established conceptual currency of theism, since its classical doctrine of creation is of creation *ex nihilo*. Mundane efficient causation can't apply to creation *ex nihilo*. This is apparent on standard personalist accounts, where God's creating *ex nihilo* isn't a case of an agent's *acting on* anything, and so cannot be like mundane efficient causation. Euteleology, too, appeals to a transcendent causal order distinct from the mundane. Euteleology maintains that something dependent for its existence on antecedent causes in the mundane causal order may coherently be (or be essentially implicated in) the ultimate cause of all existence, in view of its absolute priority in the higher transcendent causal order. This way of thinking challenges the assumption implicit in personalist theist metaphysics that the kind of causation involved in intentional productive agency is the ontologically most fundamental (if not, indeed, the only possible) kind of efficient causation. But that assumption, naturally arising as it does from the salience of intentional productive agency in our human experience, could be mistaken—and euteleology maintains that it is.

We conclude, then, that it *is* coherently intelligible that the most fundamental efficient causation that explains the very existence of the contingent Universe is as euteleology claims: the Universe exists because it realizes the supreme good which is, inherently, the purpose for which it exists. Things existing because they do what they're supposed to do is something familiar in mundane causation—and this familiarity provides the base for an *analogical extension* to a unique form of transmundane causal explanation for the Universe's existing *purely* because it fulfils its purpose.

Nevertheless, *how it actually comes about*, on the euteleological scenario, that the Universe exists in so far as it realizes its purpose remains mysterious. It is, of course, going to be intelligible scientifically how particular states of affairs which (according to a specific account) do in fact realize the supreme good come to exist through mundane causation within the Universe. But the 'mechanisms' involved in the operation of the implied higher transcendent causal order are not knowable—indeed, it may make no sense even to envisage that there *are* any such, essentially hidden, mechanisms. (It would not, for example, help to think of the way in which realizations of the supreme good are involved in the ultimate efficient cause of the Universe's existence as involving backwards causation, puzzling as that may be in itself. If there could be backwards causation, it would still count as causation, however unusual, *within* the mundane causal order. That some feature of the Universe itself causes the Universe's overall existence—past, present, and future—is causation of a completely different order from a future event causing an event in its past.)[22] It is important to emphasize, then, that euteleology's ultimate explanation for the existence of the contingent Universe—'it exists because it does what it's for'—is not an explanation that appeals to the exercise of *any* kind of power distinct from the Universe and capable of producing or controlling it. The higher, transmundane, causal order implied by reality's euteleicity doesn't operate in any such, mundanely comprehensible, way.

3.12 No Mystery about Mystery at the Limit of Human Understanding

Euteleology's ultimate explanation for the Universe's existence posits, then, a transmundane causality whose operations are in principle incomprehensible. In this respect, however, it is on a par with any rival proposal for a genuinely ultimate explanation of existence—of why there is something rather than nothing. It might, of course, be objected that no real explanation of the Universe's existence has been given if we have to admit that it must remain unexplained how it could be that the Universe exists because it

---

[22] Some interpretations of the so-called 'Strong Anthropic Principle' seem to suggest that it's the existence of conscious life—our existence—that explains why there's a Universe with life-permitting features. See, e.g., John Barrow and Frank Tipler (1986, especially chs. 7 and 10). If one is working only with the mundane causal order, this is clearly back-to-front: it's the 'anthropic coincidences' that (partly) explain how complex intelligent life could come to exist. If backwards causation is ruled out, a defence of the Strong Anthropic Principle would need to appeal to the kind of higher, transmundane, causal order made available by euteleology (or any similar 'purposivist' appeal to overall teleology inherent in the Universe)—and that, of course, takes it beyond the status of a scientific hypothesis. In other words, it would at least be intelligible that the existence of conscious life explains why the Universe exists if it were made explicit that the Universe has the inherent purpose of realizing conscious life as essential to its overall telic good.

contains within itself realizations of the ultimate purpose for which it exists. To claim that the Universe is there 'because it does what it is supposed to do' might therefore seem to make no advance on Bertrand Russell's reply to Fr Fred Copleston in their 1948 BBC debate: 'I should say that the universe is just there, and that's all!'.

Yet any metaphysics that offers an ultimate explanation of the Universe's actuality will need to respond to this charge of mystery-mongering, since—as we have been emphasizing—it is part and parcel of any purported explanation of why anything exists at all that it appeals to a kind of causation *outside* ordinary causation within the Universe, causation whose 'operations' must remain inscrutable. One clearly available response is to hold that, since human understanding has necessary limits, it is only to be expected that ineliminable mystery will attach to ultimate metaphysical explanations for the existence of something rather than nothing. The importance of recognizing the limits of human understanding (and criticizing attempts to trespass beyond those limits) is familiar—from Kantian critical philosophy, in particular. It need not, then, be 'unphilosophical' to hold that certain fundamental explanatory posits are such that their holding true is not only not in fact further explained, but could not in principle be so. Posited causation of the Universe's existence *ex nihilo* is a case in point. Such transcendent causation may be made intelligible by an analogous extension from familiar forms of causation and causal explanation—but no inkling of how such transmundane causation 'works' could even be conceived.

This defence of impenetrable mystery does require accepting, however, that ultimate explanations of the Universe's existence belong to a different explanatory category from scientific explanations. While all scientific explanations have to rest on foundations that are not themselves explained, they never do so at a point where it's to be accepted as an in principle ineliminable mystery how it is that the relevant foundational claims hold true. Some basic physical law, for example, might, in fact, remain unexplained through the entire future of empirical scientific inquiry, but this will never be because it could not be explained as a matter of principle. Basic explanatory posits deployed in *ultimate* explanations of the existence of something rather than nothing, however, are *necessarily* not open to further explanation: to return specifically to euteleological ultimate explanation, the status of the Universe's concrete realization of the supreme good as efficient cause of there existing anything concrete at all is necessarily not further explicable. Similarly, though, for *any* ultimate explanation of the Universe's existence: there is a necessary mystery about how whatever is invoked as ultimate efficient cause 'does its causing'—whether it be, to mention our two other examples, agent-causing by a supreme immaterial agent (on a typical personalist theist account), or the ethical requiredness of existence (on an extreme axiarchist account).

Personalist theists might retort that our experience of our own agency enables us to render non-mysterious the mode of causation posited by their ultimate explanation of the Universe's existence—namely as produced through agent-causation by an immaterial supernatural agent. That explanation might make less appeal to mystery than its rivals, however, only on the assumption that our familiarity with our own agency is familiarity with it *as construed on a mind-body dualist account*. But, even if a dualist account is granted, it remains incomprehensible how agent-causation of physical events by an immaterial mind actually 'works'. Personalist theists who are mind-body dualists thus seem as much committed to an appeal to mystery at the limits of human understanding as are rival accounts: the appeal to mind-body dualist interactionism confers on the ultimate causation of the Universe's existence only a specious comprehensibility, based as it is on the mystery dualism locates ubiquitously in natural agency itself.

3.13 Theological Metaphysics as Ethical Posits

A further way to vindicate ultimate metaphysical explanation as resting on posits whose truth is necessarily mysterious is to argue that those posits are motivated by their practical, ethical, utility, rather than by purely theoretical considerations. Inscrutable mystery at some specific foundational level may offend the theoretician; but it need not offend those concerned with the way a stance on ultimate reality supports the rationality of living according to relevantly related values.

This more pragmatist approach to foundational metaphysical posits is especially apt in the context of ultimate theological explanation. Theism is committed to the claim that what humans need to know (or, at least, accept) about the ultimate nature of reality and its bearing on human existence *has to be specially revealed* to finite minds. Accordingly, human minds may understand the nature of God—of ultimate reality and its purposes—only to the extent that they need such understanding in order to live and flourish as God intends. Attempts to understand what it is for reality to be 'the God-way'—that is, proposals for theist metaphysics—may thus be understood as having, from the perspective of theist commitment itself, the status of posits that reflective theists make with practical effect through reflection on what they believe has been revealed, rather than the status of explanatory theories potentially constituting intellectual mastery of ultimate reality.

Arguably, then, from a theist perspective, although ultimate reality as it is in itself may not be theoretically knowable, posits about its nature based on reflection on what is believed to have been specially revealed may be made *for practical and ethical reasons*. The theist traditions offer rich accounts of what it is for human persons to live well, individually and collectively. Theism also affirms that ultimate reality's being the God-way makes reasonable steadfast and hopeful human commitment to theist ethical ideals. To live well (the theist traditions assume) people need to believe that there are 'objective' ideals for living well, ideals that are really achievable and whose realization is conducive to, and at least partially constitutive of, human fulfilment. And the theist traditions affirm that reality meets these conditions, filling out the material details by appeal to their particular traditions of special revelation. It seems reasonable, then, to hold that theist metaphysics are not independent of theist ethics—indeed, the point of theist metaphysics seems *primarily* to reside in the service of theist ethical practice.[23]

In any case, it seems clear that criticism of supposedly specially revealed theist metaphysical posits needs to be driven, not only by essential considerations of logical coherence and metaphysical possibility, but also by further judgements as to their aptness for supporting reasonable practical commitment to theist ethics.[24] Appeals to mystery and incomprehensibility (= lack of intellectual mastery) at alleged necessary stopping points for explanation may then be brought within the ambit of this ethical critique. It may be argued that we need to understand only enough about reality (its nature, its purpose, its ultimate efficient cause) as required to support reasonable and continuing practical commitment to the ethical ideals.

---

[23] It is, of course, much debated whether ethics actually does need metaphysical support of this kind. Our point is only that it seems essential *to the theist worldview* to regard such support as essential—a point backed up by the fact that philosophers who defend an ethics that lacks supporting metaphysical commitments (a non-cognitivist ethics, for example) often see themselves as clearing away metaphysical baggage left behind by the receding tide of theist faith.

[24] There is plenty of room for debate about the ethical aptness of different accounts of theist metaphysics, as well as about the content of the presupposed theist normative ethics. For example, it might or might not be considered an advantage of the personal-omniGod account that 'objective' ethical truths may be understood as simply constituted by divine command, or that 'the triumph of the good' can ultimately be guaranteed by the exercise of all-controlling personal power. Our own 'normatively relativized' version of the Logical Argument from Evil is itself a case for rejecting a certain kind of theist metaphysics on the basis of claims about the 'right relationship' commitments of theist ethics (see Chapter 1, Section 1.8).

That principle then opens the way to an argument for the conclusion that it should not be counted against any account of ultimate theological explanation that the higher order of causation to which it appeals must remain mysterious. Hence, it should not be counted against euteleology, in particular, that it cannot be explained *how* the Universe's actuality is due to its containing within it realizations of the supreme good. On this more pragmatist account, the necessary absence of any such further *theoretical* explanation is unproblematic, so long as it does not impair the support that key theist claims about ultimate reality provide for reasonable and hopeful *practical* commitment to the pursuit of theist ethical ideals.

3.14 Euteleological Metaphysics and Euteleological Theism: Does God Have a Place?

A euteleological metaphysics, then, has these features: first, it proposes that the Universe has an overall, unifying, purpose ('purposivism'), and that the essence of reality is *inherent* directedness upon the fulfilment, in concrete contingent existence, of this overall purpose which is the good *for reality as such and as a whole*, the supreme good; second, it claims that the Universe does indeed concretely fulfil its purpose ('it does what it's for'); thereby it makes available an ultimate explanation of the Universe's actuality ('why there is something rather than nothing') in terms of the fact that the supreme good is concretely realized within the Universe ('it exists because it does what it is for').

We have developed this euteleological metaphysics in the search for a non-personalist way of understanding the fundamental ontology of theism. We do not altogether exclude, however, the possibility that a euteleological metaphysics might be thought apt in other contexts outside the Abrahamic theist traditions. Perhaps philosophers seeking a 'spiritually and ethically interesting' form of atheism might be attracted to the idea that the Universe has an overall, unifying, purpose. Such philosophers obviously won't appeal to Abrahamic special revelation, and will need some other account of how we may (within limits) know what the Universe's overall purpose is, or is not. They might also be inclined to a purposivism that rejects any ultimate explanation for existence, holding it to be an unexplained contingent fact that there is something rather than nothing. But that claim may not, perhaps, be consistent with accepting that the Universe has an overall *telos*, which may arguably itself provide *a kind of* ('final cause') ultimate explanation for its existence. Arguably, too, although final causes are generally not themselves also efficient causes (our dwelling in our house does not explain why our house is actual), in the unique case of the entire concrete Universe its final and its efficient cause may have to coincide.[25] It's worth noting that this coincidence of ultimate final and ultimate efficient cause will follow from a Leslie-style extreme axiarchism, given that the Universe's final cause is *the good* for reality as such and as a whole. And if (*pace* Leslie) that supreme good is thought too abstract to be itself an ultimate efficient cause, one may then have recourse to a euteleological efficient causal explanation of the Universe's existence as actual because it contains concrete manifestations or 'incarnations' of the supreme good which is its *telos*.

But could euteleology's purposivist metaphysics together with the ultimate explanation of the Universe's existence that we have argued it makes available really serve as a metaphysics *for Abrahamic theism*? Or might our hope to find in euteleology a viable alternative to the standard personalist theist metaphysics be misplaced, forcing us to accept that euteleological metaphysics cannot sustain more than an 'interesting atheism'?

Euteleology's prospects as an adequate account of theism seem favourable at the start, since euteleology begins from claims essential to theism, namely, that reality as such and as a whole is purposive, and that its overall purpose, the realization of the supreme good, is achieved. But euteleology's proposal that reality's directedness upon the supreme good is *inherent* breaks with the widespread account of theism as holding that reality's purposes derive from the purposes of its supernatural personal creator. And euteleology offers a startlingly different account of the Universe's ultimate efficient cause, albeit one which may plausibly have precedent in the Christian tradition. We have argued that euteleology's claim that the Universe exists ultimately because it contains realizations of its own telic good is coherent—provided it is acknowledged that a higher, transmundane, causal order is here being posited. That explanation admits that the Universe 'comes from nothing' in the sense that, not only is there no prior material, there is also no being ontologically prior to the Universe as its producer. Yet euteleology's

---

[25] Aquinas makes this claim—that God is both ultimate final and ultimate efficient cause—so, if this is 'interesting atheism' it has an impeccable theist champion! Note that, in defending this claim against the objection that, if the claim were true then before and after must exist in God and he must thus be prior to himself, which is impossible, Aquinas (at *Summa Theologiae*, I, Q44, a.4) replies that the first principle of all things is one in reality, though there's a distinction of reason: some things about God we come to know or think before others.

explanation still meets the theist expectation that the causal principle (or the principle of sufficient reason) should apply to the contingent existence of the Universe as a whole. To explain the actuality of the Universe as existing because it contains within itself realizations of reality's inherent telic purpose is not to leave the Universe 'coming from nothing' in the sense of lacking altogether any cause of its actual existence. And once it is appreciated that theist metaphysical posits have an essentially practical and ethical role, the impossibility of explaining any further *how* it could be that the Universe exists because it realizes the supreme good may be treated as a point at the necessary limits of understanding.

Here is an urgent question, however: euteleology as outlined so far seems to lack any place for *God*. Euteleology's core claims make reference to reality as such, to the whole of reality, to the Universe's transcendent and necessary *telos*, the supreme good, and to realizations of the supreme good, but there is no mention of God. Is it not, then, clear that euteleology is an atheist metaphysics? How could a euteleological metaphysics make true (for example) the creedal claim that *God* is 'maker of heaven and earth, and of all things visible and invisible'? Euteleology has no place for God as maker in the sense of a producing agent, even in the attenuated sense of a producer who neither produces from anything pre-existent nor (if time itself is created) through any temporal process. Euteleology takes 'the creation' to be *ex nihilo* in a strong sense that excludes its being produced and sustained 'from' or 'by' anything else. What, then, could a euteleological theism retain of the idea of God as creator of the Universe? Theism, furthermore, ascribes a range of attributes—omnipotence and omniscience, for example—to God. To what, though, could such attributes attach on a euteleological metaphysics?

Maybe a euteleological theism could be feasible, but many will think that this could be conceded only if there is something identifiable as God in the fundamental ontology of a euteleological metaphysics, where that identification can be shown to fit the key claims that theism makes about God. This question of how to identify—or how not to identify—God on a euteleological account is the question which we take up next, in Chapter 4.

4
God, the Divine, and the Divine Attributes

Euteleology holds that reality as such and as a whole has an inherent purpose or *telos*, which is the realization of the good for reality and, therefore, of *the supreme* good. Furthermore, euteleology proposes that the ultimate efficient causation of concrete existence rests on the Universe containing within itself instantiations of the supreme good: the contingent Universe exists because 'it does what it's for'. But if these commitments are supposed to capture the basic ontological commitments of Abrahamic theism, surely it must first be explained where *God's existence* fits into the envisaged ontology? For, as so far expounded in our previous chapter, the key claims of euteleology seem to make no explicit mention of God at all. Theism has God at the heart of its worldview, so, surely, it will be said, God has to make an appearance in any adequate account of theism's basic ontology. To defend a euteleological theism, then, we need, on the face of it, to explain *what God is* in basic euteleological ontology.

The force of that apparent requirement might be weakened, perhaps, by reiterating that euteleology is an account only of the *metaphysics* of theism—that is, it's an account of how we may reflectively understand, within the limits of our human understanding, what ultimate reality is like when theism is true. But there's a difference between that sort of metaphysical talk, and talk that is religiously and psychologically apt for human persons as they relate to God. It may, accordingly, be metaphysically mistaken to understand God as a supreme personal being, or even as any kind of 'being amongst beings', yet perfectly psychologically apt to use language about God as a personal being in prayer and liturgy, scriptures, and creeds. A non-personalist euteleological theism, then, need not propose (and we certainly do not propose) wholesale replacement or revision of scriptural, liturgical, creedal, or doctrinal claims about God.

If we say no more, however, about how a theism based on euteleological metaphysics makes room for God—no more, that is, than to emphasize that personal God-talk may be psychologically apt even though God makes no appearance as a personal being or any kind of entity in the underlying ontology—a strong suspicion may remain that euteleological theism is a version of theological non-realism, which many regard as atheism in thin disguise. After all, the non-realist idea that, though God doesn't exist in reality, it's beneficial to talk of God as a character in a fiction deploys this same distinction between what's psychologically apt and what's metaphysically acceptable on reflection.[1] However, as we made clear earlier (see Chapter 2, Section 2.1), our euteleological proposal is intended as a theological *realism*; it is a proposal for understanding *the way reality is* if theism is true. We need to do more, then, to meet the challenge that euteleology will be inadequate as a realist account of what ultimate theist reality is like unless its basic ontology can be shown to include some—suitably impressive— referent for 'God'.[2]

We do agree that it is essential for reality to be the God-way that it should be true that God acts 'by intellect and will' in creating and sustaining the Universe and, with salvific effect, within the creation. But we deny that accepting that it is true that God knows and acts is enough to secure a metaphysics in which God is a personal being.[3] In proposing euteleology as a metaphysics for theism, we are thus committed to the view that a euteleological metaphysics provides an ontology in which claims about God's acting in creating and within creation can be made true. But how could that possibly be the case, unless something in the euteleological ontology—if not a supreme person, then at least *something* suitably supreme and exalted— may be identified as God?

We'll attempt an answer to this question in the present chapter. First, we'll consider whether, even though God does not appear for euteleology as 'a being amongst beings', something suitably exalted in euteleological ontology may yet be identified as the unique secure referent for 'God'. Our conclusion will be that no such identification may be made. We will then argue,

---

[1] For this reason, in some previous work where we emphasized the distinction between metaphysical understanding and psychological aptness (e.g., our 2016b and 2016c), we may not have pursued our defence of euteleological theism as a theological realism far enough.

[2] This kind of charge has often been levelled at those who attempt an understanding of theism that goes beyond the personal omniGod. See, e.g., Alasdair MacIntyre's (1963, 222) criticism of Tillich.

[3] For philosophers who make the assumption we are here denying, see, e.g., Norman Kretzmann (1997, 197) and Brian Leftow, who suggests that 'a being that has knowledge and will is person enough for philosophical and theological purposes' (2009, 299). Eleonore Stump (2013), too, argues that whatever has mind or will must be an *id quod est* (a 'that which is', an entity, a concrete particular): Stump claims that, for Aquinas, God is both *esse* and *id quod est*.

nevertheless, that claims about God's existing and acting with great power, understanding, and goodness, can properly be regarded as made true under a metaphysics of ultimate reality such as that proposed by euteleology which has no particular item or feature, however exalted, which may be identified as God.

We'll be maintaining, then, that it is coherent to accept the truth of theological claims in which God is a personal subject, has personal attributes, and acts as a personal agent, while also holding that the underlying metaphysics is the non-personalist metaphysics of euteleology. We'll claim that personal theological language is understood by *a radical type of analogous extension or projection* from our understanding of personal language as applied to human agents. But a euteleological reflective understanding of what makes this language applicable holds God to be neither a supreme person nor identifiable with any specific item or feature in the fundamental ontology. If theism is true, personal talk about God is apt for conveying truths; yet, for a euteleological metaphysics God's reality quite transcends all categories of things that instantiate kinds and possess properties. For any theist metaphysics that holds God to be thus non- or trans-categorial, referring to God as an entity possessing properties must *itself* be an analogizing construction: in order to speak about ultimate reality as theism holds it to be, God-talk deploys a radical form of analogizing which goes beyond mundane analogy in which some *thing* has attributed to it a property understood by analogy with things in a different category. This point about a radical form of analogy involved in God-talk, going beyond mundane forms of analogy, is very important, and we will elaborate it in what follows in order to dispel any impression that there is an irresponsible play on words or equivocal use of terms involved in holding that expressions of the form 'God is F' or 'God φs' can convey truths while denying that 'God' refers to any item in fundamental ontology.

We are, of course, proposing euteleology *as an improvement* on standard personal-omniGod metaphysics—and also on alternatives to a personal-omniGod account that retain a supernatural personal being. Even if (as we'll be arguing in this chapter) euteleology is coherent as a non-personalist metaphysics that nevertheless supports personal talk about God, the question remains whether, overall, euteleology is more religiously adequate to the theist traditions than personal-omniGod or other personalist accounts. We'll reserve this question for the next two chapters, where we will focus, first (in Chapter 5), on whether euteleology offers a better understanding of divine goodness in the face of horrendous evils than do personalist accounts, and, second (in Chapter 6), on the objection that prayer and worship make no sense unless talk of God as a person not only conveys truth but is also backed by an underlying metaphysics which understands the object of worship and the addressee of prayer as a personal being.

4.1 'It's God-ing All Over': A Pantheist Identification?

To return, then, to the top of our agenda for this chapter: may some suitable, non-personal, referent for 'God' be found in euteleology's fundamental ontology?

Euteleology rejects identifying God as a person or a personal being, and goes further to deny that God is any kind of particular 'being among beings'. Accordingly, euteleology affirms divine simplicity in the apophatic sense explained earlier (Chapter 1, pp. 21–2): God lacks the 'composition' of essence and existence, and so is not 'a' being of any kind, however exalted and unique. But won't the truth that God exists imply a metaphysics that identifies God with *something*—or perhaps we should write *someThing*, using a capital 'T', to convey the unsurpassable greatness that a suitable referent for 'God' must uniquely possess? If so, what *is* that 'someThing' on the euteleological account?

According to euteleology, for reality to be as theism claims it to be ('the God-way') is for reality to have inherently an ultimate *telos*, the supreme good, and for the Universe to exist ultimately just because that *telos* is concretely realized within it. There seem to be a number of candidates here for someThing to serve as the referent for 'God'. There's no particular being amongst other particular beings that counts as God; instead euteleology depicts reality as, so to say, *God-ing all over*, since everything real has, just in virtue of its reality, the property of existing for the sake of the realization of the supreme good and only because that ultimate *telos* is realized. The most obvious someThing to suggest as euteleology's referent for 'God' is surely, then, reality itself as a whole 'God-ing all over'. Indeed, it might be suggested that 'God exists' (for a euteleological theism) is to be analysed as having the meaning of the feature-placing statement 'It's God-ing all over' (by analogy with indexically limited feature-placing statements, such as 'It's raining' or 'It's Tuesday').[4]

---

[4] Some philosophical theologians have suggested that 'God' is a verb rather than a noun—e.g., Mary Daly (1985 [1973], 33): 'Why indeed must "God" be a noun? Why not a verb—the

Now, there's nothing wrong with using a grand feature-placing statement—'It's God-ing all over'—to express the claim that all that exists inherently aims at the realization of the supreme good and owes its existence ultimately to the fulfilment of that end. According to euteleology, reality's inherent *eutelicity* (as we said in the previous chapter that we would call it) is an essential feature of everything that's real. And euteleology may reasonably describe that feature, and the whole of reality as possessing it, as *divine*, since eutelicity and reality as possessing it are essential to euteleology's account of what it is for reality to be the God-way. But is God actually to be *identified* with the eutelicity that pervades all that is real, or with reality as thereby unified? If it were held that 'God exists' *just means* 'It's God-ing all over', wouldn't that amount to a *pantheist* identification of God as the Whole of Reality, unified by its eutelicity? And, surely, if a euteleological metaphysics did make that identification, it could not then be a genuinely *theist* metaphysics?

Pantheist elements are not in fact as foreign to theism as often assumed. This is because theism shares with any serious religious pantheism the claim that the Universe of concrete existents constitutes a unified whole in a way that matters for human existence.[5] For theism, what constitutes the Universe as a unified whole is its status as God's creation.[6] A euteleological theism understands the creation's unity as arising from finite existents having their reality constituted by an essential relation to reality's *telos* and its concrete fulfilment. Accordingly, since it doesn't derive creation's unity from the intentional action of a supernatural being, euteleological theism might seem closer to pantheism than standard personalist theism. Yet, for adequacy as an understanding of theism, a euteleological theism must reject the identification of the Universe (= all that exists) with God. For theism, God must be quite 'other than' creatures, including their (unified) totality. Euteleological theism must therefore somehow retain God's 'otherness' from the creation,

---

most active and dynamic of all?'. Sharon Welch (1990, 176) seems to go further: 'Divinity is not a noun or even verb but an adjective or adverb—it connotes a quality of relationships, lives, events, and natural processes', and she cites Gordon Kaufman (1981, 28–30). See also, from a Kabbalist perspective, Rabbi David Cooper (1997, e.g., 65–75), who says that the closest we can get to thinking about God is as a process, and uses the term 'God-ing'.

[5] For a defence of this claim, and a full discussion of pantheism as a religious alternative to personal-omniGod theism, see Michael Levine (1994). For a more recent discussion of some core conceptual and ontological issues related to pantheist conceptions of God, see Andrei Buckareff (2022).

[6] For discussions of the relation between theism and pantheism (and in particular whether classical theism entails a version of pantheism), see, e.g., a series of papers by Robert Oakes, and replies to him, beginning with Oakes (1977).

while rejecting the treatment of that otherness as the supernatural distinctness of a unique personal being, or, indeed as the distinctness of 'a' being of any kind at all. How this may be done is a topic we will take up in what follows (see Section 4.5).

Although an adequate euteleological theism will not *identify* God with the Universe as a whole, or with its unifying eutelicity, it may nevertheless count both of these as essentially *divine* (as essentially 'of, or pertaining to, God'), since, for euteleological theism, it is essential to reality's being the God-way that the Universe has this unifying eutelicity. But the Universe is not *God*. This is because any 'Thing' adequate as a referent for 'God' would have to *exhaust* the divine: there couldn't be anything essentially 'of God' that didn't belong to such a Thing's reality. But, for a euteleological theism, neither reality as a whole nor its eutelic principle of unity exhausts the divine.[7] There are other features of euteleological metaphysics that a euteleological theism *also* recognizes as essentially divine, as we will shortly be elaborating in considering further suggestions for an identification for God in the euteleological ontology.

4.2 God as Ultimate *Telos*, the Supreme Good?

Might an identification for God be implied by euteleology's ultimate explanation for the Universe as existing because it contains concrete realizations of the supreme good which is reality's *telos*?

In previous work, we introduced euteleology in a way that did suggest an identification of God as ultimate cause, albeit different from the standard one where God is the supernatural producer of the Universe. We said, for example, that '[t]he core of the euteleological conception is that God's being the ultimate supremely good *telos* (end, purpose) of the Universe *is the very same thing* as God's being its ultimate cause', going on to observe that '[t]he Universe may then count as a cosmic unity even though it has *no*

---

[7] This idea that reality as a unified whole is divine but does not exhaust what's essential to divinity suggests that euteleological theism, though not pantheist, may be a form of panentheism. We take up the question whether euteleological theism is a panentheism in Section 4.12 below. Using 'divine' to mean 'of, or pertaining to, God' accords with the standard *Oxford English Dictionary* definition. Only God 'himself' is *fully* divine, of course: something divine that essentially pertains to God cannot then properly be identified with God unless it exhausts all that essentially pertains to the divine.

supernatural producer' (Bishop and Perszyk 2016a, 119–20).[8] Marilyn Adams accordingly criticized our view by asking the question, 'What does it mean to identify alternative-God as ultimate end?', and then posing objections for each of a range of possible answers (2016, 130). In fact, however, our euteleological theism does *not* claim that God just is reality's ultimate *telos*.[9] When we canvassed that suggestion we were (as we now see it) making only an opening move, signalling that a theological ultimate explanation lacks any significance for human existence unless and until *the ultimate purposes* of creation are specified. That God is 'Alpha' doesn't count for much (save as a purely theoretical tenet) except in so far as we have some appreciation of the (telic) 'Omega' that God is also. There's not, in other words, much significance for us in believing that our world has an ultimate source unless we also hold some beliefs about the ultimate purposes implicated in this 'sourcing'.[10]

It's essential to euteleological theism, then, that reality has an overall *telos*, but euteleological theism does not *identify* reality's *telos* with God. Reality's *telos*, and the supreme good that constitutes it, certainly are *divine*, since they are essential to reality's being the God-way according to a euteleological account. And the nature of the supreme good may be understood as the divine 'character', with claims about the revelation of the supreme good to humanity accordingly understood as claims about the disclosing of that divine character. A euteleological theism thus affirms the nature of the supreme good as the unchanging distinctive character of the divine. The supreme good is not *identified* with God, however, because the supreme good, reality's *telos*, is, as such, an abstract ideal, and any reasonable understanding of theism must take God's existence to be more than the abstract existence of an ideal—though, of course, theism holds a realist or 'objective'

---

[8] In another context we wrote:

What the euteleological conception emphasizes is that God is creator, not just in the sense that God is the source of all that exists, but also in the sense that God is the ultimate purpose, end, or *telos* of all that exists (where 'all that exists' is here intended to include all that ever has or ever will exist).

We noted in a footnote that the idea of God's being the ultimate *telos* is suggested in scripture: at Revelation 22:13 the angel speaks on behalf of the One who is 'coming soon' saying, 'I am the Alpha and the Omega, the first and the last, the beginning and the end (*to telos*)' (Bishop and Perszyk 2016b, 207). See also our (2014, 3 and 8).

[9] Despite opening remarks (as just quoted) in which we seemed to be making a specific identification for God, a marked caution about *any* such identifications was a feature of our earlier accounts of euteleology—see Bishop and Perszyk (2014, §3, 2016a, 120–1, and 2016b, §11, 217). That caution, in any case, is the theme of our present discussion.

[10] For further argument for the centrality of specifying ultimate purposes for theological explanation see Bishop (2018a).

view of the absolute good's being what it is. Furthermore, on the euteleological account, reality's being the God-way does indeed require essential *concrete* features beyond ideal goodness being what it is.

4.3 God as Realization of the Supreme Good?

In particular, on the euteleological account, goodness as an abstract ideal does not exhaust the divine because it's essential that ideal goodness *is concretely realized*. It might be suggested, then, that a euteleological theism might identify God with *realizations* of supreme goodness (and thus, on our Christian example of the revealed supreme good, with perfectly loving, agapeistic, relationships).

According to a euteleological theism, for this (or any) concrete Universe to exist it is necessary that it contain some realizations of the supreme good. No *particular* realization is necessary; it's necessary only that there be *some* such realizations. Yet there can be *some* realizations of the supreme good only through the existence of *certain particular* such realizations. For euteleological theism, then, those particular existents or relations amongst existents that do realize the supreme good not only manifest the character of the divine, but—it seems fitting to say—are also a precious component in reality's being the God-way. They participate in the fulfilment of reality's *telos*, and (on the euteleological account) nothing would have existed had contingent existents such as they not done so.

Realizations of the supreme good, then, are divine ('of God') in the sense that contingent existents such as they have an essential place in reality's being the God-way; yet they do not exhaust the divine, and therefore cannot be identified as the unique secure referent for 'God'. All the concrete realizations of supreme goodness, taken as a whole, may perhaps (on suitable mereological assumptions) make up an impressive aggregate existent—and there might be infinitely many such realizations if the Universe is itself infinite, perhaps in the form of an infinite multiverse. Nevertheless, for a euteleological theism, even an infinity of contingent realizations of the good cannot exhaust what's essential to the divine, since reality's eutelicity is a divine feature transcending all concrete existents. *God* is not to be identified, then, with the totality of the realizations of the supreme good that emerge within the Universe. That identification would amount to an emergentist understanding of the divine of the kind we earlier rejected as inadequate for theism on the grounds that it would make God contingently dependent on the long history of the evolving Universe (see Chapter 2, Section 2.10). We also reject a view that Marilyn Adams suggests may be ours, namely, to identify God with perfectly loving relationship understood as an Aristotelian immanent universal (see Adams 2016, 135–6). God as emergent, or God as immanent universal—these proposals cannot, we think, properly accommodate divine transcendence; our proposal for euteleological theism is to be distinguished from both of them.[11]

4.4 A Theist Ontology without a Specific Referent for 'God'?

We conclude, then, that God, that which is unsurpassably onto-ethically great and the fit object of worship, does not appear *as a specifically identifiable item or feature* in fundamental euteleological ontology. As we argued in Chapter 1, the concept of God is the concept of that which fills the 'God-roles' (see Chapter 1, pp. 15–16). Yet we are now saying that there's no specific item in euteleology's fundamental ontology which fills the God-roles. We are saying, that is, that a euteleological metaphysics for theism can identify God neither with eutelic reality as a whole, nor with reality's principle of unity (its eutelicity), nor with the supreme good which is reality's *telos*, nor with the concrete realizations of reality's *telos*, nor with the Universe that contains those realizations. Each of these essential features of euteleological metaphysics does count, however, as 'of God' (that is, as divine) in so far as it is a necessary feature of reality's being the God-way on a euteleological account of what that means. Another such necessary feature is the existence of powers *within* the Universe capable of giving rise to realizations of the supreme good; a euteleological theism will thus count these powers as divine, and their exercise as divine activity. Again, though, these features are divine in the sense that they are essentially *of* God, they are not identifiable *as* God.

To the human mind seeking theoretical mastery, then, euteleology renders God metaphysically somewhat elusive. That is not particularly surprising, however, since a euteleological theism foregrounds theism's affirmation of the overall purposiveness of existence, and human life within it, as revealed

---

[11] A euteleological theism should be distinguished, then, from the emergentist theology of Samuel Alexander (1920), as well as from more recent varieties of pantheistic emergentism found, e.g., in Philip Clayton and Arthur Peacocke's (2004) volume. For a defence of Alexander against recent emergentist theologies, and especially Philip Clayton's criticism of Alexander, see Emily Thomas (2016).

in the Abrahamic religious traditions. Euteleology thus offers an alternative to a theist metaphysics focused on God as a personal supernatural being, but an alternative which, rather than specifying some *other* identifiable item or feature of ultimate reality as God, instead resists the attempt to pin God down in that way.

But isn't the absence of any fundamentally real individual entity that can be identified as God an embarrassment for any attempt to defend euteleology as a fit metaphysics for theism?[12] On the face of it, a theist ontology needs a unique secure referent for 'God' in order to satisfy a number of key claims—in particular, that the Universe is God's creation and that God, as Creator, is wholly distinct from it; that God acts intentionally in creating, and also, to salvific effect, within creation; that God has the attributes of omnipotence, omniscience, and omnibenevolence, which seem to be personal attributes; and, finally, that the basic claim that God exists is true, and *is made true* in virtue of that fundamental ontology. Since, as we have just argued, no real item or feature in euteleological ontology could properly be identified as the secure referent for 'God', it might be claimed that euteleology provides no basis for understanding God's distinctness as Creator, or for God's agency, or even for the basic truth that God exists. It might therefore be objected that euteleological metaphysics is plainly not adequate for theism.

We believe this objection may be met. We will argue that a euteleological metaphysics *can* secure God's distinctness from creation, as well as accounting for truths about God's action and the basic truth of God's existence, even though no item identifiable as God appears in its fundamental ontology. Omnipotence, omniscience, and omnibenevolence obviously cannot be accommodated if they have to be understood as attributes of a supreme personal intentional agent; we will argue, however, that a euteleological theism may secure adequate alternative construals of these attributes which do not imply that God is a personal being. We will be arguing, then, that God's

---

[12] Mikael Stenmark (2015) describes as 'alterity theism' the view that God is 'beyond or without being'. Stenmark contrasts alterity theism with personal theism; this contrast, he thinks, marks one of the most important dividing lines among philosophers of religion and theologians today. He thinks that both personal and alterity theists face challenges. In particular, in his view, alterity theism runs the risk of exaggerating transcendence to the point where it struggles to account for God's immanence and salvific action in the world. Stenmark notes that a common objection to alterity theism is that a God who isn't a being is no God at all. See, e.g., Peter van Inwagen (2006, 19), where the shamed target, Gordon Kaufman, is unnamed. Stenmark (2015, 209, citing C. Stephen Evans 1996, 64) points out that Plantinga is reported to have said, when asked whether God was a being: 'Of course, what else is there to be?'.

being 'no-thing' in euteleology's fundamental ontology is not an indication that euteleological metaphysics is atheist or theological fictionalist metaphysics; instead, euteleological metaphysics fits theism's classical theme that God's supreme reality (than which nothing greater can even be conceived) transcends (or 'goes beyond') the ontological status of 'a' being (however great) amongst other beings. God is not an individual entity or particular item 'in' an ontology; one might rather say (taking a deep breath, for fear of raising other misconceptions!) that, for theism, God *is* ultimate ontology itself (for more on this last point, see pp. 119–21 below).

4.5 A Euteleological Account of Creation *Ex Nihilo* and God's Distinctness from Creation

The Universe's theistic status as a creation—and of the beings within it as creatures—is essentially correlated with something that confers creatureliness. Creatures have to be not only part of something 'bigger', but also ultimately dependent on the Creator who transcends their own creaturely existence. As we argued in Chapter 3 (Section 3.7), euteleology makes available an ultimate explanation of the Universe's existence. Euteleology explains the Universe as existing because 'it does what it's for'. For euteleology, contingent concrete existence depends ultimately on reality's inherent euteliicity and the Universe's containing realizations of reality's *telos*, the supreme good.

The question now, however, is whether euteleology's ultimate explanation may count as an adequate *theological* explanation of the Universe as a creation with a Creator properly distinct from it, given that fundamental euteleological ontology admits no individual being or entity that could be identified with the Creator God. We'll defend a positive answer to that question: we'll argue that a euteleological theism can accommodate the Universe as a divine creation in virtue of its fulfilled inherent direction upon reality's overall *telos*, the supreme good.[13]

---

[13] Compare Fiona Ellis, who observes that 'God's action is not confined to his role in getting things going, but is to be understood in terms of *its broader teleological aim which is to turn human nature towards its end in God*' (2014, ch.7, online Abstract; emphasis ours). Of course, theism characteristically holds that God is a sustaining creator, not merely an initiating one; but we think that Ellis's positive characterization of God's creativity conveys something similar to our euteleological proposal, namely the idea of the divine creation as existence unified under an overall teleological aim.

The theist doctrine of creation is, as noted earlier (Chapter 3, p. 79), classically the doctrine of creation *ex nihilo*. God doesn't create the Universe *from* anything pre-existent—though on the standard personalist account God's own necessary existence is 'prior' to the contingent existence of the Universe. Even on that standard account, however, the phrase '*ex nihilo*' has apophatic force, and proponents of the doctrine are thereby committed to accepting an incomprehensible mystery. As David Fergusson says about creation 'from nothing',

> 'nothing' simply denotes 'not something'. It is not a shadowy primeval substance suspended between being and nonbeing. Instead, we should regard [the creation *ex nihilo* doctrine] merely as a way of saying what is not. In other words, the cosmos is *not* formed from eternal matter, nor does it emanate from the divine being. (2014, 20)

A euteleological theism takes this apophatic reading a step further: it holds that the Universe is not formed from pre-existing eternal matter, nor does it emanate from the eternal divine being, *nor* is it the product and continuing production of a Supreme Producer.

Euteleology may thus be understood as accommodating creation *ex nihilo* in an especially pure form. Now, it may, of course, be said that 'a Universe out of nothing' is precisely what atheist 'naturalism' maintains in holding that 'something rather than nothing' is just brute fact. And it's true that a euteleological theist agrees with atheists who claim that there is nothing concrete 'external' or 'prior' to the Universe, for the Universe is, indeed, *all* that concretely, and wholly contingently, exists. But euteleology utterly rejects the Universe as 'brute fact', affirming the distinctively theistic claim that the Universe exists for the sake of an overall purpose, and explaining the Universe's existence through appeal to a higher, transmundane, causal order grounded in the necessity of reality's essential directedness upon realizing the supreme good, but having no recourse to any necessarily existent concrete *being* (see Chapter 3, Section 3.11, for our defence of the coherence of this account).

Concrete existence inherently directed upon reality's overall good, and existing ultimately because it contains realizations of that supreme good, is, we maintain, entirely fit to be described as a divine creation *ex nihilo*. This description does, though, involve *an analogous extension* from the 'base' notions of a creation as a product and the creative agent as its producer. A euteleological theism counts every existent as 'made' in an analogically extended sense, given that it admits no 'maker' in the sense of an intentional agent who produces it. On a euteleological account, creatures manifest 'the handiwork of their Maker' in so far as their reality participates, in limited characteristic ways according to their kind, in reality's overall inherent directedness upon the realization of the supreme good, and each creature is actual only because it belongs to a Universe in which that good is realized.

It might be complained, then, that a theist doctrine of creation can be defended on a euteleological theist account only as holding 'by analogy'. Outright objection to recourse to analogy can hardly be warranted, however— not, anyway, by anyone whose account of theism endorses creation *ex nihilo*, since *any* such account must make appeal to analogously extended senses of creation and creating. The qualifier '*ex nihilo*' is a clear signal that here we have creation of a unique type, intelligible only by analogy from ordinary creative production, and, in some not fully comprehensible way, violating the mundane empirical principle that you cannot get something from nothing. On any account of it, in creation *ex nihilo* there is nothing prior on which God acts, so something comes 'from' nothing in the sense that there is nothing from which it is made. As Fergusson makes clear (2014, 16), the *ex nihilo nihil fit* principle was originally used to argue against the emerging doctrine of creation *ex nihilo*—in favour of the eternity of the world or creation/emanation out of something (that has always been). Creation *ex nihilo* is thus unique, and violates the *ex nihilo nihil fit* principle as it applies to mundane experience, since there is (in scholastic terms) no passive potency (prior substance or prime matter) on which God acts and which is changed in creating. It seems to us, then, that it would be somewhat arbitrary for defenders of creation *ex nihilo* to object to our extended apophatic reading of that doctrine purely on the grounds that it offends the principle that 'nothing comes from nothing'.

Nevertheless, it might more reasonably be objected that, though some analogous extension from mundane creative production is essential in making creation *ex nihilo* intelligible, analogizing has gone too far if (as on our euteleological proposal) the Universe is supposed to be a creation in the absence of any individual being that could be identified, even in some analogous sense, as its creator. Theism requires that the Creator be distinct from the creation: how can that be ensured if God is not an individual being, and, therefore, *a fortiori*, not an individual being distinct from all creaturely beings?

If God's distinctness does not amount to God's separate existence *as a being*, God's distinctness from creation may yet be understood *apophatically*. For euteleological theism, God is not 'a' being of any kind, and is beyond all categories of existing things (as the doctrine of divine simplicity affirms, on the account we have given of it—see Chapter 1, pp. 17–18 and pp. 21–2). As many theologians have said, God is 'no-thing'—a sure way of being absolutely distinct from the world of things![14]

Resting God's distinctness from creation on God's 'no-thing-ness' won't seem challenging if this startling talk may be defused as a way of pointing out what every interpreter of theism will accept, namely, that God is no-*created*-thing. But euteleology's rejection of God's 'thing-ness' goes deeper, since a euteleological theism *also* rejects the identification of God with an *uncreated* (and necessarily existent) supernatural thing (again, as we maintain, in accordance with the doctrine of divine simplicity).

That deeper 'no-thing-ness' will seem tantamount to atheism if one is taking it for granted that God's distinctness from creation must amount to the distinctness *of a particular being*.[15] But that's the very assumption we are here rejecting! We've just been articulating an alternative to the standard personalist understanding of creaturely dependence on God in which God's distinctness from creation does *not* consist in being 'himself' a particular concrete, necessary, existent belonging uniquely to a distinct ontological category. Some further grounds for finding that articulation wanting will be needed, then, if the objector is to avoid simply begging the question.

4.6 Talk about God and God's Action as Analogical

One further objection arises from a consideration of divine action, which, on the face of it, does seem hard to make intelligible if God is 'no-thing'. Even if the Universe's being a creation and God's transcendence over it are not as such essentially linked to God's being a concrete supernatural being, this link may nevertheless seem required for it to be true that God *acts*, both

---

[14] The view that God is no-thing seems widespread amongst theologians (for a recent defence of this view, see Rupert Shortt 2016). Few contemporary analytic philosophers of religion, however, would be prepared to follow Herbert McCabe in saying 'whatever God is, he is…not a thing or kind of thing' (1987, 6). Mark Wynn (2013, 66) recalls McCabe's comment in lectures that 'God and the world do not make two.' And, as Janet Soskice (2005, 32–3) puts it, 'Two "things" can only be so near—but God is not a thing. The non-thingness of God means, as Augustine says, that God can be nearer to me than I am to myself.' (On this last point, compare our own reservations about the adequacy of accounts both of God's immanence and of God's transcendence when God is understood as a personal being—Chapter 1, Section 1.6.)

[15] As is assumed, e.g., by H. P. Owen (1971, 122f).

in creating, and in bringing God's purposes to fulfilment within creation. Does it not follow, then, that any adequate theist metaphysics must include *something* identifiable as the secure referent for 'God' which may properly be described, at least by analogy, as knowing, willing, and acting?

No, that conclusion does not follow. It *can* be true that God acts, yet without theism's fundamental ontology including *any* item or feature identifiable as God. This is because talk of God as acting may be understood as analogous in a radical way in which the very use of 'God' as a referring term is understood only by analogy. We'll now elaborate and defend this claim.

First, a brief general reflection on the way analogy is involved in personal talk about God. Theists hold that God's nature, as it is in itself, cannot be humanly 'comprehended'. Reality's being the God-way does, however, become intelligible to us—though only in limited ways and only because what we need to know (or, anyway, accept 'by faith') is *revealed*. Our articulation of what's revealed is—obviously—constrained by the limits of human thought and language. Essential to that articulation is the language of God as a personal being, acting 'by intellect and will': according to theist traditions, otherwise unavailable truths are disclosed through the use of that language. Reflective faith, however, may come to recognize (not least by pondering scriptural passages which convey God's transcendence) that this personal language applied to God does not transparently disclose to human mastery the nature of ultimate reality as theism claims it to be. It may be true that God knows, wills, and acts, but our understanding of what claims of this kind mean rests on analogizing from our understanding of what such claims mean in our own case. What it *actually is* for it to be true that God acts cannot be understood as just the very same thing as what it is for a human being to act; the precise way in which truths about God's acting are made true is thus, in significant degree, beyond our understanding.

This 'doctrine of analogous predication' is familiar enough: we find it in Augustine, elaborated by Aquinas, and discussed (and its details much disputed) by various medieval philosophers.[16] But the general idea is uncontroversial—the meaning of personal attributes ascribed to God is understood *by analogy* with what they mean when applied to human

---

[16] For a survey of medieval theories of analogy, see Jennifer Ashworth (2017). Analogical predication allows us to say some things about God that are true, even though what they mean is strictly incomprehensible in the sense that we cannot gain cognitive mastery of what is meant. Pursuing any detailed scholarship about the history of theories of analogy is well beyond our scope here, though we do think it is worth noting that Christopher Hughes (2010) argues that Aquinas's views on analogy depend on his doctrine of divine simplicity.

persons. Proponents of standard personalist accounts of theism will agree that God's agency is, in certain respects, uniquely unlike human agency. As already noted in Section 4.5, creating *ex nihilo* is unlike any human act of creation; describing God as creating 'from nothing' must thus involve an analogous extension from our grasp of what it means for a potter to make a pot, for example.

Accounts which hold that God is *not* ('literally') a person, however, will need to regard talk of God as knowing, willing, and acting as involving a more stretched analogous extension, in which attributes themselves understood as applying by analogy attach to something that is not actually a person, but nevertheless to be understood as analogous to one (or 'more like a person than a non-person'). However, for any account of theist metaphysics where no entity in fundamental ontology is identified as God (where God is 'no-thing'), a still more stretched form of analogizing must be involved in personal talk about God, as, indeed, in *any* predication of attributes to God treated as an entity referred to using 'God' as the grammatical subject of predication.

It's beyond our present scope to offer any general theory of analogy and its types; yet we will describe the kind of radical analogizing that we think must be involved in meaningful attributions to God on any account of theist metaphysics which (like our own euteleological proposal) lacks God as an entity in fundamental ontology. We will thus press a point highly salient for understanding how our euteleological proposal may be accepted as religiously adequate for theism, since it is a *desideratum* for adequacy that an account be given of how the proposed metaphysics can support personal talk about God as able to convey truths.

Here's the point we wish to press. In speaking and thinking of God as a being who knows, wills, and acts, we are not engaged merely in the mundane use of analogy in which something has attributed to it a property understood by analogy with things in a different category (as, for example, when a chemistry teacher describes atoms of the elements sodium and chlorine as wanting to complete their outer electron shells and so disposed to combine to form common salt). In attributing to God properties understood through their application to persons, we are stretching our analogizing beyond applying personal predicates to some *thing* in a different category: the very thought of God as 'a' thing, entity, or substance to which properties may be attributed is *itself* a kind of analogizing. That is, thinking of God as an entity that may possess properties may be regarded as extending by analogy our 'thing-property' schema from its ordinary use to the unique context of the nature of ultimate reality as theism holds it to be.[17] Accordingly, a proposed metaphysics may not fairly be rejected as inadequate to theism just because no specific item in its fundamental ontology is identifiable as the unique secure referent for 'God'. Such a metaphysics may be consistent with its being true that God wills and acts, since 'God wills and acts thus and so' describes ultimate reality in personal terms, and, indeed, in thing-property terms, *only by an analogous construction*. What that ultimate reality is *in itself* is something that cannot be fully comprehended by finite minds: yet an analogous extension of our mundane thought categories can make accessible to us truths about ultimate reality and the practical, ethical, implications for humans of our relation to that ultimate reality.

A euteleological theism, then, holds that thinking of God as a particular entity with personal attributes is a constructive extension by analogy of our ordinary thing-property understanding of talk about persons from its mundane context to that of ultimate reality. This claim is importantly distinct from the claim that God is a uniquely special entity to be understood as like or analogous to a person, which is the way personal-omniGod theists commonly interpret the idea that personal attributions to God involve predication by analogy.[18] Our claim is more radical. We are claiming that the very thought of God as an entity amongst entities is itself possible only by a process of extending by analogy our mundane 'thing-property' schema to apply to ultimate reality itself. In this process God-as-a-thing gets constructed as a subject for the attribution of properties as a means for conveying truth-claims about ultimate reality as being the God-way. All such truth-claims (of the form 'God is F', 'God φs', etc.) rest on this analogizing construction; their 'surface' ontology does not, then, disclose to human comprehension the nature of God's reality, even when they do state truths. According to this thesis of God's 'thingness' as itself an analogizing construction, God is an

---

[17] Our view that personal talk of God involves an analogous extension of the 'thing-property' schema has been influenced by Thomas Harvey's claim, made during the oral defence of his doctoral thesis (Harvey 2018), that Aquinas's doctrine of analogous predication *itself* deploys a, higher order, analogy. If analogy is defined as applying to something of a different category a predicate whose meaning is understood from its application to things in its 'base' category, then, given divine simplicity, analogous predication couldn't (literally!) apply to God (since God's reality transcends all categories of entity): so, speaking of God as willing and knowing, etc., can only be *analogous to* analogous predication. This elegant point alerted us to the radical nature of the analogizing involved in personal talk of God, though we are here expressing what we take to be radical about it in a different (less elegant, but perhaps more perspicuous) way.

[18] Examples include Swinburne (1993 [1977], part 3) and Hugh McCann in his reply to an early version of our (2016a), which was presented at a conference in Birmingham in 2012.

entity only in the broadest sense that there are truths expressed in sentences with 'God' as grammatical subject. An analogizing construction is needed to make that mode of expression possible, and so the truths so expressed are not made true by any property-bearing entity identified as God in fundamental ontology. Instead, in ways we cannot fully comprehend but may within limits make reflectively intelligible, the truth-makers for these analogously constructed claims (when they are true) will be (some aspect of) ultimate reality itself being the God-way, the way it is when theism is true. (We have already defended this kind of appeal to incomprehensibility—see Chapter 3, Sections 3.12 and 3.13.)

We are not, of course, suggesting that believers themselves generally understand their personal God-talk as involving an analogizing construction. Nevertheless, we think that in practice believers *are* typically sensitive to something uniquely special in talk about God. Such talk, paradoxically, 'names' the unnameable,[19] even though believers seldom make any such reflection, and do not scruple to continue to use personal God-talk if they do. Furthermore, from the perspective of the theist traditions themselves, speaking about God and to God is encouraged, even mandated.[20] Thus, using personal 'thing-property' language with 'God' as subject is seen by theists as a matter of providential divine dispensation. God's revelation, in other words, *includes* the revelatory worth of and need for personal address to, and personal language about, God. Theists hold (using personal God-talk at the meta-level) that God *wants* us to speak of and to God in this way.

Believers accept scriptural narratives about God's personal interactions with God's people. These narratives often depict God in human ways, as having feelings and emotions and even occasionally undergoing a change of mind—indeed, sometimes they go so far as to describe God's person in corporeal terms. From the believer's perspective, the true personal claims about God are to be accepted, so to say, at face value. Accepting at face value personal descriptions of God is not, however, tantamount to accepting a personalist metaphysics of the divine.[21] For—to ascend to the meta-level

---

[19] We have already referred to God's unnameability and its significance in honouring divine transcendence (see Chapter 1, pp. 25–6).

[20] 'Lord, open my lips, and my mouth will speak out your praise' (Psalm 51:15), to give but one example.

[21] The Islamic jurist Malik Ibn Anas is reported to have said, referring to God 'sitting on the throne' (Qur'an 7:54, 20:5), 'The sitting is known, its modality is unknown. Belief in it is an obligation and raising questions regarding it is a heresy' (as cited by Majid Fakhry (2004, xix)). Our thanks to Imran Aijaz for drawing this quotation to our attention: Aijaz comments (in personal correspondence) that the standard Islamic view (in Sunni Islam) is that

again—believers may accept that *God also wants* us to recognize our intellectual limitations in relation to God's own absolute and unlimited reality. What's divinely revealed in human language is necessarily subject to the limitations of human language and thought, however clearly the miraculous beauty of that language may be held to indicate its divine origin.[22] Theists may say, then, that God wants us to think of God as willing and acting, but not to run away with the idea that we thereby understand God's nature as it is in itself. Thus, in the revelations claimed by the Abrahamic faith traditions, God may rightly be understood as conveying the value of relating to God through the exercise of our personal and inter-personal faculties and powers and, accordingly, of using personal language in address to God and in talk about God: but God does *not* thereby reveal that God may be understood in reality as a person or personal being. From this insider theist perspective, then, we maintain that it is consistent to accept the truth of revelations made to human beings as expressed in language that speaks of God as a personal being, while also (as on our proposal for a euteleological theism) adhering to a metaphysical understanding of ultimate divine reality in which, not only is God not literally a person or a personal being, but there's *no entity* in fundamental ontology identifiable as the referent for 'God'.[23]

We are claiming, then, that truth-claims about God that depend on the analogizing construction of God as a (uniquely great) thing can be true when God is 'no-thing' in fundamental ontology. But how could that possibly be so? Is it not clear that our thesis of the analogizing construction of God as a thing entails that God is unreal, or, at most, real only 'in' a fiction?

---

anthropomorphic descriptions of God are to be accepted 'without asking how'. Accepting at face value that God sits on the throne need not to be regarded, then, as requiring or entitling the believer to accept, at the level of a comprehensible fundamental ontology, that God is any kind of personal being, let alone that God has what Grandma taught us to call a 'sit-upon'! Compare also the Christian affirmation that Christ is raised to 'the right hand' of God (see, for one of many such references, Romans 8:34).

[22] We have in mind the Islamic belief that the Qur'an itself is the miracle that confirms Mohammed's status as the Prophet—and the beauty of the Arabic in which the Qur'anic revelation is expressed is an essential part of this.

[23] Wesley Wildman (2006) draws a distinction between 'ground-of-being theologies' and 'determinate entity theism(s)'. If (as is evident) a euteleological theism doesn't belong in the latter category, it might then be supposed to belong to the former. It is true that some who agree that God is not 'a' being amongst or alongside other beings then go on to make a 'higher identification'—e.g., of God as Being itself, or as the ground of being. Euteleological theism, however, resists any such identification at the level of fundamental ontology, holding instead (as we have just been explaining) that God is an entity only in so far as there are truths expressible using 'God' as subject which we understand by a constructive analogous extension from our understanding of mundane 'thing-property' attributions.

Our appeal to 'God as a construction' is, surely, the currency of naturalist-atheists and non-realist theological fictionalists?

In response to these critical queries, we will, in the rest of this chapter, reaffirm our commitment to theological realism. We'll defend our use *as realists* of the thesis that talk of God as an entity results from an analogizing construction. And we'll make intelligible the idea that a euteleological ontology, lacking a God-entity, may yet provide truth-makers for personal talk about God as knowing, willing, and acting, as well as for characteristic theist doctrinal and philosophical claims about God. As already indicated, we are reserving for our final chapter (Chapter 6) a response to the overriding objection that, for essential theist practices such as prayer and worship to make sense, God has to be an entity that counts as a person or personal being at the level of fundamental ontology and not merely according to an analogizing construction.

4.7 Euteleological Theism, Robustly Realist!

It is, we think, clear that understanding talk of God as meaningful through an analogous construction does *not* entail that God, as thus constructed, must be an unreal, purely fictional, entity. There's no doubt, though, that the thesis of God's thingness as an analogizing construction is *the very same thesis* that theological non-realists (and, for that matter, naturalist-atheists) will endorse in giving their account of what humans mean in talking about God. The alleged inference to God's unreality does not follow, however, because of *the different context* in which theological realists may situate this 'constructivist' or 'projectivist' thesis—a context wider and richer than the one in which atheists and theological non-realists situate it.

For this 'constructivist' thesis to be true, there must be *some* human cognitive, conceptual, mechanism capable of constructing the idea of God as a 'higher' being not available to ordinary sensory perception. This cognitive mechanism won't involve any deliberate or conscious actions on the part of human individuals or groups; rather, it will be an evolved feature of human social psychology, open to empirical investigation. Various theories about the nature and development of cognitive mechanisms that yield religious beliefs have been put forward in contemporary evolutionary psychology and cognitive science of religion (CSR). Perhaps, for example, belief in the God of the Abrahamic traditions is an instance of a group fitness-enhancing elaboration of beliefs in 'gods', invisible agents with memorably special features (for example, being present in multiple locations in time and space, knowing what is otherwise hidden, etc.), beliefs which themselves form as a side-effect of evolved human cognition of the presence and activity of intentional agents in the environment.[24] The empirical specifics, interesting and controversially speculative as they are, are not relevant for our argument here, however; all we need for present purposes is agreement that, if the 'constructivist' thesis about God as an entity is correct, there must be *some* way in which human psychology accomplishes this construction, and this process (and its origin) will be open to a 'naturalist' explanation.

In philosophical discussion of the implications of religious belief being open to naturalist explanations such as those proposed in CSR, it emerges that different general perspectives may be taken on these natural scientific causal explanations of our construction of 'gods'. There is, of course, a naturalist-atheist perspective which interprets these explanations as explaining why belief in gods is so ubiquitous, even though (as it supposes) all such beliefs are erroneous. If there are natural cognitive mechanisms which lead us to construct gods and, by analogy, attribute personal properties to them, then such belief will occur generally in human communities even if it is systematically false (a *consensus gentium* argument for the reasonableness of belief in higher beings is thus undermined). Theological non-realists essentially share this naturalist-atheist perspective, but maintain that continued belief in gods or God is worthwhile, even though strictly erroneous: it's beneficial to invest in the religious fictions which get woven on the frame constructed by evolved cognitive mechanisms.

There is, however, another perspective on our construction of gods which is neither atheist nor anti-realist. If we have a realist theological perspective, human cognitive mechanisms that construct gods may be seen as enabling human beings to gain truths necessary for fit practical alignment of their beliefs and practices with ultimate reality and its overall divine purposes as they really are. Naturalist explanations of theist belief need not be 'debunking', then, since they may be interpreted as describing ways in which divine purposes are revealed (within limits) to humanity.[25] It is this kind of perspective on the analogizing construction of God-as-a-thing that we believe

---

[24] See, e.g., Justin Barrett (2004) and Ara Norenzayan (2013). For recent surveys of research in CSR, see, e.g., Hans van Eyghen, Rik Peels, and Gijsbert van den Brink (2018) and Robert McCauley (2020).

[25] For an example of a defence of the claim that, while CSR explanations are clearly compatible with atheism, they need not be incompatible with theism, see David Leech and Aku Visala (2011).

a realist euteleological theism can take. We may affirm the very same 'constructivist' claim about the way God-talk gets its meaning as made by theological fictionalists, yet retain a realist account of what distinguishes theism from atheism, albeit an account for which reality's being the God-way necessarily does not, at the level of fundamental ontology, include the concrete existence of 'a' supreme being with great-making properties.

We remain adamant, then, that our account of a euteleological theism is robustly realist: it is an account of how *reality* is if theism is true. The euteleological claim that reality is inherently directed upon the supreme good, and that the Universe exists ultimately because it realizes reality's *telos*, is not an account of a humanly constructed fiction with advantages for those who invest in it; it is an account of how 'the world' is, of how things really are. If reality is the euteleological God-way, that is the case without its being made so in virtue of any fact about the beliefs, attitudes, or cognitive capacities of any finite mind or minds. It is true that we are holding that talk of God *as an entity* is humanly constructed: but we are insisting that what makes claims of the form 'God is F', 'God φs', etc., true when they are true *is something about how reality is* independently of any human belief about, or construction of, how reality may be. (Yes, we are saying that talk of God *as a thing with properties* results from a human cognitive construction. No, we are emphatically not saying that God's reality is a humanly constructed fiction.) We may thus affirm (as any adequate account of theism must do), that—though, for euteleology, God is no-thing—our talk about God can connect us with *how things ultimately really are* in existentially vital ways. Our view is not, then, open to the objection commonly made against theological non-realists that it's ethically questionable to defend adherence to theism if (as non-realists imply) believers are basing their lives on a (beneficial) pretence. Reflective understanding may show—as we maintain—that God's reality transcends being a 'thing' however exalted; but that by no means implies that sentences in which the term 'God' functions as subject for predication are systematically false or true only in a fiction, as our defence of such sentences as involving a radical analogizing construction has been intended to show.[26]

---

[26] It might reasonably be asked what is the real, practical, difference between taking talk of God to be capable of conveying truths about ultimate reality through an analogizing projection from mundane categories of thought (as on our euteleological theological realism) and taking it to describe a fiction worth treating as if real because of the beneficial consequences of so doing. It's beyond our present scope to enter into a wider debate about how our 'constructivist' realism about God-as-a-thing compares with theological fictionalism. We will, however,

Of course, a euteleological theism will persist in seeming non-realist on the assumption that theological realism requires accepting that 'God' refers to some identifiable entity in fundamental ontology. But it is that very assumption we have been challenging by arguing that there can be a realist account of theist metaphysics that at the level of fundamental ontology lacks any identifiable referent for 'God'. We have argued, in other words, that we are giving an account of what it is for *reality* to be the God-way—an account which nevertheless rejects the claim that God is 'a' personal being or individual entity of any kind.[27] A theological realism, we maintain, is an account of the content of the theist worldview which takes that content to be made true (if it is true) by the way reality ultimately is, independently of any human beliefs about, attitudes to, or cognitive constructions of, how reality may be. A euteleological theism is therefore a theological realism: reality's being inherently directed upon the realization of the supreme good and the Universe's existing ultimately because that good is realized within it is a claim about how reality ultimately is in the 'mind-independent' way just specified. Yet, on this euteleological account, God is 'no-thing' in fundamental ontology, even though analogizing claims about God convey vital truths about ultimate reality and its implications for human existence.[28]

---

venture the opinion that a theological non-realism tends to prove unstable because it surely has to be some feature *of what's real* that accounts for its being beneficial to invest in the fiction, and then 'the fiction' may not be merely fictional after all. It's also worth observing that the question of the religious adequacy of the personal omniGod will arise in their own terms for theological fictionalists, since the question of how the fiction about God is understood may affect the benefits of investment in that fiction. Won't acting *as if* there were an all-powerful morally perfect being (for instance) confront a similar difficulty in the face of horrendous evil as a commitment to such a being's reality? We believe that there is scope for arguing, then, that theological non-realism results from a failure to recognize that the analogizing construction of talk about God may be understood as conveying truth-claims about ultimate reality as it relates to human existence.

[27] It is often maintained, as Joshua Hoffman and Gary Rosenkrantz write, that 'Western theism is... committed to the idea that God is a maximally great *entity*, or being of any sort whatsoever [where]...[e]ntity is the *summum genus*, or most general kind, of all categories' (Hoffman and Rosenkrantz, 2002, 14). We are rejecting that claim, adhering instead to what we believe is the more authentically classical theist stance—namely, that God's unsurpassable ontological greatness places God beyond the status even of a maximally great entity in the most general category of beings.

[28] Our stance on what constitutes theological realism is consonant with that of Christopher Insole, who gives four criteria for a realist understanding of religious discourse:

> [T]here is an indispensable core of religious utterances [statements] that are fact-asserting, not merely expressive; statements are made true by a non-epistemic state of affairs (the way the world is, rather than standards of 'ideal justification'); what is the case is independent of human cognition; and we can, in principle, have true beliefs about what is the case independent of human cognition.
>   (2006, 2; letters 'A' to 'D' deleted from the original)

A theological realism in which God is 'no-thing' is, we believe, exactly what is needed properly to honour theism's commitment to God's absolute transcendent reality as that than which a greater in being and worth cannot even be conceived. It does follow, however, that a realist ontology such as euteleology's, in which God is not an entity, must be capable of providing truth-makers for claims attributing properties and actions, and, indeed, existence, to God. More needs to be said to show truth-making of that sort to be intelligible.

4.8 Truth-Making for God-Claims When God Is Not 'a' Being

Critics might, perhaps, grant that there's no obvious contradiction in the claim that 'constructed' talk of God-as-a-thing may convey truths when fundamental ontology lacks God as an entity amongst other entities, as is the case with our euteleological proposal. An active doubt might yet remain about whether such an ontology could possibly be adequate for a realist theist metaphysics. To dispel that doubt we need to take a further step—namely, to make it intelligible that claims made using God as analogously constructed could be *made true* in an ontology lacking God as any kind of being or entity. We'll now attempt that task.

We begin with a caveat. To make it intelligible how God-claims could be made true on a euteleological ontology where God is 'no-thing', it is not necessary to provide wholesale translations of those God-claims into terms admissible in euteleology's basic ontology.[29] It won't be necessary to redefine 'God' as having some meaning acceptable in euteleological terms. Indeed, we effectively ruled out any such redefinition when we examined, and

---

Insole acknowledges his indebtedness to Alston (1995) in formulating these criteria. Insole thinks there is much confusion in the literature on religious realism/non-realism, in which (non-)realism is often characterized as 'a doctrine concerning the (non)existence of an entity "God"'. He goes on to say that by accepting his four criteria 'we are able to carve up the realism/anti-realism debate, not primarily in terms of the existence of a divine object, but rather in terms of what it is which constitutes a religious statement's truth' (Insole 2006, 2). That way of treating the realism/anti-realism issue is the approach we are taking here.

[29] The assumption that we were committed to offering 'translations of or replacements for some typical claims about God' in terms admissible at the level of fundamental euteleological ontology was made by Dean Zimmerman in his comments on our exposition of a euteleological theism in a symposium at the APA Pacific Division Meeting (1 April 2016) (later published as Bishop and Perszyk 2017). An anonymous reader also called for us to offer translations of personalist theistic statements into non-personal euteleological language so as to help readers judge the adequacy of our view.

rejected, all the likely candidates in euteleological ontology for a 'someThing' fit to be identified as God (see Sections 4.1–4.3). Furthermore, our claim that talk of God as an entity in the broadest sense (namely, as subject for predication) is itself understood only by an analogizing construction entails that God-talk is *sui generis*, strictly not translatable into other terms. No such 'reduction' of analogizing God-talk is possible: as we emphasized at the start of this chapter, a euteleological theism generally leaves in place traditional scriptural, liturgical, and even creedal and doctrinal personal language about God. A euteleological theism will reject or revise personal language about God only when it is being interpreted or proposed as conveying a literal metaphysical understanding of ultimate divine reality. (We'll illustrate this point below, in discussing how euteleology understands the traditional 'omni-attributes'—see Section 4.10.)

What it means to say, for example, that God hates nothing that he has made, and forgives the sins of all who are penitent, has its meaning understood only by analogy. Here the analogy is twofold; first, there is the analogy that applies personal relational attributes (attitudes and actions) to that which is not a person; and, second, there is the more radical analogous construction of God on the 'thing-property' model as a means for expressing vital truths (if Abrahamic theism is true) about ultimate reality and how we should relate to it in order to live well. ('That which is not a person'—to which personal attributes are applied at the first, mundane, level of analogy—is not in reality any kind of thing at all and is spoken of as such only by a second, deeper, analogy intrinsic to all God-talk.) But there's no translating or reducing such a claim about God into what it 'really means'; what it really means can be understood only by analogy.

It follows that *actually specifying* the truth-makers in basic euteleological ontology for claims such as 'God hates nothing he has made' and 'God forgives the penitent' is impossible. We may take the *via negativa* and specify that the truth-maker is *not* a supreme immaterial anthropomorphic personal being possessing certain psychological attitudes and moral policies. And we may emphasize that this apophatic claim is not to be read as implying that the truth-maker for God's forgiving penitents (to continue the example) is something *less* than personal, less than a person showing mercy. God's *not* being a person, nor any kind of being in fundamental ontology is not a lessening of God's being but, to the contrary, a consequence of the absolutely unsurpassable onto-ethical greatness of divine reality that transcends these categories of being which are characteristic of the limited, creaturely, natural world. But just precisely *how* it is, positively, that some feature of this transcendent theistic ultimate reality makes these claims true is not something we can grasp. This is not, in practice, any kind of deficit, since the truths that we can grasp through using the analogizing construction of God as an entity with properties analogous to personal agents are entirely sufficient for us to have the right religious and ethical practical orientation to reality if theism is true. To make the point in terms of the example, penitent believers who trust that God forgives them will thereby (if theism is true) be rightly related to how things really and ultimately are. It's worth reemphasizing then, that, while euteleological theism is 'non-personalist' in the sense that it does not have God as a personal being in its fundamental ontology, it is *not* non-personalist in the broader sense that it doesn't value personhood or that it takes God to be something impersonal, a force like the force of gravity, for example. And a Christian euteleological theism hardly 'depersonalizes' theism when it takes the supreme good to consist in *agapē*-love.

We do need to make it intelligible, however, *that* claims of the form 'God is F', 'God φs', etc., could be made true by truth-makers that fit euteleological basic ontology, even though (as we have been urging) the radically analogical status of these claims correlates with an in principle inability to comprehend precisely *how* they are made true. If it could not be made intelligible that this kind of truth-making is possible, then it would remain open that claims about God as an analogously constructed entity may simply float free of reality, belonging only to a fiction, as theological non-realists maintain.

4.9 Divine Will, Freedom, and Action (When God Is Not 'a' Being)

We'll return, then, to the 'hard case' of divine willing and action, with the aim of making it generally intelligible that claims about God's agency and its exercise could be made true in basic euteleological ontology.

God is said to will and act freely, but basic euteleological ontology lacks a supreme being with a personal agent's 'free will'. Yet we can make it intelligible how analogical talk of God's will could express truths by appeal to euteleology's core claims, namely, that everything that exists does so inherently for the sake of realizing the supreme good, and that this ultimate *telos* is fulfilled—from which it follows that there are powers capable of achieving this fulfilment, powers whose exercise brings about concrete realizations of reality's supreme good. The claim that God's will is unchanging, then, can be understood as made true by reality's unchanging directedness upon the realization of its good. But the manner in which God's will is fulfilled is varied and contingent: the supreme good is in fact instantiated in the Universe in particular states of affairs; but it could have been realized differently, in ways both imaginable and unimaginable. This modal feature may be identified in euteleological metaphysics as what makes it true to describe God as acting freely—as choosing how to fulfil God's unchanging will in the concrete Universe. Particular claims about God's willing and acting effectively within the creation are made true, then, not by the exercise of the powers of a supreme personal agent, but by the exercise of those powers which are capable of contributing to concrete realizations of the supreme good. As noted earlier (Section 4.4, p. 95), these powers may be counted as divine—but what does euteleological metaphysics take these divine powers to consist in?

Realizations of the supreme good are natural states of affairs, arising through the operation of the powers of nature. Natural powers, then, must be understood from the euteleological theist perspective as amongst the divine powers, thus honouring the sense of nature pervasively imbued with divine purpose, as expressed in Psalm 104, for example.[30] Accordingly, a euteleological theism sustains the view that the natural sciences impart *some* knowledge of what it takes to be, in fact, fundamentally divine operations. Of course, the natural sciences *themselves* don't posit an overall *telos* for the natural Universe. Yet, from the perspective of a theism based on a euteleological metaphysics, natural powers are divine powers in so far as they are essentially implicated in producing realizations of the supreme telic good. On a euteleological account, natural powers are fundamentally *God's* powers, and every exercise of a natural power is fundamentally an exercise of divine power.[31]

---

[30] For the full effect, the whole psalm needs to be read. But here's a verse (Psalms 104:24) epitomizing its theme:

> How countless are your works, Yahweh,
> All of them made so wisely!
> The earth is full of your creatures.
> (*The New Jerusalem Bible*)

'Yahweh' is the English rendition of the Tetragrammaton, used (though having no descriptive meaning itself) as the 'name' of the unnameable as revealed to Moses.

[31] Compare Aquinas, *Summa Contra Gentiles*, III, ch. 67, whose chapter heading is 'God is cause of activity [another translation has "operation"] in all active agents', and which affirms that 'every agent acts by the divine power'.

That bold claim must, of course, be read in the intended euteleological way. The assertion that all power is God's is not to be read as the claim that God is the only being who is a genuine productive agent, with creaturely action merely a matter of appearance (as occasionalism holds). That is what the claim would mean for a metaphysics where God is a supreme personal agent—a metaphysics for which there is a tension, arguably irresolvable, between God's sovereign agency and the free agency of creaturely persons.[32] No such competitive tension arises for a euteleological theism. On a euteleological account, natural beings have, and exercise, genuine powers of productive agency. Those powers ultimately owe their existence, however, to the fact that reality's *telos*, the supreme good, is concretely realized. Those powers exist for the achievement of specific ends, proper to the kinds of beings whose powers they are—but all within the scope of reality's ultimate end. In this sense, then, all creaturely powers may be understood as, fundamentally, divine powers; in rightly exercising powers properly described as their own, creatures participate in, without competing with, the exercise of divine power.

Does this understanding of divine action as exercised in and through creaturely powers leave room for *special and miraculous* divine action of the kind which seems essential to theist narratives about God's revelatory and saving acts? We've just argued that creaturely powers may be understood as, fundamentally, divine powers; but surely there must be more to divine power than the creaturely powers (even when somehow aggregated or combined)? Personalist understandings of theism may take divine power to include a power of intervention—though this is resisted by some personalist theists.[33] A euteleological metaphysics obviously cannot understand special divine power as a power of intervention in the natural causal order by a supernatural agent. Nevertheless, if it is to be adequate as an account of theist metaphysics, a euteleological ontology for which God is neither a person nor any kind of being does need to accommodate special divine power *within* the natural Universe. Somehow it needs to be made intelligible that claims about God's revelatory and saving acts (analogical as they are) can be made true by truth-makers admissible in basic euteleological ontology.

[32] As one of us (Perszyk) recalls from seminars at the University of Notre Dame, David Burrell would often lament that contemporary discussions of divine sovereignty and human freedom typically picture God and free creatures as if competing in a zero-sum game. See Burrell (1993, 2).
[33] Peter Forrest (1996) is a case in point: he denies that God intervenes in the natural universe while retaining a metaphysics of God as a personal being. Forrest's title, *God without the Supernatural*, is perhaps misleading, since, as Creator, God must be supernatural in the sense that he is a being in a distinct ontological category from the natural world, even if he makes no supernatural interventions in it.

God's revelatory acts—for example, in giving the law to Moses on Mt Sinai—may be understood on a euteleological account as conveying to humans (so far as is needed) the nature of reality's telic good and its implications for how we should live and the stance we need to take on ultimate reality. The general question how it is possible for reality to become known in limited ways by finite minds is a large question about the metaphysical foundations of epistemology. It suffices here to note that a euteleological theism must deny any claim that reality's revealing itself occurs through the actions of a personal creator who designs creaturely cognitive capacities with the proper function of producing (in the right circumstances) true beliefs.[34] Euteleological theism shares this denial, of course, with a natural scientific worldview—but, by contrast, holds that humans *may* acquire truths about the ultimate purposes of existence and of humanity's relation to those purposes. The processes through which this is possible will count, for euteleological theism, as divine processes operating *within* the Universe. The same applies to God's saving actions (anyway closely linked to revelatory ones). So, we need an enhanced account of divine power within the Universe—which we'll postpone until the following chapter (see Chapter 5, Section 5.6), when, in the context of a 'non-perfectionist' soteriology, we'll deploy the Christian idea that the special divine power operating within the world is the emergent power of *agapē*-love.

But for that last promissory note, however, we think we have shown that it *is* generally intelligible that analogical claims about God's willing and action may be made true within the ontology of euteleological metaphysics in the absence of any supreme being possessing personal agential properties.

4.10 A Euteleological Account of the Divine Attributes—The 'Omni-Properties'

We are claiming, then, that scriptural, liturgical, and creedal claims about God's knowing, willing, and acting gain their meaning through a twofold analogy—first, by analogously applying personal psychological and agential

---

[34] Alvin Plantinga (1993, especially ch. 11) is well known for defending a 'proper functionalist' account of knowledge, and for criticizing atheist-naturalism as unable to support any such account. It is beyond our scope to try to close off an argument for personalist theism along these lines, though we will observe that, if our reservations about the religious adequacy of personalist theism as expressed in Chapter 1 are indeed weighty, that may itself be some reason for doubting that a personal omniGod is needed at the metaphysical foundations of epistemology.

properties to that which is not in reality a person or personal being, and, second, in the very construction of God-as-a-thing by analogy with our mundane 'thing-property' schema in describing an ultimate reality in which God's reality absolutely transcends all categories of things. And we have argued that it is generally intelligible that some such scriptural, liturgical, and creedal claims may be made true under euteleology's account of what it is for ultimate reality to be the God-way. We'll now consider how euteleology may accommodate the truth of traditional theistic claims about God's attributes, beginning with the 'omni-'properties—omnipotence, omniscience, and omnibenevolence.

On a standard personalist account, God's possessing the omni-properties is understood as extrapolating from our understanding of power, knowledge, and goodness in creaturely persons. And this extrapolation, it may be conceded, involves some analogous extension of our grasp of what it is for persons to have and exercise power, knowledge, and goodness. After all, it must surely be agreed that we cannot comprehend what it is to possess these capacities without any limitations (save, perhaps, for purely logical ones).[35] By contrast, a euteleological account denies that God's omnipotence, omniscience, and omnibenevolence are to be understood as (uniquely special) instances of a thing—whether a person or something analogous to a person—having agential power, knowledge, and goodness. Where God is

---

[35] William Alston (1985) makes the suggestion that attributing personal power, knowledge, and goodness to God uses these terms *partially* univocally. Alston argues that God's otherness from finite persons is secured by *the different way in which* these personal properties are realized in God, and he cites Aquinas's distinction (e.g., in *Summa Theologiae*, I, Q13, a.3) between the thing/property signified and the mode signified (see Alston 1985, note 1, 229-30). For some predicates that are applied to God and creatures, says Aquinas, the property signified is the same but not the mode signified. Alston retains, however, a theist metaphysics in which God is a particular person amongst persons: indeed, Alston's account of analogous predication as partially univocal predication is an attempt to argue that a personalist metaphysics can secure sufficient divine 'otherness'. But we think Alston's personalist metaphysics will still face all the problems of religious inadequacy we set out in Chapter 1 (Section 1.6–1.8). Besides, we doubt that partially univocal attributions—especially of goodness—could be acceptable with God understood as a person: a partially univocal use of a term must thereby also be partially *equivocal*, so it would have to follow that in attributing, e.g., goodness to a personal God we would be, at least in part, meaning something different from what we mean when attributing goodness to a finite person. We incline to the view, then, that Aquinas's distinction between the thing signified and the mode signified is not well explicated in terms of partially univocal attributions. It seems to us, rather, that Aquinas, in making this distinction, was explaining that, though we are using the relevant terms univocally, in doing so through their analogous extension to that which is most ultimately real, we have only (very) partial understanding of the way in which those terms apply and how it is that truths thereby accessed are made true. Such an account, of course, takes Aquinas to be a proponent of a non-personalist metaphysics for theism.

'no-thing' in fundamental ontology, God's infinity (or unlimitedness) cannot be understood as finite being infinitely extended (if, indeed, such an understanding is even a coherent one).

God's being all-powerful, then, is not, for euteleology, the all-controlling power of a supreme agent; nevertheless, it may be accepted that 'God is all-powerful' is true in a context where God is analogously constructed as a being possessing personal properties analogous to those possessed by human persons. But how can it be made intelligible that God's being all-powerful should be made true within the resources of euteleology's ontology? It may be granted that agential power is being attributed to God only by analogy, but it still remains to be explained what it means to attribute 'all' power to God and then to make intelligible this claim's being made true under euteleological metaphysics. A similar line of questioning—it may readily be appreciated—may apply to attributions of omniscience and omnibenevolence, resulting in the same need to explain what attributing unlimited knowledge and unlimited goodness mean when attributed to God, and to show that it is intelligible for these attributions to be made true under a euteleological ontology.

We have, in fact, already provided a euteleological understanding of divine omnipotence in the previous section (Section 4.9) in discussing how a euteleological theism may accommodate divine will, freedom, and action. Divine omnipotence amounts to all power being, at root, God's power. For a euteleological theism, 'God is omnipotent' holds true in virtue of the fact that every power, and every exercise of power, exists for the sake of realizing the supreme good and only because that end is fulfilled.[36] And reality's eutelicity—its inherently aiming at realizing its *telos*, the supreme good—makes it intelligible what it means to say, by analogy, that the 'will' that exercises these divine powers is a 'wholly good will' (that is, that God is omnibenevolent). God's omniscience is made intelligible by analogy with the 'know-how' a person exercises in intelligently selecting and bringing about the means to fulfil an intended goal. Since its overall *telos* is achieved, reality may be said to embody the 'know-how' needed to fulfil the ultimate 'project' of realizing the supreme good. And that know-how may reasonably be held to be ultimate, all-encompassing, knowledge—hence, omniscience.

---

[36] It is worth recalling that we are thinking of the realization of the ultimate *telos* in terms of potentially many, even infinitely many, repeated manifestations of the supreme good and not—or, at least, not as necessarily requiring—a final consummation in which concrete existence consists in a flawless and incorruptible manifestation of the good (see Chapter 3, pp. 66–7).

A further analogy may be implicated in divine omniscience, while also providing a way of understanding divine omnipresence. Euteleology holds that every existent exists ultimately for the sake of realizing the good and only because the good is realized—and that all-pervasive feature provides some intelligibility for the analogous attribution to God of total 'knowledge by acquaintance' of all that exists. That attribution presupposes that God is always and everywhere present, so God's omnipresence may also be analogously affirmed. Reality's essential eutelicity implies various real constraints on how the 'project' of realizing the supreme good may be achieved—constraints which arise from the nature of the supreme good itself and from limitations (in particular, logical ones) on ways in which the good may be concretely realized. These constraints cannot be fully known to us, but we may analogously attribute to God total knowledge of what those constraints are. There are no limits on God's knowledge of what the good is, or on God's knowledge of what constrains its concrete realization, and, hence of the myriad real possibilities for the concrete existence of the supreme good.

It is, of course, a problem to reconcile the co-attribution to God of omnipotence, omniscience, and omnibenevolence with the existence of evil—a problem which, as we argued in Chapter 1 (Section 1.8), can (given certain normative assumptions) generate serious doubts about the religious adequacy of a supreme personal being as the fit object of theist worship. Now, it would obviously be a mistake to suppose that, just because it understands the omni-attributes not as the attributes of a personal being but only as applicable by analogous extension, a euteleological theism faces no such problem of evil. This is because the question of compatibility with existing evil may be raised at the level of the features in euteleological theist metaphysics in terms of which the analogous attribution of the omni-attributes is supposed to be made intelligible. If all powers exist and are exercised for the sake of realizing the supreme good, and only because that good *is* realized, how could it be possible for some (indeed, many) exercises of power to result in horrendous evils? Yet, of course, we know that in fact horrendous evils do sometimes occur, so it seems that some form of Argument from Evil may readily be constructed against a theism grounded on euteleological metaphysics. This issue is so important for a defence of euteleological metaphysics as religiously adequate for Abrahamic theism that we will devote a full chapter to its consideration—the next chapter, Chapter 5. But, first, we have more to say about a euteleological understanding of the traditional divine attributes—including the most basic one, existence itself.

4.11 God's Existence, and the Classical, 'Metaphysical' Attributes

A euteleological theism is robustly realist (see Section 4.7): evidently, then, it holds that 'God exists' is true, and made true by the way ultimate reality is. As explained in Section 4.6, however, we are able to speak and think about the ultimate reality of God's existence only through using the term 'God' in a manner analogously constructed from our use of referring terms for things belonging to kinds which possess properties. We cannot think about divine reality without thinking true propositions in which 'God' functions as a referring term in the grammatical subject position—and God is therefore an item or entity *in that very broad sense*. But it need not follow that God is in any stronger ontological sense 'a thing amongst other things', and, for euteleological theism, God does *not* appear as an item or entity (however great) amongst other items or entities at the level of fundamental ontology.

Stephen T. Davis writes:

> I have always thought that the English term 'thing' is almost infinite in what it ranges over. A 'thing' is just anything whose name or referring term can appear in the subject position of a coherent sentence, is a property bearer and has an identity apart from other things. Is God a thing like other things? Of course not. Is God a thing among other things? Of course, or so I would say.   (2008, 164–5)

Davis's reasoning here would, we think, be widely shared. Yet the idea of God as a thing, but a quite unique and ultimate thing, overlooks the possibility we have been urging, namely that, in the unique case of 'God', its occurring as a referring term in sentences taken to be true results from a radical analogizing of ultimate reality. God is then 'a thing among other things' only in the very broad sense that 'God' can occur as grammatical subject in true subject-predicate sentences. *Pace* Davis, it does *not* follow that God is 'a thing among other things' in a stronger sense linked with 'being a property bearer' and having 'an identity apart from other things'. In this unique context, due to the analogous stretching of the notion of an identifiable thing with properties to apply to (in itself incomprehensible) ultimate reality, God is a thing (= referring term that can take the grammatical subject position) while (as a matter of fundamental ontology) altogether transcending thinghood in the sense of a thing that possesses properties and has an identity apart from other things. By this analogous construction, however, we *can* convey truths about divine reality by speaking of God in just this way.³⁷

But what, then, is the truth-maker that makes it true that God exists in basic euteleological ontology, given that no entity in that ontology can be identified as God? That truth-maker is nothing less than the overall state of ultimate reality existing concretely as it does and having the highly general features articulated in euteleology's core claims—namely, being inherently directed upon the realization of reality's *telos*, the supreme good, with the concrete contingent Universe existing ultimately just because it contains such realizations. And that overall state, if it obtains, is reality as it is— ultimate reality *in* its being the God-way, *divine* reality. Thus 'God exists' has a concrete truth-maker—but that truth-maker is not 'a' supremely great concrete being, but ultimate reality as it concretely is. We make this truth-making relation intelligible by appeal to the eutelic features reality necessarily has (articulatable as they are only at high levels of abstraction): but it's not something abstract or merely ideal that makes 'God exists' true, it's reality's sheer concrete existing. Aquinas's *ipsum esse subsistens* comes to mind as apt for referring to reality's sheer existing, but should not be read as identifying God (*qua* entity) either with the totality of existents or with a universal, whether Platonic or immanent. *Ipsum esse* may indeed refer to the truth-maker for 'God exists', but it does not follow that 'God' *means* 'being itself'.³⁸ Understanding being itself as euteleological does, we think,

---

³⁷ Accordingly, we view with some sympathy remarks like that of 17th-century German mystic and religious poet Angelus Silesius: 'God is a pure Nothing. In him there stirs no Now nor Here. The more you reach for it, the more it escapes from you.' (Thanks to Amber Griffioen for drawing our attention to this quotation.) There is also the idea, which has a long pedigree, that God is beyond being and non-being (see Plotinus, *Enneads*, on the One). Caution is needed, however, in interpreting such remarks: properly understood, they do not imply that theists cannot truly affirm that God exists. Rather, we suggest, these insights from the mystical tradition convey recognition of God's living reality as transcending entity-hood at the level of fundamental ontology.

³⁸ In general, an assertion's truth-maker is not to be identified with what the assertion means. As John Heil puts it, '[t]ruthmakers...are features of the world in virtue of which assertions are true. There is no reason to suppose that competent speakers, owing solely to their being competent speakers, need to know very much at all about the nature of the truthmakers for assertions about everyday objects' (Heil 2005, 503). Of course, the way in which the meaning of assertions about ordinary objects—Heil's example is a table—fails to amount to the obtaining of its truth-maker ('a dynamic arrangement of particles with a particular history and standing in particular arrangements to other dynamic arrangements of particles') is quite different from the God case: God is not a composite object! Nevertheless, the general message does apply; as Heil says, philosophers should avoid being 'beguiled by a conception of language according to which we can "read off" features of reality from our styles of representation. This is the linguistic tail wagging the ontological dog' (Heil 2005, 508). Thanks to Andrei Buckareff for drawing our attention to Heil's article.

at least make it intelligible *that* (if not precisely *how*) ultimate reality (so characterized) makes it true that God exists.

Taking 'God wills' and 'God acts' and 'God exists' to involve thinking of divine reality through an analogous projection from mundane thought categories removes the air of paradox that may seem to attach to the metaphysical divine attributes of classical philosophical theology. Traditionally, God—the living God, who sustains the creation and acts with salvific effect—is held to be atemporal, immutable, impassible, necessary (not contingent), and simple (not 'composed'). On the face of it, however, 'God wills' and 'God acts' imply that God changes, making it paradoxical to hold that God is unchanging and 'outside' time. But the paradox dissolves once it is accepted that willing and acting are ascribed to God only by analogy. As we argued above (Section 4.9), euteleology's combining reality's unchanging essential directedness on realizing the ultimate telic good, with the contingent diversity of ways and possible ways in which that supreme good may be realized, supports the attribution to God (analogously constructed as a possessor of properties) both of an unchanging and of a free will. The truthmaker for the attribution of unchanging will is an essential feature of reality as such, while the truth-makers for attributions of the exercise of free will are contingent facts relating to the natural/divine powers that exist for the sake of realizing the supreme good. God's freedom, then, is to be understood as a freedom to determine the ways in which God's unchanging will actually is fulfilled.[39]

Further high paradox looms with the use of 'God' as subject-term in the sentence 'God is simple'. That sentence appears self-defeating since its grammatical form presupposes the 'composition' involved in predication, along with the existence of a particular referent for the subject-term, which, in turn, presupposes the 'composition' involved in a particular's having an identity as instantiating a certain kind of thing.[40] This apparent paradox may be dissolved, however, by recognizing that God-as-a-thing is only a construction by analogy with things that have properties (including existence) and that simplicity is an apophatic property. Still, that God is simple *is made true* by divine reality being as it is. Our predicament in the face of ultimate divine reality, transcending all categories of being as it does, is that,

---

[39] It seems, then, that a euteleological theism will not endorse a philosophical theology which holds that God is free to do evil. The question of how a euteleological theism deals with problems of evil is our topic in the next chapter.

[40] See our earlier discussion of divine simplicity understood apophatically, in Chapter 1, pp. 21–2.

if we are to speak of it at all (or think of it in linguistically articulated ways), we have to deploy our 'thing-property' schema in so doing. As personal beings, it is entirely natural for us to use specifically personal language when thinking and talking about God and our relation to God (indeed, as noted earlier, p. 104, the aptness of this way of talking about God is something theism views as itself under divine revelatory providence). Yet we are able reflectively to appreciate that, in using this language about God, we are deploying an analogous construction of God as an individual personal being, so that the truths we express through its use do *not* convey that ultimate theistic ontology consists in an individual personal being with maximal great-making properties.

A metaphysics of theism that takes God to be a personal being will struggle, as we noted at the outset (Chapter 1, pp. 18–19), to accommodate the traditional metaphysical divine attributes. That is understandable, since being a person seems conceptually tied to being temporal, passible, and mutable, and the idea of an absolutely 'non-composite' person seems nonsensical. A non-personalist metaphysics—such as provided by euteleology—has no such struggle, and can follow classical precedent by reading these attributes apophatically (as conveying an understanding of what God is not) and understanding them as attaching to a subject (God) which is 'a thing' only through an analogous construction. There is thus no implication that *there is an individual entity* that is atemporal, immutable, impassible, necessary, and simple. Notice that the *predicates themselves* are not applied analogously when we say, in apophatic mode, that God is atemporal, impassible, etc., since we *do* literally mean that God isn't temporal, doesn't suffer or undergo anything, and so on. Nevertheless, their attribution *to God* depends on describing ultimate reality through the construction of God as a thing by an analogy with the mundane category of things possessing properties.

Euteleology admits no unchanging, atemporal, and necessary individual *being*; yet there are essential elements in euteleological metaphysics that are unchanging, eternal, and necessary. These may be described as euteleology's *ideal* elements—namely, reality's essential purposiveness and the nature of the supreme good which is reality's *telos*. Euteleology takes a realist view of these unchanging and necessary ideal elements: they are real, and belong to 'how things really are' independently of human beliefs, preferences, or 'constructions'. The reality of the concrete Universe, including particular realizations and incarnations of the supreme good, is, by contrast, wholly a changing and contingent reality. Euteleology may thus be seen as drawing a distinction in its overall view of reality as between the reality of unchanging and necessary ideals (such as the nature of the supreme good) and the changing and contingent concrete reality in which reality's inherent purposes are fulfilled in manifestations of supreme goodness. Euteleology wouldn't admit a Platonic reading of this distinction, however, since Platonism, as usually understood, gives ontological priority to the reality of the ideal, treating the concrete contingent world of particulars as the realm of 'appearance'. By contrast, euteleology holds that realizations of the supreme good, though limited and passing, are not thereby mere reflections of, or partial sharings in, the good; rather, they participate in the (eternal) reality of supreme goodness in its full character, and without the existence of such as they nothing real would exist at all, save the bare (unrealized) ideals. Unchanging ideal euteleological realities, then, transcend concrete existence, yet without constituting a distinct ontological category of beings. They might, then, be said to be abstract realities, just in the sense that they are not concrete existents and without implying any abstraction from the concrete by any act of mind.

What of the metaphysical attributions familiar from natural theology—that God is First Cause and Necessary Being, for example? These attributions seem not to be purely apophatic. Can these be sustained, then, as positive attributes of God by a euteleological metaphysics? Euteleology lacks any individual *entity* that stands at the head of a vast chain of causal relations and exists as a matter of logical necessity. Yet, as we have explained, euteleology does provide an ultimate explanation for the existence of contingent concrete reality. That the Universe exists because 'it does what it's for' may, then, make intelligible the attribution of status as 'first cause' to God, given that it's only by an analogy from mundane 'thing-property' thought that we think of God at all as something to which such a status could attach.[41] Once again, there's no translating the meaning of 'God is first cause' into the terms of the euteleological ultimate explanation of contingent existence: but it is intelligible that 'God is first cause', whose meaning is only analogically grasped, is made true in virtue of that explanation holding true (if it does hold true).

Explaining the Universe as existing because it 'does what it's for' implies that the Universe contains within itself the reason for its existence—though only by virtue of reality's transcendent euteliocity (its inherent directedness on the supreme good as its end), which is a necessary and unchanging ideal

---

[41] This clarifies a remark we made in earlier work (2016b, 218) when we said that euteleology may retain the essential theist commitment that God is the efficient cause of all that exists.

feature of how things ultimately are. We think there's the material here to make intelligible for a euteleological theism the attribution to God of aseity and necessity (as positive attributes)—though there's no individual being that is *a se* and existing from necessity. If ultimate reality is as euteleological theism claims, then that is a matter of necessity; and it's intelligible that, accordingly, God—in the analogous construction of God-as-a-thing—exists necessarily. Furthermore, if ultimate reality is the euteleological God-way, its being so does not depend on anything else: hence it's intelligible to attribute aseity to God. However, though for euteleology the concrete Universe is wholly contingent, if euteleological theism is true it follows that there is *some* contingent concrete Universe, and, indeed, a Universe in which the supreme good is realized (see our earlier discussion, Chapter 3, p. 78). God's existence is thus, for euteleology, conceptually and logically related to the existence of a created world. We'll complete our exposition of a euteleological theism, then, by considering whether it assists an understanding of our proposal for a euteleological theism to see it as a version of panentheism.

4.12 Euteleology—A Panentheism?

Broadly speaking, panentheism is the idea that all that exists is 'in' God (and thus inseparable from God), though God is 'more than' the Universe and is identical neither with it nor with its principle of unity. Pan*en*theism thus implies a contrast with a *pantheist* metaphysics, for which (in some sense) God and the Universe coincide. As made clear earlier (Section 4.1), a euteleological account resists identifying God with the Universe—although it does share some characteristic features of pantheism. In particular, a euteleological theism affirms that the Universe exhibits an overall principle of unity, since every existent exists for the sake of realizing the divine purpose and ultimately only because that purpose is realized. Euteleological theism therefore sides with pantheism in taking our changing natural world to have more than passing or merely humanly conferred worth. Indeed, since it holds, further, that some parts of our world actually realize the supreme good, manifesting the divine character fully, euteleological theism takes the natural world to be capable of incarnating that which is of ultimate worth—something seemingly impossible (other than through 'miraculous' supernatural incursion) on a standard personalist picture where God, and eternal life with God, belong to a supernatural realm from which the natural world may appear ultimately dispensable. The pervasive immanence of the divine in the natural Universe seems well accommodated, then, under a euteleological theism. Is this enough to make euteleological theism panentheist?

The panentheist claim that all is 'in' God might be read rather literally as a claim that the Universe is a (proper) part of God. It is plain, however, that panentheistic being 'in' God is typically understood metaphorically, as connoting some inseparable connexion between the Universe's being and God's being while retaining the idea that God is 'more than' the Universe. Process theologies are thus paradigm examples of panentheism in so far as they posit an essential inter-dependence between God and the Universe.[42,43]

Now, since a euteleological theism doesn't posit a personal God, *a fortiori* it doesn't claim any inter-dependence between a personal God and the Universe. Furthermore, as we have been arguing in this chapter, euteleological theism makes no specific identification in fundamental ontology for God as a particular being. So, if panentheism suggests a metaphysics in which the concrete Universe is somehow (metaphorically) 'in' the being of God where God is thought of as a 'grand item' in fundamental ontology, then euteleological theism is *not* panentheist.

However, a euteleological theism may hold that the concrete Universe, with its all-pervading eutelicity, is *divine* (in the sense that it is 'of God'), while also claiming that reality's being the God-way is 'more than' the contingent existence of the Universe as a whole (even when you add that it is unified by its eutelicity). Reality is 'more than' the contingent Universe because reality is *necessarily* eutelic. Inherently aiming at realizing the supreme good would still have been of the essence of reality, even if nothing in this

---

[42] Process theists tend to self-identify as panentheists, following the lead of one of their 'founding fathers', Charles Hartshorne, who also labelled his view 'neoclassical theism'. He thinks Whitehead is panentheism's chief representative among philosophers (see Hartshorne and Reece (1953, vii and 273)). We briefly discussed process theologies earlier: see Chapter 2, Section 2.5.

[43] There are those, such as T. J. Mawson (2019), who want to maintain theism (*as opposed to* panentheism) while *also* claiming that the Universe is literally God's body. Anyone who claims that the Universe is God's body can hardly be happy with the idea that God is completely ontologically separate from the Universe, and they must therefore think that *in some sense* the Universe is 'in' God (even if it's not a 'proper part' of God, since bodies seem not to stand in the part-whole relationship to the persons whose bodies they are). *Pace* Mawson, then, such a view *does* seem to count as a kind of panentheism—and, if offered as an interpretation of theism, as a panentheist interpretation of theism.

R. T. Mullins (2016) tentatively suggests a way to demarcate panentheism from its rivals that illuminates its otherwise vague core claim that the universe is 'in' God: The universe is literally in God because absolute (or metaphysical) space and time are attributes of God. More recent attempts to find literal meanings of 'in' include Karl Pfeifer (2020) and Joanna Leidenhag (2020).

actual Universe had existed as it does, and even if (*per impossibile*, if euteleological theism is true) nothing concrete had existed at all. In this way, then, a euteleological theism seems to fit the panentheist theme that the Universe is divine but God is more than the Universe (though 'God is more than the Universe' must be recognized as resting on an analogizing construction in the way we've explained all 'God is F' statements have to be for euteleology). Furthermore, as we've noted, euteleological theism is clearly in the camp of those who hold (as panentheists must do) that there is an essential connexion between God's existence and the existence of the—or, rather, a—creation.[44] If theism on a euteleological account is true, it's impossible that there should have been no creation at all in which to realize the good concretely—even though the actual creation, with its particular instantiations of the good, is wholly contingent. It appears, then, that, with some caveats, euteleological theism *can* wear the panentheist label.

A euteleological theism might also be described as 'the-en-pan-ist', to mark its view that God's power is exercised in and through all natural exercises of power. The thought that 'God has no hands but our hands' is familiar (probably originating from a 14th-century poem by St Theresa of Avila): its implication that creaturely agency is (potentially) divine agency may be understood euteleologically as holding true in virtue of the fact that creaturely agency exists only for the sake of realizing the supreme good and because that end is actually achieved. Again, there's an obvious problem of evil: how can it be that it is with the hands that are, or are potentially, God's hands we often enough obstruct goodness and destroy what is created for the sake of realizing goodness? As already indicated, we'll take up the problem of evil in a eutelic Universe in the following chapter.

---

[44] The common view that for theism, unlike panentheism, God need not create anything has been contested. For example, the idea that God must create has been endorsed by Timothy O'Connor (2008, 2012, ch. 5), who maintains that, given God's omnibenevolence, there is a plenitude of love that inevitably leads God to create an infinite number of universes. According to Thomas Oord's 'essential kenosis theology', which combines elements from open and process theologies, God's self-giving in creation is necessary and involuntary: God has everlastingly been creating out of that which God previously created because God's nature is love ('*creatio ex creatione a natura amoris*'). See, e.g., Oord's (2010, chs. 4–5). Michael Lodahl (1992, 52f) introduced the phrase '*creatio ex amore*'. While he doesn't think *creatio ex amore* and *creatio ex nihilo* are necessarily mutually exclusive, he does think (see e.g., Lodahl 2014, 100) that God 'has never been without some kind of creation, some sort of world or another'. David Basinger (2013) also disputes the claim that theism must deny the necessity of a creation; open theists, he thinks, can endorse it. According to Norman Kretzmann (1997, 223f), God is bound by God's nature to create some world or other. The idea that God must create appears to have a long pedigree in the Christian tradition, with at least hints of it in Pseudo-Dionysius, Bonaventure, Abelard, and Scotus Eriugena.

This concludes our exposition of euteleological metaphysics and its potential for making intelligible what it is for reality to be as theist faith claims it to be, the God-way. According to a euteleological metaphysics of theism, reality is inherently directed upon the realization of its *telos*, the supreme good, and the Universe exists because the supreme good is indeed realized within it. God is an entity only in the broadest sense implied by 'God' functioning as a referring term that can take the subject position in true sentences. But God is not 'a' being, however unique and great, nor any kind of item amongst the items and features of fundamental theist ontology. Our talk of God as a personal being with properties involves a radically analogous extension from our thinking about mundane things to permit thought about ultimate reality as revealed (according to the Abrahamic traditions). We believe it is a mistake to treat that talk as needing to be supported by an underlying metaphysics in which God is a personal being. We explained our reasons for regarding this standard metaphysical understanding as problematic in Chapter 1, placing the emphasis on several ways in which (we claimed) a personalist metaphysics is *religiously* inadequate to the lived-out faith of believers in the Abrahamic traditions. Our task now, in the remaining chapters, is to consider whether euteleological metaphysics counts as an improvement on standard personalist accounts of the metaphysics of theism, since, as we have already noted, doubts may be raised about the religious adequacy of a euteleological theism, especially in relation to key practices such as prayer and worship and the question of how a metaphysics that understands reality as inherently directed upon the supreme good can accommodate the existence of evil.

5
The Religious Adequacy of a Euteleological Theism
The Problem of Evil

Euteleology interprets theism as holding that reality as such and as a whole is *purposive*—that it has, and has inherently, an overall purpose (*telos*). This ultimate *telos* is reality's good, the good *for* reality, and, therefore, the supreme good. Furthermore, euteleology claims that the contingent Universe exists for the sake of realizing that supreme good, and only because that supreme good is realized within it. Euteleology thus offers a non-personalist metaphysics as an alternative to the personalist theist metaphysics widely taken as standard amongst analytic philosophers. According to that 'standard' metaphysics, we are to understand God as a supreme personal being, like ourselves only vastly greater in power, knowledge, and goodness. But, as we argued in Chapter 1, reasonable doubts may be raised about the adequacy of that standard account, doubts weighty enough to motivate exploring, from within the perspective of faith, alternative ways of understanding what it is for reality to be the way theist faith accepts it as being ('the God-way'). The euteleological metaphysics we have presented in the last two chapters is just such an alternative for *fides quaerens intellectum*.

But how good is that proposed alternative? To be any good, a proposal for making intelligible what it is for reality to be 'the God-way' will at least have to succeed in just that—it will have to be *an intelligible* account. We think we have shown in the last two chapters that the euteleological proposal *is* adequately intelligible. Where understanding comes to an end, as, of course, it must, we think that euteleology's intelligible limits are no more constraining than those of standard personalist divine metaphysics and are, anyway, in accordance with the limits *fides quaerens intellectum* must expect given the 'incomprehensibility' of the divine. Accusations of sheer unintelligibility against euteleology seem to us typically to be question-begging—as, it must be admitted, similar blanket accusations are when directed against the coherence of standard personalist theist metaphysics.

The doubts about personalist accounts that we took (in Chapter 1) to motivate a search for an alternative were not, however, so much philosophical doubts over questions of intelligibility and coherence. Those motivating doubts were, rather, about the *religious* adequacy of an understanding of God as a supreme personal being. We argued that taking God, the creator, to be a personal being leaves us with a God who is, paradoxically, at once insufficiently transcendent and too remote. And we argued that—relative to certain reasonable normative commitments, anyway—a personal God with ultimate control over creation may not be regarded as perfectly good in the light of the existence of horrendous evils. For these reasons, God according to a personalist metaphysics may be judged an unfit object of worship. We concluded that there is at least *a* reasonable internal theist perspective from which understanding God as a uniquely great person proves religiously inadequate, and, therefore, that *fides quaerens intellectum* may have a lively interest in considering alternative ways of understanding what it is for reality to be as theism claims it is. In our two preceding chapters, we have set out and defended as coherent a euteleological account of reality's being the God-way—the way it is if theism is true.

Any alternative to standard personalist accounts of theism would, of course, be satisfying only if it clearly improved upon perceived religious inadequacies in those personalist accounts while not introducing further inadequacies which, all things considered, outweighed those advantages. We will now consider whether a euteleological theism can meet these conditions. We won't attempt here a full defence of the improved religious adequacy of euteleological theism over standard personalist accounts. We'll focus instead, in this chapter and the next, on two topics which seem to present the most pressing obstacles to the adequacy of a euteleological theism. In the next chapter (Chapter 6), we will consider how a euteleological theism can make sense of prayer and worship when its fundamental ontology lacks a supreme personal being—or, indeed, any supreme entity analogous to one. In the present chapter, we will tackle the question of how a euteleological theism understands evil. To set the scene for the problem of evil as it affects a euteleological theism, we'll begin with an obvious objection that may be raised at a point where a euteleological theism supposedly improves on personalist accounts, namely its honouring of absolute divine transcendence.

5.1 Transcendence, Immanence, and Evil

One respect in which personalist accounts of theism may be held to fall short of religious adequacy is their compromising divine transcendence by understanding God as a person 'amongst persons', a being 'amongst beings'. A euteleological theism makes no such compromise: for euteleological theism, God's reality altogether transcends being an entity, however uniquely great, of any kind. It might be objected, however, that euteleological theism emphasizes transcendence at the expense of immanence. How can a God that 'absolutely transcends entityhood' be present to believers, and be at work in the world bringing reconciliation and salvation?

In the previous chapter, we believe we showed that this objection is ill-founded. We noted that a euteleological theism generally *leaves in place* scriptural, liturgical, and creedal language as able to convey truths about God's presence and action in the world. We argued that, although its fundamental ontology lacks God as a personal being, a euteleological theism accepts the aptness of believers' engaging their inter-personal faculties (including their personal God-talk) in relating to God. We claimed that euteleological theism offers a reflective (and itself, of course, limited) understanding of personal claims about God's knowing, willing, and acting as deploying an analogous construction from our ordinary thinking about persons, things, and their properties in order to articulate what theism reveals about our ethically significant practical relation to that which is ultimately real, and, in itself beyond comprehension. Furthermore, we maintained, euteleological theism makes intelligible a more intimate divine immanence within the creation than personalist metaphysics can accommodate. According to euteleological theism, all existents exist for the sake of realizing the supreme good and because it is realized, and God's agency in the world isn't externally 'super-added' to the agency of creaturely agents but effected in and through their agency.

An obvious problem remains, however. Euteleological theism is clearly committed to holding that such intimate divine immanence obtains in the midst of suffering, wrongdoing, and, even, deliberate opposition to the divine purposes. The euteleological theist surely needs to accept, then, that (for example) the torturer deploys what is ultimately *divine* agency in inflicting anguish on his victim—anguish which exists (as supposedly everything does) for the sake of realizing the supreme good, and only because that good is realized. Thus, although a euteleological theism doesn't face the difficulty of holding morally perfect an all-powerful personal agent who sustains a torturer's powers, for euteleology 'the problem of evil' may seem to be even worse than it is on standard personal-omniGod theism. The problem may seem worse because accounts which take God to be an independent person seem to have the advantage of placing God at some 'personal' distance from the evil will and deeds of creaturely persons who do wrong. No such 'distancing' seems possible when—as euteleological theism claims—all agency is divine agency in a world where everything exists for the sake of realizing the supreme good, and, ultimately, only because that goal is achieved.[1] Our topic for this chapter, then, is to consider whether euteleological theism can provide a religiously adequate understanding of evil in a world that it claims exists for the sake of realizing the supreme good.

5.2 Theism's 'Privationist' Notion of Evil

The existence of evil in the created order provides significant grounds for doubting the religious adequacy of personalist theism (as we argued in Chapter 1): do equally or more serious doubts arise if we shift to an account of theism based on a euteleological metaphysics?

It is useful to begin an answer to this question by reflecting on what evil is—or, rather, on what evil is taken to be in the context of theist commitment. Euteleology, as we have explained, gives central place to the key theist theme of an ultimate, unifying, purpose—the supreme good for the sake of whose realization all that is real exists. Theism accordingly has a notion of evil as the lack of the good that ought to be given reality's purposiveness: theism's concept of evil is thus a *privationist* one. For theism, evil is not simply the absence of what's good—it's not just what's bad or wrong, or even what's seriously bad or wrong. Rather, evil is the absence of the good *that there ought to be*.[2]

---

[1] Whether personalist accounts really do have this advantage is far from clear, however. On strong accounts of divine providence within the personalist camp, God must (for instance) concur at every step of the way in the torturer's actions, sustaining the torturer's resolve, the victim's continued consciousness, and whatever physical and other conditions are necessary for the torture to occur.

[2] In standard contemporary discussions of the Argument from Evil, focused as they are on the significance of evil for the existence of the personal omniGod, the classical privationist doctrine (evil as *privatio boni*) is typically set aside or downplayed; instead, evil is understood, as Peter van Inwagen puts it, as 'the real existence of bad things' (2006, 12). This side-lining of the significance of privationism about evil amongst personal-omniGod theists is for understandable reasons, on which we'll remark below (see note 24).

Evil exists in this privationist sense only when there is something good which ought to be but is not. A privationist concept of evil thus gets a grip only when it's a given that certain states of affairs ought to be—so, for example, lack of sight is a privation in a mature animal that is normally sighted in the environment to which it is adapted, but lack of sight is not a privation in (say) a stone.[3] Evil as privation is thus *relative* to goods which are 'purposed'. Such privations are therefore *conditional* on the telic status of the relevant goods. But if—as theism claims—there is an *overall and ultimate* divine purpose for all existence, there can be privations which are categorical rather than only conditional, since reality's overall *telos* is that which *unconditionally* ought to be fulfilled.

5.3 Soteriology: Responding to an Existential Problem of Evil

Now, theism certainly does accept that there are evils which are categorically, unconditionally, evil: they are privations of the overall good that categorically ought to be, the good that God purposes. And we are looking for an answer to the question how, if God's purposes are good and the creation is fit to fulfil those purposes, any privations of those good purposes can exist at all, let alone the horrendous evils of our human history.

To tackle that question properly, we need first to discuss *soteriology*—that is, the aspect of theist teaching that has to do with 'salvation'—and to consider the kind of soteriology that could be admitted by a euteleological account of theism. A soteriology seems essential to theist belief—even if, as Brian Leftow argues (2016, 69), it is at least thinkable that the God of theism might not bring salvation. In practice, theist belief is vitally concerned with accepting that evil exists, recognizing what evil is (and what it is not), and learning how to deal with it and overcome it.[4] Theism proclaims that,

---

[3] This example is Aquinas's (see *Summa Theologiae*, I, Q48, a.5, ad.1). Aquinas here (*ST*, I, Q48) develops the doctrine of evil as *privatio boni* as found in Augustine (see *Enchiridion*, 11; 2014, 278–9). The doctrine has its roots in neo-Platonism (see Plotinus, *Enneads* I, 8; 1956, 66–78).

[4] It is therefore mistaken to read theism's privationist understanding of evil as a doctrine about the unreality or illusory status of evil. Yet that kind of interpretation has often enough been adopted—e.g., by J. L. Mackie, who takes the doctrine of evil as *privatio boni* to amount to the claim that 'evil that would really be opposed to good does not exist' (1955, 201). As a lack of the good there ought to be, evil cannot be on an onto-ethical par with the good (there cannot be any *evil* that ought to be!), but this does not imply that evil isn't real, or that evil is not 'really' opposed to the good.

despite the existence of evils, there is a way for humans to 'become what they were created to be' by achieving fulfilment in accordance with God's good purposes. And that 'way' towards realizing the human good and the good for all creation crucially includes salvation from obstacles to the achievement of that goal—that is, ways of coping with and overcoming evils. God is a God who 'saves', who 'liberates', ultimately defeating the evils that oppose the fulfilment of the divine purposes and thus ensuring that these purposes are indeed accomplished.

The really fundamental 'problem of evil' in the context of theist commitment is, therefore, the *existential* problem of maintaining faith in the worth of hopefully pursuing the supreme good (and our human fulfilment in it) in the face of suffering, weakness, failure, and the various forces, both within ourselves and outside ourselves, which may operate to undermine the capacities needed for achieving and participating in the good, or which are even directly antagonistic to that goal. It's an essential function of belief in the theist God that it is belief in something which provides resources for dealing with this existential problem of evil. Accordingly, a theist worldview offers an account of how, by divine dispensation, humans may be 'saved' from all that opposes their participating in the enjoyment of the good for which God creates them.

Evidently, any account of how to attain salvation presupposes some understanding of what it is to 'be saved'. At its most general, the state of salvation for humans, individually and collectively, is constituted, for theism, by the state of fully realizing humanity's *telos*, the purpose for which God created humankind. Some may prefer to talk just in terms of 'ultimate human fulfilment', perhaps because, for them, 'salvation' carries specific traditional connotations that seem narrow or even ethically problematic.[5] Yet the Abrahamic theist traditions certainly hold that there are pervasive, even universal, obstacles to human fulfilment, and therefore that ultimate human fulfilment is possible only through our 'being saved' from what opposes that fulfilment. One may say, perhaps without too much fear of controversy, that Abrahamic theism understands salvation as requiring transformation from a natural tendency for self-centredness to a flourishing

---

[5] For example, some may find problematic the idea prominent in some Christian theories of atonement that salvation requires 'paying the price' for 'original sin'. Appropriating and extending the insights of Hannah Arendt, Grace Jantzen (1998) sharply distinguishes between a model of salvation (based on what she calls 'a symbolic of mortality') and a model of flourishing (based on 'a symbolic of natality'), and claims that they lead to very different accounts of the human condition and our relations to one another and to the divine.

God-centredness—a transformation that must work itself out both individually and socially. Beyond that, however, the details of how ultimate human fulfilment is understood, and what is needed for salvation from what opposes its achievement, are varied and often controversial, and a matter for systematic theology in each theist tradition. But we are not doing systematic theology here. Our present concern is only with the question of the religious adequacy of proposals for theist metaphysics, that is, with proposed ways of understanding reality as being the God-way. There is, of course, no possibility of deriving an entire soteriology from just the underlying theist metaphysics. Still, the underlying metaphysics will set limits for the soteriology. A religiously adequate theist metaphysics must therefore be 'soteriologically fitting' in the sense that it is consistent with the truth of a religiously viable soteriology. We need to consider, then, whether a euteleological metaphysics could be soteriologically fitting. Euteleology won't be a religiously adequate account of the basic metaphysics for theism if it cannot admit an account of how humanity may achieve ultimate fulfilment which may reasonably be judged religiously satisfying.

5.4 Can Euteleological Metaphysics Cohere with a Viable Soteriology?

What do we need for a religiously satisfying theist account of how humanity may achieve ultimate fulfilment? As we've already acknowledged, there's room for reasonable disagreement about the answer to this question: indeed, soteriology is one of the most contested theological topics. A soteriology that may satisfy some may not satisfy others. It follows, then, that one's judgement of the religious adequacy of a particular account of theist metaphysics may be affected by one's attitude to the kind of soteriology that the account may or may not be able to support. We'll be content to argue, then, that the kind of soteriology that euteleological metaphysics can support is *a* viable soteriology that may reasonably be judged satisfying—in particular by those who find standard personalist metaphysics religiously inadequate (as we have maintained—in Chapter 1—that it is quite reasonable for them to do). But it will be no surprise that those who do not share these qualms about the religious adequacy of personal-omniGod (or near enough) accounts of theism may *not* find satisfying the kind of soteriology that is available to euteleologists and other non-personalist interpreters of theism. (It may be helpful to remind our readers here that we aren't trying to persuade personal-omniGod theists to become euteleologists; rather, we want to persuade analytic philosophers generally that euteleology provides *a* viable way of understanding theism in a context where it's reasonable, if not rationally obligatory, to reject the personal-omniGod account as inadequate.)

It does seem uncontroversial, however, that a religiously satisfying theist soteriology has to affirm that God's good purposes in creation considered as a whole—across all time and space, and all spatio-temporal universes, if creation is a multiverse—are fulfilled, and that humans (though not necessarily only humans) may participate in and enjoy this fulfilment. And it has to affirm, accordingly, that evil is defeated—and especially that antagonist evil is ultimately frustrated in its aim to undermine the fulfilment of God's purposes. A viable soteriology must therefore affirm *a way* for humans, through God's grace, to overcome obstacles to their fulfilment that arise from their own limitations through ignorance, weakness, and deliberate wrongdoing.[6] A theist soteriology will thus proclaim a path through which individuals may overcome the self-centredness that (on a theist diagnosis) gives rise to evil, so as to be transformed into aligning their wills in accordance with God's good purposes.[7] Furthermore, human groups and institutions exhibit 'systemic' evils, so a satisfying soteriology ought also to proclaim the means by which these collective and social evils may be defeated so that the peace and justice God wills may be accomplished in human existence. Since collective evils, though they supervene on the actions of individuals, may occur independently of what those individuals (even obliquely) intend, it is not obvious—though some will find this controversial—that a focus on salvation by the overcoming of individual selfishness will alone suffice. Social and political ways of behaving may need transforming too.[8] (Indeed, in our era of anthropogenic climate change, this imperative may have an urgency which we humans are struggling to manage at the needed global collective level.)

---

[6] We think what we say here can remain neutral on the contested question of what balance there is between human efforts and God's gracious, enabling, initiatives in the process of overcoming obstacles to human fulfilment in accordance with divine purposes.

[7] John Hick has argued (1989) that the effecting of a transformation from self-centredness to what he calls 'Reality-centredness' is a key element, not only in theist soteriology, but also in all the great world religions.

[8] As affirmed, e.g., in liberation theologies. The term 'liberation theology' was coined by Gustavo Gutiérrez at a Conference of Latin American Bishops held in Medellín, Columbia in 1968. Gutiérrez is often seen as the father of the movement, and his (1971) is widely considered its foundational text.

But what exactly is required for the 'victory over evil' that a theist soteriology proclaims? Here there is much to contest. Must there be a guarantee of an ultimate consummation in which finite existence instantiates the supreme good *in toto*, with everything standing to everything else in perfectly just and right relationship in such a way that nothing but the good can be manifested ever again (save, perhaps, where divine justice may require that some beings remain excluded from everlasting enjoyment of the good)? If that is indeed what the victory over evil requires, then there needs to exist a Power that can ensure such an ultimate triumph. A euteleological metaphysics, however, cannot admit such a Power if, as seems plausible, a Power that *guarantees* the triumph of the good would have to be the agential power of a being distinct from, and, ultimately, in complete control of, the created world.

By contrast, standard personalist metaphysics do seem to support a 'triumphalist' and 'perfectionist' soteriology since the personal omniGod can serve as the required Power to ensure total victory over evil and institute an incorruptible 'heavenly order'.[9] There are, of course, well-known difficulties about human participation in an immortal incorruptible order, relating to questions not only about how such participants could be identical with denizens from mortal history but also about the worth of unending finite personal existence as ultimate human fulfilment.[10] If those difficulties are set aside, however, the perfectionist soteriology that standard personalist metaphysics can support might seem to give it the advantage over non-personalist, and, in particular, euteleological metaphysics.

---

[9] Whether the personal omniGod can in fact ensure this on particular personalist accounts has been contested. For example, Molinists often criticize open theists on the ground that there's no guarantee for a risk-taking God that things won't get so out of hand that God gets stuck with soteriological disaster. How can a God not armed with middle knowledge (or something stronger) guarantee that any creatures will (freely) accept him? Open theists think this is scare-mongering. They tell us we should rest assured that all will be well in the hands of an infinitely resourceful God; their critics doubt the grounds for such confidence, however.

In addition, if a 'triumphalist' and 'perfectionist' soteriology requires or implies universalism (the thesis that all will be saved), and especially necessary universalism, it's difficult to see how the personal omniGod can ensure this if creatures have libertarian freedom, even with post-mortem chances to accept salvation. For further discussion of the points raised in this note, see, e.g., Jonathan Kvanvig (2011) and Perszyk (2019).

[10] For a lively dialogue regarding personal identity and immortality, see John Perry (1978). On whether personal immortality would necessarily be undesirable, see Bernard Williams (1973). The idea of unending perfected finite personal existence also raises tricky issues about whether the inhabitants of such a heaven are able to sin, and if not, whether they are free. See, e.g., James Sennett (1999).

5.5 Soteriology for Non-Personalist Theists

A non-personalist metaphysics for theism might try to retain the standard soteriological framing assumption of a guaranteed ultimate, incorruptibly perfect, fulfilment of Creation's overall purpose by understanding reality as evolving inexorably towards a perfect fulfilment of its own nature. Such a view is reminiscent of Hegel—and, indeed, it has been suggested that Hegel might be brought to euteleology's aid.[11] However, as already indicated in Chapter 4 (pp. 94–5), a euteleological theism does not *identify* God with some emergent feature of reality: God is therefore not, on a euteleological account, the 'yet-to-be-realized' *telos* or final stage of the Universe. Nor is euteleological theism committed to the inevitability of such an ultimate consummation. Thus, a euteleological theism might well reject the usual soteriological framing assumption: as we've said, soteriology is contestable—and, in particular, it is contestable whether soteriology has to be triumphalist and perfectionist. There may be *non-perfectionist* soteriologies that affirm a meaningful victory of good over evil without guaranteeing that finite historical existence ultimately reaches a consummation of perfection that brings history to an end. And it may be that there is a non-perfectionist soteriology which may reasonably be judged religiously adequate while also being consistent with, and supported by, euteleological metaphysics.

Euteleology certainly gets us to soteriological first base, so to speak, with its assurance that the supreme good is no mere lofty ideal but is actually achieved. (Indeed, euteleology claims that nothing contingent would have existed at all had the supreme good not been finitely instantiated.) But further assurance is needed: an adequate soteriology proclaims that evil may indeed be overcome. This can be true, however, only if there are *powers* that work towards realizing the good within finite existence, that are capable of overcoming the evils that are obstacles to that end, and that are able to operate in the lives of communities and individuals. On a euteleological account, there is no room for the idea that such powers are supernatural in the sense

---

[11] Thomas Schärtl-Trendel pursues the comparison between Hegelianism and a euteleological theism in (Schärtl 2019). An anonymous reader has also noted similarities with Hegel—e.g., in the central place given to love as the supreme good, in the concern to avoid an inappropriate dualism in the God-world relation, and in the intention to provide a true philosophical expression for Christian theism—and suggests that interested readers be referred to Anselm Min (1976). However, the question of the relation of Hegel's metaphysics to Judaeo-Christian theism is a large one, with an interesting history—and well beyond our scope for discussion here. On the Christian underpinning of Hegel's conception of God, see, e.g., Quentin Lauer (1983), Patricia Calton (2001), and Peter Hodgson (2005).

that they operate on and intervene in the creation 'from outside'. But a euteleological theism does not reject altogether the existence of such powers: it admits their existence *within* the one order of contingent, concrete, reality unified by its inherent directedness upon realizing the supreme good. These powers for good are, then, 'natural' powers, subsuming but not reducing to, physical and psychological powers of the kind accessible to scientific inquiry. Such powers, though properly described as divine, may not guarantee a final triumph of absolute perfection, but (as we will explore further in the next section) they may still be worth trusting—indeed, they may be the only thing worth trusting—in the transforming struggle against evil for true human fulfilment and the good for all creation.

5.6 The Power of Love

To illustrate this possibility—of salvific powers within the creation admissible under a non-personalist and 'naturalist' account of theism such as a euteleological one—we may deploy specifically Christian ideas about the supreme good as *agapē*-love understood as wholly just and right relationship (see Chapter 2, Section 2.10). We argued earlier that a Christian euteleological theism would not identify perfectly loving relationality (or the totality of its instantiations) with God (Chapter 4, pp. 94–5). But it does seem feasible to hold that *the power of* love may be identified as *the divine power* that operates to salvific effect within the Universe.[12] Christianity may thus be interpreted along euteleological lines as holding not just that *agapē*-love is the overall good for reality, but also that love is the highest (divine) power for good. Love is fecund, and its own sole engenderer. On such an interpretation, love is understood both as a certain kind of state of affairs and also as a power. This idea of love as dynamic may be made intelligible by appeal to the fundamental phenomenon of powers emerging from, and supervening upon, relational complexity. Emergence of this kind is familiar in the evolving material world. The claim that such a phenomenon occurs at the level of just and loving relationships amongst persons giving rise to a newly emergent power is a bold one, though arguably it does have some phenomenological and empirical support. In any case, it is a possibility which our scientific

---

[12] This is a common theme in process theism: e.g., John Cobb affirms that 'God's power is the power of love' (2011, 130).

knowledge doesn't exclude, and it may thus serve as a 'genuine option' for faith (to use William James's (1956) term).[13]

And Christianity may be viewed as proposing that genuine option. Christianity teaches that the nature of *agapē*-love is revealed to humanity in Jesus the Christ, who taught love of enemies and commanded his disciples on the night one of them betrayed him to love one another as he had loved them. The idea that the power of love is the only power which can defeat evil is plausibly, then, a key Christian idea. Indeed, this idea may be—and we use this adjective advisedly—the crucial Christian idea. As process theologians observe, the power of love is a persuasive, and not a dominating, power. Dynamic love is forgiving, reconciling. Love cannot proceed by compelling or insisting: to produce what's good (namely, the right relationality that is itself), love cannot force an outcome, since an outcome that is forced as such falls short of right relationality. The lack of a guarantee that the power of love will be effective in overcoming evil (in any particular case, let alone in arriving at an ultimate triumphal consummation) is thus intrinsic to love's very nature. Yet the lack of a guaranteed incorruptible triumph of good over evil need not lead to resignation or despair.[14] The power of love may provide solid grounds for hope in overcoming evil and achieving the good.[15] And that hope may be based on something which *is* guaranteed, namely, love's persistence. Love's engendering of itself is a dynamic that cannot cease. Thus, the vision of an ultimate consummation of perfection, which is a notable feature of theist eschatology, may be taken as symbolic of a reality in which there cannot be any limit to the potential for realization of the supreme good, which is love. In other words, there *is* a guarantee, not of final static completion, but of infinite, unlimited, potential for the supreme good (which is love) to be realized over and

---

[13] We have previously suggested that 'an understanding of the power of love, as the power of something relational, may need to rest (through analogy at least) on a scientific understanding of how powers emerge out of complex interrelation of entities' (2016a, 122, n. 41). For a good introduction to varieties of emergence, see David Chalmers (2006).

[14] Compare Sharon Welch (1990) who, on behalf of a variety of liberation theologies, speaks approvingly of the power and wisdom of struggle without any guarantees of success, rejoicing in the decision to resist and not in any final victory over evil. She reminds us (p. 113) that the expectation of certain victory often leads middle-class activists to disillusionment in the face of defeat and to cynicism when only partial solutions are found.

[15] Cobb (2011, 53) concedes that the God of process theism will seem too weak if you think God's power includes the power to make creatures act in just the ways God wants them to act. Cobb says, 'for those for whom Christian faith is the basis of the assurance of a final future outcome of history in which all is made right, process theology does not suffice'. But, as we've said, it is contestable whether soteriology must be triumphalist. Cobb goes on to say that process theists aren't optimists about the course of history, but they do have hope.

over again—and potentially, too, in fuller and more lasting ways than human history has so far achieved.[16]

Love, furthermore, sees and honours the truth. Therefore, if (as theism traditionally holds) evil is always a privation, love recognizes even the strongest antagonism to the good as itself a lack of the good that is purposed. For example, the rebellious will is, in truth, a will that exists only for the sake of contributing to and participating in the good, however horrendously destructive the exercise of that will turns out to be (Satan is traditionally a fallen *angel*). Privationism thus has soteriological implications. Overcoming evil is not a matter of taking up arms (literally or figuratively) against forces of *inherent* 'pure evil', but of seeking to restore the good that is lacking against the unchanging background of the good's overall eutelic sovereignty.[17]

Yet understanding evil as privation of the good does not downplay the seriousness of evil, nor does it fail to take proper account of systemic powers of evil which transcend individual ill-will and wrongdoing. Indeed, it is arguable that sufferings and wrongs are *more serious* a scandal for the privationist than they could be on alternative accounts of evil which do not avail themselves of the idea of the good that *categorically* ought to be.[18] Accepting a privationist understanding of evil overcomes doubts about the rationality

---

[16] A euteleological theism's commitment to the unlimitedness of the potential for realizing the supreme good raises interesting questions, which we won't attempt to settle here. For example, might that infinite potential need to be *so* unlimited as to extend necessarily beyond our spatio-temporal universe (which contemporary cosmologists generally agree is itself finite)? Would euteleological theism then be committed to the existence of a multiverse consisting in an infinity of spatio-temporal universes—and, if so, would that be a problem? Does commitment to infinite potential for contingent realization of the good somehow entail that a state of unending perfect goodness must ultimately eventuate? Or, to the contrary, might an *infinitely* persisting state of perfect goodness not be compatible with the contingency essential to the concrete realization of goodness?

[17] As Mark Larrimore observes, the doctrine of evil as *privatio boni* 'demythologises' the idea of a unitary inherently evil enemy force. It also helpfully 'disaggregates' evil into the varied particular ways in which goods may be compromised, thereby heightening our awareness of the vulnerability of goods and our need to care (see Larrimore 2008, 149–50).

[18] One of us (Bishop) writes elsewhere as follows:

> It may be argued that the scandal of egregious wrongdoing is recognizable only by understanding such evil as privative. For, it's not just that the wrongdoer exercises abhorrently a power that *could have been* exercised for the good; the wrongdoer exercises that power contrary to the way it *should have been* exercised given the purpose for which it exists. Such antagonist opposition to the good is thus always an unfitting deployment of resources that are 'given' for the sake of realizing and fulfilling the good. This is a kind of opposition to the good, then, that *perverts* what is good and what exists *for* the fulfilment of the good. It may thus be argued that it is only by understanding such evil as privation of the good that the horror of such perversion may be appreciated, and viewed with the appropriate compassion. (Bishop 2021)

of pursuing the good, including the sneaking suspicion that one might do better joining the forces of evil. This is because privationism locates evil within an overall reality whose good (the supreme good) categorically ought to be realized. To seek the good is therefore to align one's will with *reality's own telic direction*, and cannot therefore be unreasonable.

For the pursuit of the good to be undertaken *hopefully*, assurance is needed that this is not a humanly impossible project even when severe adversities (both external and internal) seem to make it so. Some may judge hopeful adherence to the good in the face of evil to be reasonable only under a triumphalist soteriology with its recourse to an ultimate perfectly good all-controlling Power. But an alternative, non-triumphalist, Christian soteriology may also be envisaged—for example, along the following lines. The love which is the supreme good is found in relation with Christ and with Christ's followers: history does not need to be wound up in a final consummation for the 'Kingdom of Heaven' to be already amongst us.[19] Hope in following 'the law of love' rests on trusting the power of that love and, in adversity, trusting that power alone as the only defeater of evil. This trust under adversity commends itself as perfectly exemplified in Jesus the Christ, crucified by an unholy alliance of secular and religious powers, and vindicated in the Resurrection—whose reality may be understood on a euteleological view, not as an exercise of 'external' all-controlling power intervening to 'set things to right', but as the supreme historical working out of the divine power of love.[20]

---

[19] Christian scriptures do, of course, present images of a final consummation focused on the triumphant 'second coming' of the Christ in glory: and the belief that 'Christ will come again' is a core element in Christian creeds. Some theologians have, however, offered eschatological theories focusing on the idea of *realized eschatology* (the term is due to C. H. Dodd 1961 [1935])—that is to say, the idea that the *eschaton* (the 'end', the 'last day', in which God's purposes are wholly vindicated) is already present within contingent history. We are arguing, in effect, that—under euteleological metaphysics and in the absence of an all-controlling Agent—only an eschatology based on realized eschatology can properly express theist hope for the victory over evil. Such an eschatology would not, of course, reduce the *eschaton* to the past fulfilment of God's purposes, but would hold that the *eschaton* is *both* already realized *and* always, *without limit*, ready to be made present again, and, potentially, ever more fully. We think it reasonable (though obviously not uncontroversial) to hold that such an eschatology is religiously adequate—and, indeed, more adequate than a literally triumphalist one.

[20] Christian theology of the Resurrection emphasizes that Jesus is raised to new, eternal, life, and that this is not a mere restoration of his former life. The sense in which the Resurrection is 'bodily' is far from straightforward. The New Testament stories of Resurrection appearances seem to stress at one and the same time that the risen Jesus is embodied (not a ghost) yet not subject to ordinary physical constraints (he appears from behind closed doors, vanishes in an instant, and is unrecognizable for a long time at close quarters until a characteristic action reveals who he is). It's beyond our scope to attempt a euteleological Christian theology of the Resurrection. Such a theology would have to rule out a raising to new life through the

Natural forces and powers enable love's operations—indeed natural powers are deployed in the physical embodiment of those operations. Those natural powers may therefore properly be described as divine, as we argued earlier (see Chapter 4, pp. 113–14). But divine powers do not *reduce to* natural powers—trusting in divine power for salvation does not come down to trust in 'the natural powers of mankind'. It's true that (on a euteleological view) divine powers do not consist in additional powers exercised supernaturally (in the 'dualist' sense of 'supernatural' which connotes agency by a being in an ontological category distinct from that of creatures).[21] Trust in divine power is not trust in 'dualist' supernatural power; but it is not therefore trust in powers which are simply on a par with the natural forces and powers known to natural science. The divine power of love cannot be recognized *by the natural sciences* as divine, nor can the extent of that power be limited by what natural science may come to know of the physical powers embodying its exercise. A Christian 'power of love' soteriology understands that divine power as transcending any purely human individual or collective powers, and so preserves the theist trope that it is *in God* that we trust, not our own unaided natural human powers.

As we have argued earlier (Chapter 3, Section 3.11), the euteleological context makes available a higher order of causality transcending the mundane causal order. A soteriology based on the power of love within the creation may therefore understand that power as operating in just such a transcendent causal order arising from love's realization being reality's ultimate *telos*. Thus, what's impossible when treated in terms of the mundane causal order may be accepted as applying at the level of eutelic reality's ultimate transcendent causality: *agapē*-love, which can emerge only at later stages in the mundane causal development of a contingent material universe, can itself (at the level of the higher, transcendent, causality) be the power that operates from the beginning in the universe's evolution.

---

intervention of God the Father understood as the personal omniGod (or similar): but we think that still leaves scope for a range of options in the much contested area of Resurrection theology which would be consistent with our euteleological account. For discussion of the main kinds of views that have been held, see, e.g., Peter Carnley (1993).

[21] Caution is needed in handling different senses of 'natural' and 'supernatural', as we have already remarked (see Chapter 2, pp. 47–8). Divine powers and their operations could reasonably be described as supernatural in so far as they are not knowable *as such* from the natural scientific perspective; but they need not therefore be supernatural in the sense that they involve intervention in the natural Universe by a being in a distinct ontological category 'outside' the natural world. A euteleological theism may thus be described, using Fiona Ellis's term, as an 'expansive' naturalist theism—i.e., a 'monist' theism which admits divine transcendence yet without a radical ontological divide at the level of beings between the supernatural and the natural (see Ellis 2014, 2).

We maintain, then, that a 'power of love' soteriology of the kind sketched here would be consistent with euteleological metaphysics and acceptable as religiously adequate. Of course, those who find they cannot regard as ultimately trustworthy anything short of divine power which *guarantees* an ultimate incorruptible triumph of the good will not find this 'power of love' soteriology (which *essentially* lacks such a guarantee) religiously satisfying. They will regard euteleology as soteriologically lacking in the same way that—as we have already noted (Chapter 2, p. 47)—process theologies may be found lacking: that is, for the reason that there's no supreme agent capable of unilaterally ensuring the perfect fulfilment of the purposes of creation. Yet, as we've emphasized, soteriology is contestable and a 'power of love' soteriology may be regarded as more religiously adequate by those who sense a whiff of the idolatrous in soteriological triumphalism. To defend fully the claim that a non-triumphalist and non-perfectionist 'power of love' soteriology is indeed an improvement would require more filling out of details and further discussion of specific questions. For example, if (as it seems) a euteleological 'power of love' soteriology does not support universalism (the claim that God's love ultimately prevails in saving all), is that a problem? More generally, how do questions about divine providence, election, and pre-destination play out when a non-personalist euteleological metaphysics is assumed? And what could a euteleological theism make of theist traditions which proclaim that ultimate human fulfilment involves eternal life? We feel sure that these soteriological and eschatological issues provide fruitful ground for appreciating important differences between personalist and non-personalist accounts of theism, but we won't undertake that further exploration here.[22] We think we have said enough here, however, to justify the conclusion that a euteleological account of theism may not fairly be dismissed as inadequate just on the grounds that it excludes anything that could count as *a* religiously viable soteriology.

5.7 Intellectual Problems of Evil

Euteleology may fit, then, with a soteriology that (though non-triumphalist) may be judged as *a* reasonable account of how the truth of theism deals

---

[22] We recorded initial thoughts on some of these questions in our (2016a)—see p. 123, including notes 44 and 45. And we have written elsewhere on the question how a non-personalist account of theism could understand the Christian promise of eternal life—see Bishop and Perszyk (2022).

with the existential problem of maintaining hopeful commitment to the pursuit of the good in the face of evils. But, of course, intellectual problems about the truth, or possible truth, of theism arise from the existence of evils. It's endemic to theism that its soteriology for coping with evil, based as it must be on the overall sovereignty of the divine, raises the intellectual question how evil could have come to exist in the first place if divine power and goodness are to be trusted in overcoming evil and securing human fulfilment. Indeed, any proposed interpretation of theism for which no such intellectual problem of evil arose would *thereby* count as an inadequate interpretation. Unsurprisingly, then, a euteleological theism faces intellectual problems of evil.

Two different types of intellectual problems of evil for theist commitment need to be distinguished. The first is that evil's existence counts as evidence against the existence of whatever supposedly enables evil to be overcome. In other words, evil provides *prima facie* grounds for doubting that theism is true. Put in euteleological terms, the point is that the existence of evil gives us reason for denying that reality is inherently directed upon the supreme good and that the Universe exists ultimately because the good is realized. But, of course, evil may tell against the truth of theism while other forms of evidence tell in its favour. Provided there is *enough* good in the overall mix of good and evil in the world as we experience it, the *overall* balance of evidence may then favour theism, making it more reasonable to accept theism than to reject it or suspend judgement. Alternatively—a view we find more plausible—the publicly available evidence, including as it relates to good and evil, may, when assessed from a neutral starting-point, be not simply counter-balanced but *ambiguous* in the sense that it is equally coherently interpreted from a theist as from an atheist point of view. Then, commitment to theism's truth requires a faith-venture which cannot be certified as rationally required under wider inter-subjective evidential practices—a faith-venture that is understood from within faith's perspective as itself mediated by divine grace. On either of these overall evidential scenarios, the fact that the existence of evil provides *some* evidence against theism is, by itself, no barrier to the reasonableness of theist belief.[23] These considerations apply equally when theism is understood euteleologically: provided it

---

[23] Natural theological evidence for the truth of theism is obviously salient in this context. Note that, on the 'evidential ambiguity' scenario, natural theological arguments may still serve to articulate theism as *a* reasonable stance given the overall evidence even though these arguments may fail to make theist commitment rationally compelling (i.e., the *only* rational position to take given the evidence).

is acknowledged that there is enough good in the world, it could, overall, be reasonable to accept that reality is inherently directed upon the good while *also* accepting that evils, of the types and amounts and distributions in which they actually do exist, provide *prima facie* evidence that reality does *not* have that telic direction. Indeed, one may reasonably be committed to the truth of a Christian euteleological theism while agreeing that, when the overall evidence about good and evil is considered from a neutral perspective that makes no appeal to Christian sources of (alleged) special revelation, suspension of judgement or even outright denial is the evidentially justified attitude to have towards the claim that everything exists for the sake of realizing *agapē*-love and only because *agapē*-love is realized.

The second type of intellectual problem of evil for theism arises from the suspicion that the existence of evil—or, more specifically, the existence of certain types, amounts, degrees, or distributions of evil—is *logically incompatible* with reality's being the way theism claims it to be. If some fact about evil is logically incompatible with the facts as they would need to be for theism to be true, then accepting that fact about evil makes theist commitment irrational, and therefore renders such commitment unjustifiable. This holds even from the perspective of faith so long as it is accepted—as, of course, we think that it should be—that God's grace doesn't operate to enable us to believe what is contrary to reason in the strong sense of being self-contradictory.

In Chapter 1, pp. 31–2, we argued that, given the acceptance of certain norms for goodness as a person in relation to other persons, the existence of horrendous evils is incompatible with an account of theism which takes God to be a personal being with unlimited power, knowledge, and goodness. That argument evidently no longer applies on the euteleological account of theism, since euteleology admits no such supremely powerful morally perfect being at the level of fundamental ontology. Does a suspicion of actual evil's logical incompatibility with a euteleological theism nevertheless still arise?

Euteleological theists might try appealing to the classical theist understanding of evil as always the privation of the good that ought to be in the hope of dispelling any suspicion that actual evils could be logically incompatible with eutelic reality. That appeal is certainly euteleologically apt, but by itself it won't be enough. It is certainly true that, on a privationist account, the existence of evil as such could not be strictly logically incompatible with reality's being inherently directed upon the supreme good. If evil is always the lack of the 'purposed' good that there ought to be, nothing counts as evil save in a context where the good ought to be. The existence of evil thus *presupposes* the purposed status of what's good, and so (obviously) is logically compatible with reality's inherent directedness upon the good. Reality's being inherently directed upon the ultimate telic good seems, therefore, to be clearly logically compatible with the actual existence of some states of affairs that fail to realize that good, or fail to contribute as they should towards that supreme good's realization. A doubt obviously may remain, however, as to whether the actual existence of bad things—especially horrifically bad things—is compatible with reality's being as euteleological theism says it is: sure, if horrors *are* all privations of the good there ought to be, then there's no logical inconsistency with euteleology (since the key euteleological claim is *written into* their very description as privations). But *is* it coherent to describe horrors in that privationist way? Might horrors (or even any bad things) be such that it's logically absurd to describe them in a way which presupposes an overall directedness of all that exists on the realization of the supreme good?[24]

It may remain puzzling, then, how it can be possible for privations of the good to exist in the Universe in the types and amounts that they actually do—or even at all—if reality's very essence is eutelic and the ultimate explanation for the Universe's existence is that it realizes the supreme good. There's no contradiction in the idea of something which exists to contribute in its characteristic way towards realizing the supreme good nevertheless failing to do what it should and thus instantiating evil. Nevertheless, we may wonder how such an, in itself, logically possible state of affairs could possibly arise, and arise as often and severely as it evidently does, if the Universe does exist for the sake of the supreme good and because that good is realized within it.

5.8 A Euteleological 'Theodicy'

The only way to dispel these doubts about the coherence of a euteleological theism that acknowledges actual evils is to provide a coherent explanation

---

[24] Notice how ineffectual the mere appeal to evil as privation is in replying to the Argument from Evil against the existence of the personal omniGod: that Argument tells as much against the existence of privations of the good as it does against the existence of (very) bad things in a world governed by the omnipotent power of a morally perfect supreme agent. It's unsurprising, then, that personal-omniGod theorists have usually downplayed the doctrine of evil as *privatio boni*. Euteleologists, too, need to do more than merely appeal to that doctrine; as we are about to explain in the next section, we think they fare better in the further task of explaining how privations of the good can arise in a world as euteleology understands it than do theorists for whom Creation's overall good purposes are those of an omnipotent agent with perfect personal goodness.

of how evils—privations of the good there ought to be—may possibly arise when the Universe supposedly exists to realize the ultimate good and because that good is indeed achieved. An explanation of this kind constitutes *theodicy*—or, at least, plays a broadly similar role to it—for the non-personalist context of euteleological theism. In that context, there is, of course, no question of speculation about what God's agential *reasons* could be for causing or permitting evil in the creation, nor of justifying or 'excusing' a God who is ultimately *personally* responsible for evils.[25] Nevertheless, there is a need to explain how evil may exist compatibly with divine goodness in creation. And that need is not satisfied by appealing *purely* to the vital theist trope that evil is always a privation of the purposed good.

We think it can be explained how evil could arise in an essentially eutelic world by deploying resources familiar from 'standard' speculative theodicy. Evils may be necessarily implicated in a 'higher' good—though obviously a euteleological theodicy makes no reference to an agent who is supposedly, but problematically, morally justified in causing or permitting evil for the sake of achieving that outweighing good. Nevertheless, in euteleological theism's non-personalist context, we may still make use of the idea that, for all we know, evil may *somehow* be inherent in what's needed for the finite realization of the supreme good which is reality's *telos*. It may be the case that, because it is what it is, the supreme good requires for its concrete instantiation *a process* in which levels of concrete complexity emerge that have the capacity to instantiate it. (To continue with our Christian example, if the ultimate telic good essentially is or includes *agapē*-love, then personal beings may need to evolve who are capable of entering into loving relations.) Scientific knowledge of the evolution of the cosmos and of life on Earth provides an understanding of what such a process is like. Of course, that process as we actually have it could, from a euteleological perspective, have been different in an unknowable number of ways. Yet euteleological theodicy may maintain that any such process capable of yielding instantiations of the ultimate telic good will have essential limiting features which give rise to privations of the good there ought to be. Evil may thus be

---

[25] The provision of such justifications or excuses is often assumed to be essential to theodicy, and some philosophers promote 'anti-theodicy' as a reaction against what they see as a morally flawed speculative endeavour (see, e.g., Nick Trakakis 2018). In our view, however, there's a broad notion of theodicy as an account of the justice of God in the face of evil that can apply in non-personalist accounts of theism.

inherent in the very 'project' of concretely realizing the supreme good—a project quite beyond human comprehension.[26]

This proposal may apply both to 'moral' and to 'natural' evils—that is, both to evils whose causes include morally significantly free actions by finite persons and to evils lacking any such causes.[27] Any possible set of natural forces needed for the eventual evolution of beings capable of realizing the supreme good may be inherently limited in various ways, including the uniformity of their operation under the laws of nature. Due to these limitations, physical forces and powers—though they exist for the sake of making their specific contributions to the realization of the supreme good—may sometimes fail to make that contribution. Worse still, the regular operation of natural forces may sometimes positively undermine the development of capacities needed for the supreme good to be instantiated, or impair or destroy already developed capacities of that sort. Indeed, natural powers may operate to curtail participation in the supreme good: for example, a just society may fall vulnerable to pandemics and disasters just as readily as a corrupt one. In these ways, 'natural' evils may be inherent in a eutelic Universe.

'Moral' evils may also arise from limitations inherent in such a Universe. For the ultimate telic good to be achieved, creatures capable of making significantly free moral choices may need to exist: evidently, this is so if the good essentially includes agapeistic relations. But morally free agency may be exercised contrary to the supremely good purpose for which it exists. Choices are made which are not in accordance with love, which impair existing just and harmonious relationships, or which even deliberately oppose the formation and maintenance of loving relationality. And the collective, social, and institutional behaviour of free finite persons exhibits

---

[26] The idea that humans cannot comprehend what's involved in God's creative activity is the theme of God's rebuke to Job 'from the heart of the tempest': 'Where were you when I laid the earth's foundations?' (Job 38:4). God's repudiation of the counsel of Job's friends (42:7) further conveys the idea that privative sufferings are inherent in the creative 'project', and may certainly not be attributed (as those friends had said) to the dispensation of divine justice or discipline. Authentic divine justice and mercy perhaps becomes more apparent when God doubles Job's former prosperity 'while Job was interceding for his friends' who had incurred God's anger (42:10).

[27] This distinction has become commonplace in standard discussions of theodicy. It is a somewhat technical distinction, since it implies (for example) that harm done by well-intentioned agents inculpably ignorant of the nature and consequences of their actions or omissions is 'moral' evil even though no one is blameworthy. Ordinary parlance, however, would tend to associate the idea of moral evil with attributable moral fault. Furthermore, the distinction is not clear-cut: e.g., if people have chosen to live near known fault lines the devastation they suffer in an earthquake (which seems a paradigm 'natural' evil) may technically be a 'moral' one.

emergent powers which, though they exist to produce and maintain just relationships amongst persons and with the wider environment, evidently sometimes operate in ways which fail to achieve that purpose, or, indeed, directly oppose it, yielding 'systemic' evils.

It doesn't seem *logically* impossible, however, for the 'project' of concretely realizing the supreme good to go wholly 'according to plan'. There seems to be no logical contradiction in an evolutionary process in which every existent plays its proper part (and thus is fulfilled and flourishing) in yielding, eventually and without limit, instantiations of the ultimate telic good. We agree that the total absence of evil in a eutelic Universe may be a bare logical possibility; yet we think we may readily explain the existence of actual evils as consistent with the claims of euteleological theism. Those claims offer no guarantee that evils won't occur in a process capable of realizing the supreme good. Indeed, those claims are consistent with its being the case that any such process has inherent limitations which render it statistically, if not logically, inevitable that evils will occur.

The finiteness of the evolutionary process towards the required complexity may necessarily involve matter-energy dynamics indifferent to the harm and suffering they sometimes cause to sentient creatures (think, for instance, of the debris of the Solar System's formation with its threat of meteor strike, the movement of tectonic plates on the Earth, the phenomena of animal predation and parasitism, or the mechanisms of cellular growth potentially turning malign in cancers). The matter-energy substrate needed for the good's concrete realization may thus aptly be regarded as possessed of a certain inertia (or even recalcitrance) in fulfilling its destiny.[28] The fact that some creatures suffer in ways that undermine their flourishing may then indeed be a statistical inevitability in any type of finite evolutionary process that would be capable of yielding instantiations of the supreme good. Yet no particular lack or undermining of flourishing will ever, as such, be logically necessary for the sake of realizing the ultimate telic good. No being's harmful suffering ever becomes 'meaningful' because it 'had to be' for the sake of achieving 'higher' good: yet suffering, together with its meaninglessness,

---

[28] Is there a hint here of the idea of matter as inherently evil—an idea often attributed to neo-Platonists? Not really. All the present proposal has in common with that idea is the general notion that the limitedness of physical matter-energy imposes constraints on how the supreme good can come to be made concretely real. There is no privation of what ought to be that attaches *to the nature of physical matter-energy itself*: to the contrary, euteleology understands matter-energy as just what it needs to be to function as the substrate for the supreme good to be 'incarnated' in it.

may be unavoidably present in a world where the supreme good comes to be concretely instantiated.

This kind of response may make sense for some forms of 'natural' evil: can a similar approach cover 'moral' evil also? It is indeed a bare logical possibility for all free creatures always, but freely, to choose the good. With a morally perfect agent who has agential power limited only by logical possibility supposedly on the scene, it needs to be explained how it is possible for this happy outcome not to be actual (see Chapter 2, Section 2.3). In the non-personalist context of a euteleological theism, however, it may suffice to argue that finite creatures with the capacity for free agency necessarily have a strong disposition (under certain commonly occurring conditions) to exercise their agency contrary to its purpose, and that it is, therefore, only to be expected that they will sometimes freely do wrong.

A version of the doctrine of 'original depravity' may here be invoked: finite agents will take the satisfaction of their own desires as the purpose of their capacity for agency, and will be naturally disposed to assume, in many situations, too narrowly self-focused a view of what's to be desired. This self-centred disposition stems, it may be thought, from the limitations intrinsic to an embodied being with agent-control and self-consciousness. Embodied agents naturally assume, by default, that they are each *themselves* the proper object of their highest concern. Accordingly, the moral evil of selfish thinking and acting in a eutelic Universe is coherently explicable, even though it is not a *logical* consequence of the existence of finite free agents that such evil should occur. Nevertheless, it seems 'bound to happen' that free agents sometimes freely make the wrong choice. But the existence of moral evil is a matter of statistical (and, in a certain sense, historical) rather than logical, inevitability.[29] Of course, for euteleology, there is no supernatural agent standing by with a power that could have been used to stave off or minimize the damage from the statistically (though not logically) inevitable moral

---

[29] There are different kinds of statistical inevitability, some of them having the status of probabilistic natural laws (e.g., the half-life of radio-active elements). But the statistical inevitability of narrowly self-centred behaviour by finite free agents is clearly not a fundamental probabilistic law of nature. Furthermore, from a theological point of view, it may be problematic to hold that finite free agents act selfishly (at least on some occasions) as a matter of nomic necessity. For Christianity, it is important that Jesus the Christ—the fully human 'second Adam'—was 'tempted in every way as we are, but without sin' (Hebrews 4:15). Jesus's (supposed) uniformly unselfish focus on doing God's will would be inconsistent with his humanity if the inevitability of selfish behaviour amongst humans were a kind of natural *necessity*. Nevertheless, the (strong) *tendency* towards self-centredness may be necessary for humans, as, indeed, for any self-conscious finite intentional agents.

evil, and whose reasons for not doing so then need to be speculatively interrogated.

Perhaps it may be objected, however, that, even though the existence of *some* evil is consistent with the Universe's euteicity, *the degree and amount of (horrendous) evil and the unfairness of its distribution* are incompatible with the Universe's having the supreme good as its *telos* and existing because that *telos* is fulfilled. We agree that inconsistency would result if evils somehow dominated to the extent that they extinguished the potential for realization of the good. But no evils can possibly have that power if the privationist account of evil that a euteleological theism endorses is correct. If whatever exists—even existents which exhibit a privation of their 'purposed' goods—exists ultimately for the sake of realizing the supreme good, then 'while there is life (indeed, while anything exists), there is hope', hope based on the directedness upon the good that belongs to the what-it-is of reality itself.[30]

Admittedly, at times there arises in human experience a sense that adversity and injustice dominate to the extent that they *do* extinguish the potential for any kind of good in which humans may participate. If one endorsed such a sense of things, then, evidently, that would give grounds for rejecting euteleological theism (along with its account of adversities and injustices as evils that are privations of a human telic good). But, as we have already noted, it need not be a problem for an account of *the content* of theism that it allows that theism may reasonably be rejected on certain available evidence. What's problematic for an account of theism's content is for the actual evidence about the existence of evil to threaten to make that account *internally contradictory* if (as it must) it incorporates that evidence. We have argued that an *agapē*-focused Christian euteleological theism can resist that threat, by affirming the classical view that evils are always privations of the good that ought to be, and by appealing to the claim that any finite natural processes capable of yielding instantiations of the agapeistic supreme good will inherently have limiting features which make evils of the kind found in

---

[30] There seems, then, to be an argument from a privationist account of evil to the conclusion that it is impossible for existence to consist in nothing but evil. If evil is always the privation of the good there ought to be, then the potential for good must exist whenever evil exists. It then follows that where evil exists there is something with the potential for good, and that thing must thereby be good *in that respect at least*, so that it is impossible for there to be nothing but evil. Of course, given euteleology's ultimate explanation of why anything contingent exists at all, there has to be something which realizes the good—so it's impossible, given a euteleological metaphysics, that there's nothing but evil. Euteleology thus provides two separate reasons for holding that 'purely evil' worlds are impossible.

the actual world statistically (if not logically) inevitable. In addition, if the truth of such a euteleological theism is to cohere with the actual facts about evil, it will need to affirm, not only that the potential for realization of the good remains so long as anything exists at all (which the very existence of evil implies on a privationist account), but also that there is a *sufficient* level of realization of the supreme good in the contingent Universe as a whole. There's no saying exactly how much good counts as sufficient, but it does seem clear that a Universe which could not reasonably be viewed *overall* as exhibiting a preponderance of good over evil would also not reasonably be viewed as one in which the power of love was operating in yielding (without limit) concrete realizations of the good. As we've already noted, an appeal to revelation may be needed to view the world in that way—our point is just that, to the extent that one can so view it, a euteleological theism that affirms privationism about evil will be consistent with the existence of the actual evils that blight human history. The evident fact that it seems clearly logically possible that things could have gone better won't threaten incoherence—given that euteleology posits no Agent with perfect moral goodness and power limited only by logic.

5.9 Evil and Analogizing

A euteleological theism may escape, then, the 'standard' 'logical' Argument from Evil. But can euteleological theism escape the force of that Argument altogether if it leaves in place scriptural, liturgical, and creedal personal language about God? We have emphasized that theism understood as based on euteleological metaphysics largely retains this personal language, explaining its meaning as understood through an analogous extension from our understanding of what we mean when we attribute agency, wisdom, and goodness to human persons (see Chapter 4, Section 4.6). But won't it then follow that euteleological theism remains susceptible to problems about horrendous evils with which we earlier taxed personalist accounts of theism (see Chapter 1, Section 1.8)? If, as we have argued, it is problematic to attribute perfect goodness to a Creator God who is literally a personal agent like ourselves only vastly greater in knowledge and power, will it not be similarly problematic to attribute perfect goodness to a being who, though not literally a person, is nevertheless rightly described by analogy as acting by understanding and will?

We agree that taking God to be a being who is analogous to a person may well fall into the same difficulty over evil's existence as accounts which take God 'literally' to be a person. For example, if one holds that God's being a person in an analogous sense conveys positive understanding of what God actually is—namely, a grand entity similar to a person in key respects, or properly to be treated *as if* it were a person, or the like—then horrendous evils may indeed generate doubts about how this significantly person-like being could be rightly related to suffering creatures. But on our euteleological account there is no grand entity or being that can be identified as God, and, *a fortiori*, no supreme entity that may be understood for what it is by analogy with what it is to be a person. Recall that, on our account, thinking or speaking of God as an entity possessing properties is *itself* an analogizing move. To articulate truths about ultimate reality as theism holds it to be, we have to treat ultimate reality by analogy with the mundane reality of the natural world of our experience, thus analogously constructing God-as-a-thing, to whom properties (which may, or may not, themselves apply by analogy) may attach (for our full explication of this view of the radical analogizing involved in God-talk, and our defence of this account as a theological realism, see Chapter 4, Sections 4.6 and 4.7).

Our view that personal language applies to God by analogy is not to be confused, then, with the view (which we emphatically reject) that what God is may be comprehended by understanding God as *a being* analogously like a person. Evil's existence cannot therefore generate inconsistencies with the existence of any supreme *being* that either is, or is analogously like, a personal agent for the straightforward reason that there is no such being in euteleology's fundamental ontology. Concerns *may* be raised about the consistency of evil with what *does* belong in that ontology—but we've already responded to those concerns in this chapter's immediately previous section. We've argued that it may be inherent in the 'project' of concretely realizing the supreme good that (privative) evils will occur—though no particular privations are *individually* necessary, and the occurrence of certain types of evil may be a matter of statistical rather than logical inevitability given the euteleological scenario. Using the analogizing construction of God as an entity possessing analogous personal properties, we may then say (in terms familiar from traditional theodicy) that these circumstances make it true that while God's *direct* will is wholly focused on the realization of the good, evils occur within God's *permissive* will. The analogizing character of these claims ensures, of course, that there's no implication that (in basic ontology) any personal agent is allowing or sustaining evil for the sake of higher good. Nevertheless, the theme that good may arise from evil may be retained on a euteleological account, as we'll explore further in the next section.

5.10 Maintaining Faith in the Face of Evil, and Bringing Good 'from' Evil

Believers encountering adversities, or contemplating the troubles of others, may reflect on what the love, mercy, and power of God can mean in the midst of serious suffering and injustice—and those reflections may sometimes provoke a crisis of faith. To conclude our discussion of a euteleological theism's understanding of evil, we'll note some differences in the ways reflective believers may resolve such a crisis as between 'personalists' who understand God to be a supreme person, and 'non-personalists' who do not, even though they do employ personal language in talking to, and about, God. We'll consider the resources for resolving an evil-prompted crisis of faith that are available, in particular, to a reflective non-personalist believer who endorses our euteleological account of theism. And we'll examine what it could mean, on a euteleological understanding, to bring good 'from' evil and thereby defeat it.

Reflective believers may find that trust in God in the face of evil requires accepting some kind of mystery at the heart of evil's existence—its appearing to be absurd or pointless. Many personalists will have to see that mystery as the inscrutability of God's morally adequate reasons for causing or permitting each particular evil which is apparently pointless (but actually, from the divine perspective, has an adequate rationale). Other personalists think they can admit that some evil is actually pointless, but is consistent with the personal omniGod's existence. In either case, personalists have to think that God has some morally adequate reason for not preventing any particular evil, whether it is actually or only apparently pointless.[31] By contrast, non-personalist believers will not trade in speculations about possibly

---

[31] Even if God does not have a special reason for permitting a particular evil in terms of its serving an outweighing good (or preventing a worse evil)—i.e., the evil is 'pointless'—nevertheless, God does have to have some reason justifying a general policy of permitting evils that are in this sense pointless. (One might then think that such evils *would* have point, at least at some 'higher order'.) For a discussion of attempts to argue that pointless evils are consistent with the personal omniGod's existence, see, e.g., Nick Trakakis (2007, ch. 12).

adequate reasons for a loving God's withholding what love seems, patently and urgently, to require. For them there's a mystery at the heart of suffering and evil which is a *general* feature of the momentous business of making the ideals of the highest goodness concretely real in limited, historical, existence. They may hold that particular evils, in themselves, are *always* absurd—not in the narrow sense of containing contradiction (like round squares), but in the wider sense of having no point at all. This follows from evil's privative status: there can be no point in something's failing to be or do what it is 'meant' to be or do. (Or, at least, this is so for a privative evil *considered in itself*: considered in a wider context it may seem that certain evils *do* serve a purpose—in particular, when good that would otherwise not have been achieved 'arises from' evil. We'll discuss this further in the next paragraph but one.)

If a euteleological account of theism is true, retaining hopeful trust in God in the face of—in itself, pointless—evil is reasonable because the potential for realization of the good is never, and could never be, altogether extinguished. A specifically Christian, agapeistic, euteleological theism understands that potential as resting on the power of love working within the finite world. This divine power is the light that (it is claimed) never fails—though it may seem at times to flicker only very weakly. The cross of Christ is an 'icon' for this divine power that appears weak in 'worldly' terms: while he is taunted by onlookers ('if he delight in him, let him deliver him', as Handel puts it in the Messiah), the power of love works still in Jesus to ask forgiveness for his enemies and comfort the penitent thief crucified beside him. Whether these resources are *enough* to resolve a faith-crisis of felt abandonment in adversity ('My God, my God, why have you forsaken me?' as the Gospel-writers relate that Jesus cries from the Cross, quoting Psalm 22)...well, that is a matter of experience in each such crisis, resting in fact—a Christian theologian will say—on whether or not, by God's grace, believers find they can trust in the vindication of the power of love as perfectly exemplified in Christ. All we want to claim here is that there's nothing in a euteleological account of theism that blocks resolutions of evil-prompted crises of faith. Indeed, it may be that basing theism on euteleological metaphysics provides a more fitting understanding of how it can be reasonable to retain hopeful trust in God's love under horrendous adversity than a standard personalist account does. This is because, in resting the vindication of faith on the exercise of ultimate overall power by a supernatural personal being, the standard personalist account allows to persist doubts about how that power could possibly combine with moral perfection if it was—as it must have been—ultimately responsible in the first place for those adversities in all their detailed horror.

But is evil always pointless? Isn't it a fact—and a vital theme in theist hope—that evil can be defeated in ways that bring good *from* evil? Dealing with suffering and evil can strengthen sufferers and bring them to greater psychic and spiritual maturity. And, anyway, all forms of goodness that reside in overcoming evil logically presuppose evil's existence. Is it not clear, then, that there are contexts where evils—even if absurd *in themselves*—are given real point through their relation to kinds of goodness which would not have obtained without those evils?

Yes, good somehow emerging from evil is a real and significant phenomenon: but there are different ways in which this phenomenon may be construed. A standard personalist account of theism has to construe 'bringing good from evil' as part of God's consciously and deliberately chosen overall plan for the creation.[32] God's defeating evil and weaving it into the fulfilment of God's good purposes has to count as morally *justifying* God for causing or permitting that evil to exist at all. But this may be problematic. For agents to cause evil 'that good may come' is ethically questionable, especially when, as would apply in a personal God's case, the point of doing so is to enable the exercise of their own capacity for overcoming evil with good. Personalist theists will no doubt retort that these ethical concerns may not apply, given that God is a person in a unique situation as Creator. Our point here, though, is that these concerns just don't arise on a euteleological non-personalist account. Without a supernatural personal 'supervisor of everything' on the scene, the phenomenon of goods which would not have arisen without evil simply heightens the wonder of existence's essential eutelicity. Given reality's eutelicity, evil exists only in a context where all that exists does so for the sake of realizing the good, so that powers able to achieve that *telos* are never altogether extinguished. Thus, the existence of evil—the failure, in some specific way, of the purposed good—provides the occasion for the persistence and versatility of the eutelic powers (the power of love) to become apparent as those powers operate in the quite particular circumstances of each occurrence of privative evil. Using personal language about God in the analogizing constructivist way, then, Christian euteleological

---

[32] In the absence of middle knowledge or knowledge of what God will (pre-)determine regarding creaturely free actions, the 'plan' may consist of a complex set of contingency plans God has up 'his' sleeve.

theists may affirm—to take a scriptural example—that 'this man was born blind so that the works of God might be revealed in him'.[33] For reflective Christians with this euteleological understanding, there's no supreme person planning the man's blindness in order to achieve the good of restoring his sight; rather, his blindness is a particular privation which is the occasion for the exercise, in ways specific to that occasion, of powers within the natural Universe that are capable of realizing the good.

---

[33] The scriptural quotation is from John 9:3. This chapter in John's Gospel begins with Jesus repudiating the suggestion that the man's blindness is a divine punishment for his sin, or the sin of his parents (compare the divine rebuke to Job's friends).

6
The Religious Adequacy of a Euteleological Theism
Worship and Prayer

In considering questions of religious adequacy, we argued in Chapter 5 that a euteleological theism isn't rendered religiously inadequate by the facts about evil—at least given acceptance of a non-perfectionist soteriology based on trust in a 'seemingly weak', 'persuasive' divine power within the creation that does not provide the kinds of guarantees offered by a dominating supernatural power. A theist faith which understands itself in the euteleological way may be able, then, to resolve evil-prompted crises. But, even if their implicit soteriology is non-perfectionist, it's surely essential to their religious practice that believers pray for healing and help in adversity. And when they maintain their faith in the face of adversity, they continue to believe in God, as the One to be trusted, obeyed, and worshipped. It might be urged, then, that even if evil's existence can be accommodated, no coherent sense can be made of prayer and worship under a euteleological, or any non-personalist, understanding of theism. Worship seems to imply a supreme person who is uniquely worthy of it. Petitionary prayer seems to imply a supreme person who can hear and answer. Non-personalist accounts of theism such as a euteleological one may therefore appear religiously inadequate, regardless of any theoretical virtues or practical benefits those accounts may have.

In this final chapter, we aim to meet this objection head on. We will argue that, from the point of view of making good sense of what theists are doing in worship and prayer, a non-personalist understanding of theist metaphysics may be religiously viable, and arguably preferable to personalist accounts. Our discussion will focus mainly on worship.[1] And we'll defend

---

[1] Prayer can't reasonably be considered altogether separately from worship, since some forms of prayer—such as prayers of adoration and thanksgiving and certain types of contemplative prayer—constitute forms or components of worship, while the practice of petitionary

the claim that worship can have its fit object under an interpretation of theism (such as a euteleological one) whose fundamental ontology has no identifiable God-entity.

6.1 May Worship Risk Idolatry if Addressed to a Person?

One way of supporting the claim that worship doesn't need a personal object is to argue that worship is problematic if it *does* have a personal object. Some philosophers have raised moral doubts about theist worship, making the standard assumption that its object must be a supreme person. For example, James Rachels (1971) argues that worshipping God is not an isolated act but a ritual expression of commitment to a role which dominates one's entire way of life—namely, the role of God's child. To worship is to commit to total subservience to God, since a being can be worthy of worship only if it has an unqualified claim on our obedience. But this role of worshipper, Rachels argues (appealing to a long tradition in moral philosophy), is in direct conflict with what it is to be a moral agent, namely, autonomous or self-directed. Similarly, Scott Aikin (2010) argues that worship is morally objectionable because its requirement of unconditional submission to another person's commands undermines the worshipper's own moral integrity. Aikin also finds it morally problematic to suppose that an omnibenevolent being would command us to worship him. In a similar vein, Stephen Cahn (2017) maintains that seeking to be worshipped suggests weakness of character; the virtuous are typically made uncomfortable by praise. Furthermore, if worshipping is morally flawed, no virtuous person could want to be its object.[2] These kinds of arguments are typically proposed

---

prayer (prayers of repentance seeking forgiveness, and prayers of supplication asking for help for oneself and others) presupposes that the One to whom petitions are made is worthy of worship. In some theist traditions prayer may be addressed to saints and forebears in the faith who are believed to dwell with God: yet this practice still presupposes that the response to prayer is *ultimately* in the hands of the God who is the uniquely fit object of worship.

[2] Cahn argues that, contrary to what's commonly assumed, possessing the omni-properties, whether individually or as a package, cannot render the personal omniGod worthy of worship. For further discussion of problems with justifying an obligation to worship the personal omniGod, see Tim Bayne and Yujin Nagasawa (2006). Note also that Peter Geach (1977) argues that it would be blasphemous to give God *moral* praise. As already noted (Chapter 1, p. 33), Marilyn Adams endorses the consensus of the medieval philosophers that 'God is too big to be networked to us by rights and obligations'. We think that recognizing in this way that God is not a member of our moral community significantly attenuates the notion of a person as attributed to God.

by philosophers who regard them as a moral critique *of theism itself*. But they are more precisely understood, of course, as showing (if they are sound) that a morally—and, therefore, religiously—adequate understanding of theism cannot take the object of worship to be a personal being. These arguments thus point towards the conclusion that a religiously adequate interpretation of theism must be a *non-personalist* one.

The conclusion that a religiously adequate understanding of theism must be non-personalist is, of course, what we ourselves were urging in Chapters 1 and 2—on the basis of considerations more wide-ranging than those just rehearsed about moral flaws in worshipping or wanting to be worshipped.[3] The concerns we raised there about religious adequacy may be put as objections to the worship-worthiness of the personal omni-God or of anything near enough to it. We argued that a supremely powerful person could not place itself in right relationship with created persons caught up in horrendous evils, nor could it be transcendent (or, indeed, immanent) enough to count as the uniquely fit object of theist worship. We claimed that these grounds for recognizing the personal omniGod as an idol—though not compelling on pain of irrationality—are nevertheless decisive for some, and ought, anyway, to be acknowledged by all as weighty enough to make reasonable a lively interest in ways of understanding theism without the personal omniGod. Now that we're considering the religious adequacy of our alternative euteleological account as developed in Chapters 3 and 4— and are about to defend the idea that worship and prayer do *not* conceptually require that God be a person, or even any kind of identifiable 'grand-entity'—it is worth recalling that we have already, in effect, canvassed

---

[3] We suggested in Chapter 1 (p. 14) that personal-omniGod theists are unlikely to be troubled by purely philosophical objections to the coherence of theism on their interpretation of it, and we focused instead on issues of religious adequacy. Nevertheless, we did note that many philosophers have raised doubts about the coherence of personal-omniGod theism, and it's worth adding here that some of these doubts specifically concern the coherence of worship. For example, H. J. McCloskey (1964) argues that no finite being would be worthy of worship (i.e., merit reverence, adoration, self-abasement, and total submission), and no infinite being would be worthy of worship either, because of the difficulty (following J. M. E. McTaggart, he says) of reconciling infinitude with personhood. (McCloskey doesn't provide a reference for McTaggart, but presumably he's thinking of McTaggart (1906, ch. 6, §§166-70), where he argues that omnipotence, understood as unlimited power, is incompatible with personhood.) Wesley Cray (2011) presents an argument for the incompatibility of being omniscient and being worthy of worship. No omniscient being, he argues, could be a person (because it would lack the psychological unity required for personhood), and so no omniscient being could be worthy of worship. Both McCloskey and Cray take it for granted that something is worthy of worship only if it is a person.

significant grounds for thinking that petitionary prayer is misunderstood as making requests to a person who may or may not grant them, and that worship is misunderstood as submission to a (vastly) more powerful personal being. It follows, then, that the argument that theism requires a metaphysics in which God is a personal being because worship and prayer make no sense otherwise can hardly be expected to be a straightforward 'slam-dunk' objection to a euteleological theism.

6.2 An Argument that Worship Must Have a Person as Object

Nevertheless, some philosophers evidently do think there is a knock-down argument from God's being worshipped to God's having to be understood as a personal being. For an explicit statement of such an argument, we'll turn to Brian Leftow, who writes: '[a]t a minimum, to be conceptually appropriate for worship, an item must be able to be aware of us addressing it and to understand enough of our address for there to be a point to it, and be sufficiently superior to us in some way to deserve a worship-attitude' (2016, 70). This claim rests on Leftow's account of worship as a religious practice:

> worship is a form of address: when we worship, we *say things to* what we worship. We sing hymns *to* God; we pray *to* God; we declare *to* God our belief in Him. We do not intend this as some sort of psychological self-help, or for moral improvement. The point of the practice is for these words to be heard and understood.   (2016, 71)[4]

Leftow then infers that a non-personal God would not be able to be aware of being addressed, nor have any understanding of what is said by way of address. Leftow therefore concludes that a non-personal God could not be a conceptually appropriate object of worship (2016, 70–1).

Leftow's argument is valid, but its soundness may be contested. It will be convenient to set out his argument as follows:

---

[4] Leftow is not alone in giving this kind of account of worship. Ninian Smart (1972, 11), Bernard Dauenhauer (1975, 58), Edward Henderson (1979, 34), and Michael Levine (1994, 315 and 322) all seem to agree that worship requires addressing an object, with the implication that address is typically (if not always) directed to a (distinct) person or persons.

(1) Worship is, or requires, a form of address.
(2) The form of address needed for worship requires that the addressee hears and understands what is said.
(3) A non-personal God does not (cannot) hear or understand what is said in the address involved in worship.

Therefore,

(4) A non-personal God is not a conceptually appropriate object of worship.

In what follows, we will raise questions about each of the premises of Leftow's argument.

6.3 Worship in a Broader Sense

Premise (1) in Leftow's argument—that worship involves address—may be contested on the grounds that it is true only of worship in a narrow sense. There's a sense of worship which is broader than specific acts of ritual prayer, liturgy, or private devotion. In that broader sense, worshipping God (to repeat our own words from Chapter 1 (p. 15)) is a matter of practical commitment to a whole ethos and way of life rooted in a cognitive and affective orientation to reality which places God at the centre. It is important to highlight this broad sense of worship, because worship in a narrower sense seems of little value unless set in the context of worship in this broad sense. For example, Christian worshippers believe themselves to be spiritually fed 'by Word and sacrament' *so as to become* 'the body of Christ in the world' and carry out Christ's mission; Christian ritual prayer and worship is therefore thought to be hollow if it does not issue in a way of life which holds love of God and neighbour as the overriding priority. In the broader, sense, then, believers are worshipping whenever they submit to God by following God's will in the way they live, and this kind of worship need not include any element of 'address' to God.[5]

---

[5] Compare J. V. Bartlet:

> Worship has two senses, a wider and a stricter. The wider, expressing a man's devoutness in all his living, is equivalent to piety; the narrower, denoting specific forms of devotion, personal or social, is nearly synonymous with cultus.... [S]ince

There's some disagreement, however, about whether worship in this broad sense is worship properly so-called, or, instead, the 'working out' of what worship implies for the way believers should live their lives. Nicholas Wolterstorff, for example, takes the view that loving one's neighbour and 'imitating God' by behaving justly and mercifully do not *as such* amount to worship, because (he thinks) such behaviour is not *specifically* 'Godward'.[6] This disagreement might, perhaps, be seen as purely semantic—though a Christian philosopher saying he assumes it's *false* that 'the Christian life as a whole is, or should be, worship' surely does invite a startled response.[7] But those like Wolterstorff who allow only a narrower sense of worship do still agree, of course, that worship fails in its purpose if it is not followed through with practical love of neighbour. Believers who engage in public prayers and rituals yet don't show the fruits of their Godward orientation in unselfish living are behaving hypocritically and are not worshipping or praying *well* or *effectively*.[8] It seems to us, however, that, to the extent that it's reasonable to think that 'Godward orientation' is the essential core of authentic theist worship, the idea that a life lived in submission to God counts as 'a life of worship' employs a fully legitimate broad notion of worship, which is, plausibly, *the primary* notion from which (ritual) worshipping in a narrower

---

the relation between the two senses of worship, the inward or inclusive and the external and particular, is so intimate in Christianity, it is needful constantly to bear in mind the context of "holy" or devout life in which worship is set, in so far as it is Christian at all. (1980, 763)

[6] Wolterstorff tells us that he once met a group of young Chinese Christians for whom it seemed that worship wasn't part of their lives: 'So far as I could tell, Christianity for them was a religious orientation that included love for neighbour, ... but it did not include worship' (2015, 9). Wolterstorff goes on to say:

We can acknowledge God's unsurpassable greatness by our lives in the everyday—for example, by carrying out the prophetic call to imitate God by doing justice and loving mercy. *But this is not worshipping God.* Why not? ... In our lives in the everyday we are oriented toward our tasks, toward our neighbors, toward the created world.... In worshipping God we turn ... away from attending to the neighbour so as to attend directly to God. In worship we are face to face with God. When we worship God, our acknowledgment of God's unsurpassable greatness is *Godward* in its orientation. (2015, 24, first emphasis ours)

[7] Wolterstorff closes his chapter entitled 'God as Worthy of Worship' with this remark: 'It is sometimes said that the Christian life as a whole is, or should be, worship. In this chapter I have assumed that this is not true' (Wolterstorff 2015, 39).

[8] Compare Wolterstorff, in the context of discussing the petitions of the Lord's Prayer:

Of course if we, in our daily lives, are not playing our own role in the coming of God's kingdom, if we are not promoting the hallowing of God's name in our community, not promoting the doing of God's will in our nation, not working to the end that everybody has sustenance adequate for his or her daily life, ... then our prayer is deviant, malformed. (2015, 124)

sense is derivative. That suggestion, too, fits with the fact that *false*, idolatrous, worship isn't merely (or at all) a matter of bowing down to physical idols, but of giving overall priority in one's way of living to what doesn't merit it—the pursuit of power, fame, and riches, for example.

6.4 Ritual Worship: Needed for Authentic Theist Commitment?

It might be replied, however, that engaging in worship in the narrow sense is still *necessary* for genuine theist commitment.[9] Premise (1) in our statement of Leftow's argument—namely, that worship requires a form of address—would then be upheld. Worship may involve more than activities addressed to God, but, it may be claimed, it isn't authentic theist worship unless it at least includes such activities. That claim might be resisted by holding that narrow-sense worship involving address to God is only an optional extra, so that broad-sense worship at the level of unselfish living is all the worship that authentic theist commitment really needs and premise (1) is therefore false, making Leftow's argument unsound. How plausible is this response?

We think that a reasonable defence may be made of the claim that people may be worshipping God even though they never engage in ritual worship or petitionary prayer. In the Gospels, Jesus affirms that the greatest and first commandment is to love God with all one's heart, mind, and soul; but the second commandment makes it clear that love of God cannot in practice be detached from loving one's neighbour (Matthew 22:37–40). It might be argued, then, that there isn't a zero-sum game between attending to God and attending to one's neighbour, or between having a Godward orientation and being oriented toward others. It may seem tenable, then, to hold that the Godward orientation just *is* the *authenticity of* being oriented towards

---

[9] A concern to insist on the importance of ritual worship may be what motivates philosophers like Wolterstorff to claim—injudiciously, as we've been suggesting—that ritual worship is *all* that constitutes worship properly so-called. Wolterstorff says (2015, 40): 'it has been my experience that those who declare that all of life is worship almost always downplay the importance of what I am calling *worship*, especially the importance of what I am calling *liturgical* worship'. Note, however, that address to God in liturgical worship sometimes explicitly invokes the wider notion of worship. Consider, e.g., the first verse of Horatius Bonar's 19th-century hymn (*Hymns Ancient and Modern, New Standard*, 1983, No. 200):

> Fill though my life, O Lord my God,
> in every part with praise,
> that my whole being may proclaim,
> thy being and thy ways.

others: it's *agapē* in practice that constitutes true worship. Jesus is also represented in the Gospels as asserting that 'God is spirit, and those who worship God must worship in spirit and in truth' (John 4:24)—an injunction which (however precisely one understands it) clearly goes beyond urging participation in ritual acts.[10]

These considerations are not enough to show, however, that worshipping God aright doesn't require worship in a narrower sense. According to New Testament scriptures, Jesus himself initiated a simple ritual of giving thanks for shared bread and wine in remembrance of him (Matthew 26:26–9; 1 Corinthians 11:23–7), and he taught his disciples what needs to be said to God in prayer ('the Lord's prayer', Matthew 6:9–13, Luke 11:2–4). Furthermore, the experience of theist religious communities generally strongly suggests that ritual worship, 'cultus' in some form or other, is not in practice merely an optional extra, even if the point of ritual activities is to encourage ethically desirable ways of living (which amount to worship in the broader sense). Liturgy and ritual prayer seem the inevitable expressions of the essentially communal aspect of theist commitment; they play an important role in encouraging the wider living out of an authentic Godward orientation.[11] A religiously adequate understanding of theism, then, does seem to need to make sense of worship in this narrower sense.

Worship in this narrower sense doesn't always and necessarily involve direct address to God, however. Hymns aren't always sung *to* God, but often, instead, celebrate what God is and what God has done.[12] Liturgical recitation

---

[10] According to Runar Thorsteinsson (2010), our earliest and most reliable Christian sources are Paul's letter to the Romans, the first letter of Peter, and (outside the New Testament canon) the first letter of Clement. With respect to the first of these, Thorsteinsson says (2010, 104): 'Paul wants [Christ's followers] to understand that their "reasonable worship" [Romans 12:1] embodies the moral principles presented in [Romans] chapters 12–15. To abide by these principles *is* their "living sacrifice." Their reasonable worship is in essence a moral one.' Regarding 1 Peter, Thorsteinsson says (p. 114) that for both Paul and the author of 1 Peter, 'the "sacrifices" of the gentile Christ-believers are largely to be thought to be offered through proper conduct. Sacrifice is embodied in their way of living.' Thorsteinsson concludes (p. 138) that 'all three writings stress that, rather than observing particular ceremonies, the most important kind of worship is to follow God's directions for a particular way of life'.

[11] Vigen Guroian (1995) reminds us that the word 'liturgy' comes from the Greek *leitourgia*, which connotes an action through which we come together to become something collectively that we are not individually.

[12] According to Stephen Farris (2002, 92), hymns

> most commonly speak not to God but about God. Though some hymns address God directly, they characteristically use the third person singular when speaking of God. So we read in Luke's infancy narrative, 'My soul magnifies the Lord' (1:46) and 'Blessed be the Lord, the God of Israel' (1:68). A brief glance at the Psalter will confirm the preponderance of third person speech in hymns. They offer praise for what God has done, for what he does repeatedly, or even for what he will do.

of creeds does not address God directly, and may reasonably be viewed as implicitly addressing fellow-believers in a collective affirmation of identity. And prayers of blessing or for healing often explicitly address those for whom blessing and wholeness is sought—for example, 'May the Lord bless your going out and your coming in, this time forth and for evermore', 'May the Holy Spirit strengthen in you the love of God and fill you with God's peace'. Address to God—'the Lord', 'the Holy Spirit', in these examples—is only indirect: God is not addressed in the second person.

A solely address-focused account may thus be too restrictive even for ritual worship and prayer: the point of worship and prayer is not all about God 'hearing' and 'understanding' us. Still, *petitionary* prayer clearly *is* directly addressed to God in the second person. In liturgies of intercession, common responses to specific petitions include 'Lord, graciously hear us', 'God of love, you hear our prayer', 'We beseech thee to hear us, good Lord', etc. Public *ex tempore*, 'free', prayer is typically framed by explicit second-person address to God. Personal private prayers for help and deliverance appeal to God directly or to intermediaries who will pass on requests. It seems, then, that, even if the purposes of prayer essentially have to do with transformative effects on those who pray and those for whom they pray, the truth of premise (1) in Leftow's argument should be conceded—worship and prayer that directly addresses God are typically involved in theist practice, even if worship in a broader sense (implying no such address) has primacy. A religiously adequate account of theist religious practice, then, needs to make sense of this direct address to God in worship and prayer.

6.5 'God Hears Our Prayer'

Leftow's argument for the conclusion that worship (of the kind involving direct address to God) can make sense only if God is understood, metaphysically, as a personal being might still be resisted, however. Perhaps premise (2) in Leftow's argument may be rejected? Perhaps worship and prayer involving second-person address to God does *not*—as that premise asserts—require an addressee who 'hears and understands what is said'? Wolterstorff usefully distinguishes between 'strong' and 'weak' address: in strong address the persons making address expect or hope that the addressees realize they are being addressed and are capable of apprehending what is being said; weak address lacks both these features.[13] Might direct address to God when it occurs in worship and petitionary prayer be merely weak address?

We think not. The purpose of worship and prayer may indeed have to do primarily with *our* human transformation into conformity with God's will; but it would be fallacious to infer that, therefore, when we pray we 'really' address ourselves, not God. Address to God in prayer and liturgy seems clearly to be 'strong' address that presupposes that the One addressed hears and understands. The idea that the true God is one who hears, understands—and answers—has a long pedigree. In the Judaeo-Christian tradition it is the focus of the story of Elijah and the prophets of Baal (1 Kings 18). And the psalmist asks, rhetorically, 'Does he who implanted the ear not hear?' (Psalm 94:9).[14] However, the tradition is also clearly sensitive to the idea that relationship with God is not the same as personal relationship with other humans, and, in particular, that God does not hear or understand in the way human persons do. For the theist tradition, then, the true God is one who hears and responds—but these attributions deploy *an analogous extension* from our grasp of what such talk means as applied to persons, and they do not permit us to grasp *what it is* for God to hear and respond. Indeed, scripture speaks of God's hearing in ways which make it radically unlike human hearing. Thus, for example, God hears Hannah's voiceless prayer for a child—though her lips were moving in silent speech (1 Samuel 1:13).[15] The psalmist goes further: 'Even before a word is on my tongue, you, Lord, know it completely' (Psalm 139:4).

Premise (2) is to be accepted, then—*but only on the proviso* that God's hearing and understanding are understood by analogy and not equated with

---

[13] In 'strong', unlike 'weak', address, we address 'someone in the expectation or hope that one's addressee will realize that they are being addressed' (Wolterstorff 2015, 58); 'In strong address one takes one's addressee to be capable of apprehending what one is saying; in weak address, one does not. An example of weak address would be a child saying to his goldfish, "You sweet little things." I assume that liturgical address to God is strong address' (Wolterstorff 2016, 12, note 10).

[14] Pieter van der Horst (1994, 1) points out the common practice throughout the ancient world of saying prayers out loud, with the assumption that the gods had ears that functioned in much the same way that we do; if we made no sound, we wouldn't be heard. For evidence, he points to the representations of the gods' large ears in a number of reliefs, the sheer number of prayers that were directed to the ears of a god, and the frequent references to 'the gods who listen' in ancient literature and on monuments.

[15] On the slow process whereby speechless prayer became acceptable in Judaism and Christianity, see Van der Horst (1994).

the hearing and understanding of human persons. With the significance of that proviso properly appreciated, it may then seem that premise (3) of Leftow's argument—that a non-personal God cannot hear and understand—risks begging the question. Since it's *analogous* hearing and understanding that's at issue, whatever it is *that actually does* constitute God's hearing and understanding (which is beyond our comprehending) might obtain under a theist metaphysics such as a euteleological one where God is not a personal being. Premise (3) simply asserts, without giving any reason, that there is no such possibility.

This allegation of question-begging may be filled out this way: personalist theists like Leftow accept that God's hearing and understanding are to be understood by analogy. They don't believe—*of course*, they don't believe—that God has ears and a brain to process auditory information. Yet they confidently affirm that what happens when God hears and understands is hearing and understanding by a uniquely great, immaterial, personal being. And, if they go along with Leftow's argument for the inadequacy of any non-personalist interpretation of theism that admits the need to account for practices involving strong address to God, their confidence extends to the claim that what happens when God hears and understands *couldn't be anything else* but a case of a non-corporeal personal being hearing and understanding. That confidence is presumably based on the assumption that anything to which hearing and understanding is attributed even analogously must be a conscious being, analogously like a person if not literally one. But once it's accepted that God's hearing our prayers involves an analogous extension from humans' hearing and understanding speech addressed to them, who may say without arbitrary stipulation how far this analogizing may go?

Can it be fairly argued, then, that personalist theists, who themselves think it reasonable to understand God's hearing and understanding as the immaterial hearing and understanding of a non-embodied personal being, don't have any non-question-begging grounds for denying the reasonableness of a euteleological account that *also* attributes hearing and understanding to God in an analogously extended sense? Recall that, according to euteleology's reflective understanding of the basic ontology required for ultimate reality to be the God-way, God is not only not a person, *but not 'a' being of any kind at all*. Analogous attribution of hearing and understanding to God, then, is, for euteleology, not just attribution of mental properties to something in a different ontological category from the category of finite minds, but it is attribution to... well, to 'something' that is not (in fundamental ontology) an entity of any kind at all! Proponents of Leftow's argument, then, might feel that they are hardly begging the question if they protest that, on a non-personalist account where God is not any kind of entity, claims that God hears and understands our prayers (even though they analogize from 'ordinary' human hearing and understanding) could not possibly have truth-makers. Those claims could be made true, they may hold, only by analogous predications of hearing and understanding attaching to some individual being that is person-like or analogous to a person. Any view according to which basic ontology admits no such being, they may say, can have no recourse to analogizing in attempting to preserve truths about God's hearing and understanding praise and prayer. Such an attempt, they may insist, pushes the boundaries of analogy too far, yielding sheer mystification.

The basic lines of our response to this challenge may—we hope!—already be apparent, given our elaboration in Chapter 4 (Sections 4.6–4.11) of the radical kind of analogizing that we hold to be involved in God-talk. There we emphasized that God-as-a-thing-possessing-properties is a cognitive construction, resulting from a radical analogy that applies to ultimate divine reality the thing-property schema involved in claims whose meaning we understand from their home in relation to our mundane experience. Attributions of properties to God always deploy this analogizing construction, and may also themselves involve analogous predications. We replied to the allegation that this view must imply theological non-realism, and we defended the claim that it is possible for claims about God's knowing, willing, and acting, as well as other kinds of attributions, to be made true by reality's being the God-way, where that is understood in the euteleological way as we set that out in Chapter 3. While the precise ways in which euteleological reality makes God-claims true are beyond human understanding, there's no 'sheer mystification', since it can at least be made intelligible *that* God-claims are made true in euteleological terms. Leftow's premise (3), then—that a non-personal God cannot hear and understand—*does* beg the question against our non-personalist theist metaphysics, even though that metaphysics also denies that God is any kind of individual being, and therefore denies that hearing and understanding can be attributed to something that, though not a person, is at least analogous to one. On our account, a euteleological theism provides a basic ontology in which it may indeed be true that God hears and understands praise and prayer—where not only are hearing and understanding attributed to God analogously, but it's also the case that God's being a thing which has those attributes is *itself* an analogous construction. Though we have, in effect, already provided the basics of what's needed to defend this claim, it will be helpful to revisit, clarify, and reinforce salient points, by providing a positive euteleological theist account of worship and prayer.

6.6 A Euteleological Theist Account of Worship and Prayer

We are arguing, then, that a euteleological theism provides a metaphysics which may accommodate truth-makers for the claims that God hears and understands our prayer. Indeed, euteleological theism may accommodate truth-makers for the psalmist's claim that God knows what we say even before we say it—a claim which obviously extends our ordinary understanding of what it means for a person to hear another. The analogous extension of our ordinary understanding of hearing involved in the case of God is not, however, merely 'ordinary' analogizing (as when, for example, we may say, truly, of our deaf friend that she hears what we say). On the account we have given, the claim that God hears our prayer involves a radical twofold analogizing of a type specifically needed for the case of attributions to God. On this view, the claim that God hears prayer attributes hearing to God by an analogous attribution of hearing to an entity constructed by analogy from our ordinary understanding of beings with properties to apply to a transcendent ultimate divine reality whose being 'in itself' is not fully comprehensible, but may be understood *not* to consist in the ontology of a supreme ultimate entity with great-making properties. The truth of the claim that God hears our prayer is therefore quite consistent with a basic ontology where God is not to be understood as a personal being, nor a being like a personal being, nor as any kind of entity, however exalted and unique.

This consistency claim may seem mistaken, for the kinds of reasons articulated in Leftow's argument discussed in the preceding sections. But we believe that we've rebutted that argument: in brief, we conceded that worship involves address to God (premise (1)) and argued that, while the need for the addressee to hear and understand (premise (2)) may be accepted only if God's hearing and understanding are understood analogously, on that interpretation the claim that a non-personal God cannot hear or understand (premise (3)) will reasonably be rejected by non-personalists, including those like ourselves who hold that God's being transcends being 'a thing' altogether and who understand the analogizing involved in attributing hearing and understanding to God in the radical way we've explained. (Alternatively, one might concede premise (3) is true for literal attributions of hearing and understanding, but maintain that premise (2) so interpreted is clearly false.)[16]

Perhaps our rebuttal of Leftow's *argument* might convince, and yet the intuition remain that Leftow's *claim* is still true. Leftow may not have *established* that prayer and worship require a personal being as addressee—or, at least, a supreme entity significantly like a personal being. Yet it may still seem puzzling what sense could be made of worship and prayer if, as euteleology affirms, reality's being 'the God-way' *doesn't* include the existence of any such item. What could these key activities look like on a euteleological interpretation of theism?

Well, worship and prayer in theist religious traditions are what they are! A euteleological understanding of the metaphysics of theism makes no difference to that and carries no implication that they need radical reformation. There are ritual practices of worship and prayer, public and private, which, as an anthropologist could describe, show certain functional profiles in the context of believers' characteristic individual and collective ways of living and beliefs about how they should live. These rituals, often enough, involve 'strong' address to God who is believed to hear and understand. As we've said before, a euteleological theism generally leaves in place personal ways of thinking and talking about and relating to God. The meaning of these ways of talking is usually (when not brought into service in metaphysical theorizing) just their 'face-value' meaning. It's a separate question, though, how to understand the way reality has to be when and if these ways of talking convey truths, and this is not something that can simply be read off the surface grammatical structure of the language used to articulate these truths. There's no suggestion, then, that addressing God in praise and prayer and thinking of relationship with God in personal terms are ill-founded because—as a euteleological theism claims—an adequate understanding of what it is for theism to be true has an ontology where God absolutely transcends entity-hood and is thus not 'a person amongst

---

[16] Jonathan Kvanvig (2022) holds that the heart of worship is *communication*, and that it's only a short Gricean step from that to the conclusion that worship requires that God is a personal being. We think that Kvanvig's argument will be open to rebuttal along similar lines to those we've deployed in reponse to Leftow: the attribution to God of Gricean communicative beliefs and intentions will be understood on the euteleological account as involving twofold radical analogizing, and then it will be question-begging to insist that these analogously attributed intentional states must belong to a person, albeit an immaterial one.

persons'. A euteleological theism certainly doesn't amount to a proposal for a new form of theist (or post-theist) religious sensibility with revised practices of worship and prayer somehow generated from its non-personalist metaphysics.

As we've emphasized before, a euteleological theism proposes an account of theism *from the perspective of 'faith seeking understanding'*. The phenomena of theist faith, religious practices, and ways of life thus count as given. And the real question about what worship and prayer 'look like' for a euteleological theism is a question about how these practices *are to be understood* from the perspective of *fides quaerens intellectum* if, from that perspective, reality's being the God-way is not to be understood in terms of the existence of a supreme person or person-like being, but rather in euteleological terms.

On a euteleological metaphysics, worship is not intelligible as making obeisance to a vastly more powerful personal being, nor is prayer intelligible as moral praise of, or supplication for favours or assistance from, such a being. A euteleological understanding of theism, then, won't trouble the consciences of those with ethical doubts (mentioned earlier) about praising and totally submitting to another person's greater power, or who share with us the view that (given the facts about evil, and certain reasonable assumptions about personal moral perfection) such a supremely powerful person could not be morally perfectly well related to other persons.

But what *positive* euteleological understanding may be given of worship and prayer? How may a euteleological theism understand what it is for believers to attach ultimate worth to, and rest hope for salvation and fulfilment upon, the 'object' of theist worship? Since euteleological metaphysics cannot support identifying God with any 'thing', the relation of the worshipper to the 'object' of worship isn't that of one thing to another thing. Rather, for euteleological theism, in authentic worship worshippers are rightly related to the ultimate reality of which they are a part, and under whose overall purposes their lives are subsumed. There is indeed right relationship at the heart of authentic worship, but it is not to be understood as relationship to or with any other particular thing, however great—it is right relationship to eutelic reality as directed upon realizing the supreme good. Euteleologists may thus understand authentic worship as a matter of according ultimate worth in one's attitudes and actions to that which truly merits it. Human beings who worship 'in spirit and in truth' form a right practical orientation towards reality and its ultimate purposes, and the roles that are theirs to play, both in the processes of the realization of that purpose and in its fulfilment.

This understanding of worship may seem sparse, reminiscent, perhaps, of a vague 'new age' spirituality of being 'at one' with ultimate reality.[17] Keep in mind, though, that we are here talking about a euteleological *theism*, in which the nature of reality's ultimate purposes are held to be known through the Abrahamic traditions and talk of those purposes as *God's* purposes is not merely apt but essential. Again, we stress that God-talk is not being downplayed on a euteleological understanding of what theist faith is about, only recognized for what it is—an *essential* vehicle for conveying revealed truth, but *sui generis* and radically analogical, not metaphysically transparent. Worship (in a broad sense) still needs to be characterized (to repeat our earlier description) as a matter of practical commitment to a whole ethos and way of life rooted in a cognitive and affective orientation to reality *which places God at the centre.*

Prayer fits into this euteleological picture, too, if it is understood as the work of aligning human wills with the divine will and engaging with divine action in the world—which a Christian euteleological theism may understand as the exercise of the power of *agapē*-love. Euteleologists may hold that prayer as aligning with 'the divine work' is more basic than prayer as intercessory petitioning—although prayer in this basic sense constantly makes the same petition, 'thy will be done'. For prayer like this the injunction 'pray without ceasing' (1 Thessalonians 5:17)—though a high challenge—isn't simply blankly unfeasible as incessant supplication would be.

It may seem, however, that euteleological theism would have to abandon the idea that God (sometimes) answers prayer. But that is not the case. While euteleology admits no being who, like an absolute monarch, grants or rejects petitions, it may understand God's answering petitionary prayer as the particular contingent ways in which reality's *telos* is realized in the circumstances in which prayer is offered.

To explain this further, consider a familiar puzzle about petitionary prayer. Why are some prayers answered and not others? Answering this question may be easier when there is no ultimately all-controlling person who must be supposed to have good reason for granting *only some* pleas for help—especially when equally deserving petitions appear not to be treated equally. One solution is to claim that *authentic* prayer, since it reduces to the plea that God's will be done, is *always* answered, even if not in ways petitioners expect or desire. That response will fit accounts of prayer which

---

[17] We conceded earlier that a euteleological metaphysics might be deployed in a non-theist context—see Chapter 3, pp. 84–5.

deny that prayers could 'change God's mind'—and it is therefore available in the euteleological context, where God's unchanging will is understood in terms of reality's inherent telic direction, and, as just proposed, God's answering prayer may be understood as consisting in contingent realizations of the supreme good and of conditions needed for such realizations.

That solution generates another problem, however: if we're assured that the will of God *will* be done, what's the point of praying for it? This problem seems more tractable on a euteleological account than it is on the standard personalist one. If prayer is all about influencing an all-powerful being to do what's right and good, it does seem pointless to pray if that being is, anyway, perfectly good. But if those who pray and those for whom they pray are themselves able to be crucially implicated in divine processes that yield contingent realizations of the good, the overall assurance that there will indeed be many—perhaps infinitely many—such contingent realizations doesn't make it pointless to pray for the good to be realized in every particular circumstance, since it might be that, without that prayer, the good will not *there* be achieved.

6.7 The Object of Worship

A euteleological theist understanding of worship and prayer, then, takes as primary broader notions than those that implicate direct address to God.[18] But a euteleological theism also needs an understanding of worship in a narrower sense where God is directly addressed, even if (as we are maintaining) the point of ritual prayer and worship derives from worship *qua* right practical alignment with reality's ultimate purposes.

There can be no object of authentic theist worship but God. Yet— recalling our discussion in Chapter 4—according to a euteleological theism, when we seek *to understand what God is* we cannot identify God with any entity in fundamental ontology. God altogether transcends entityhood, counting as 'an entity' only in so far as 'God' functions grammatically as a referring term in true sentences. God *is* made known *in relation to us* as (for example) the God of Abraham, Isaac, and Jacob, the God and Father of Our

---

[18] There is much more to be explored in understanding these broad notions. And one might sense in the background an even broader notion of worship not confined to that offered by human persons. If *everything* that, in its own specific way, rightly relates to reality's ultimate good purpose could be counted as worshipping, then a euteleological theism may make available a *very* broad notion of worship in which every 'spinning' quark is singing God's praise!

Lord Jesus Christ, etc. But we cannot know theoretically what God is in God-self—a common theme in medieval theology.[19] The absence of a God-entity in the fundamental ontology of a euteleological theism might be portrayed, then, as hardly surprising given God's incomprehensibility. Yet, when it comes to thinking of God as the intentional object of direct address in prayer and worship, God's absence from basic ontology might seem to imply that the object of worship is merely intentional, not real—and that *would* be surprising for a supposedly theist ontology.

But there is no such implication: the claim that *God's transcendent reality* is not to be understood as that of 'a' thing obviously does not imply that God is unreal. Euteleological theism preserves the claim that the intentional object of worship is real—but holds that this ultimate reality is not that of a supremely great personal being or entity 'amongst entities' of any kind. Though the God whom believers worship is made known ('revealed') to them, there can be only limited understanding of what God is (including understanding of what God is not).[20]

Euteleologists agree, then, that, if theism is true, when we praise God we are indeed worshipping the real, living, God, the divine substance, the divine being. But they will urge that we should not fall into the trap of supposing that these terms convey a theoretical understanding of what it is we are worshipping (such as the understanding of it as, literally, a substance, a being amongst other beings). That way risks falling into a subtle idolatry in which the worshippers' intentional object is not the living God but an entity

---

[19] Consider, e.g., Aquinas's claim in *Summa Theologiae*, I, Q2, a.3 that 'we cannot know what God is'; and, in *Summa Contra Gentiles* I, 14: '[T]he divine substance surpasses every form that our intellect reaches. Thus we are unable to apprehend it by knowing *what it is*.' It is true that Aquinas refers to the divine 'substance' here, but his key point about the impossibility of knowing what God is entails, in particular, that we cannot infer from the aptness of this term theoretical knowledge of God as the supreme individual instance of the general category, substance. As Simon Hewitt observes (2020, 7, note 22), ' to say that God is a substance is…perfectly in order as purely negative theology': it does not convey positive understanding of what God is beyond the apprehension of God's unsurpassably, trans-categorially, incomprehensibly, great reality. God is, speaking analogically, substance *par excellence*, but necessarily not comprehensible as a supremely great individual instance of the mundane category of substance.

[20] The two 'notes' Leftow affirms for a fit object of worship—that it be a thing in the right category for worship, and that it be deserving of praise in relevant respects (Leftow (2016), 71)—thus rest on an underlying assumption rejected by accounts of theism like the euteleological one that emphasize God's transcending entity-hood. On such accounts, there's no possibility that we might be worshipping the right kind of thing—a person, as Leftow maintains—but failing to latch on to a thing of that kind that's deserving of worship. On such accounts, authentic worship is never of *any* kind of thing, even though grammatically 'worship' does have an intentional object: there's no comprehending that intentional object as a particular thing of any kind or category, given the transcendence it must have to be worship worthy.

of which they take themselves to have some theoretical mastery. However, if worship is not to be, meaninglessly, worship of 'we know not what', worshippers must be able to describe the God whom they worship. They do so in ways that use 'God' as a term referring to some (supreme great) *thing*, and (if theism is true) these descriptions may convey vital truths. On the account of God-talk we gave in Chapter 4 (see Section 4.6), talk of God-as-an-entity to which attributions (both literal and analogous) may be made rests on an analogizing cognitive construction in which the 'thing-property' scheme which organizes our thought about mundane reality is applied to ultimate reality as a euteleological theism understands it. Theist worshippers think and speak of the God they worship as a supremely great personal being; they need not—and on non-personalist accounts of theism, they should not—endorse that description as a reflective theoretical understanding of what God is.[21]

Worshippers do not worship *its being the case that* or *the fact that* God exists, nor (when they are reflective) do they worship their best understanding—limited and 'through a glass darkly' as it must necessarily be—of *what it is* for God to exist. Worshippers worship *God*.[22] On our account of God-talk as deploying an analogizing cognitive construction of God-as-a-thing, won't it follow, though, that what worshippers are worshipping is a human construct or projection? If so, euteleological theism lands us in a not-so-subtle form of idolatry! As we explained in Chapter 4 (Section 4.7), however, this analogizing construction of God-as-a-thing may be viewed *in a theological realist way* as a means by which human minds, limited by the categories of thought and language, may appropriate revealed truths about ultimate divine reality and its implications for human existence. The analogizing construction of God-as-a-thing is a tool in service of making ultimate divine reality known (within limits) even though theoretical

---

[21] It is interesting to reflect on ambivalence within theist traditions over the use in prayer and worship of images—and, especially, personal images—of the divine. Islam forbids such images for the sake of honouring God's absolute transcendence, favouring instead for the decoration of places of worship abstract geometrical patterns that suggest the well-ordered goodness of the creation and the mind of its Creator. Traditions that do deploy personal images of the divine (and of saints who share in God's eternity)—such as Eastern Orthodoxy—typically stress that such icons properly function as windows through which the transcendent is approached. It seems, then, that caution about reducing God to a personal, or any kind of, being is a feature of traditional notions of how to engage rightly in ritual prayer and worship.

[22] As an anonymous reader observed, theists may (in liturgical worship) express gratitude that God exists; but we think that this does not amount to worshipping that fact rather than God. (Note that, given divine simplicity, if God does exist, the distinction between God and the fact of God's existence does not apply.)

mastery of what it is for reality to be 'the God-way' is humanly unattainable. Worship is enabled by this tool, it is not *of* this tool. We think that recognizing that God-as-a-thing is an analogizing construction is actually a guard against idolatry rather than an occasion for it. In accepting that we are able to grasp ultimate divine reality only by cognitive means which deploy radical analogizing from our understanding of the ordinary world of our experience, we acknowledge the object of theist faith and worship as a mystery beyond human comprehension, not able to be 'pinned down' by those who may say, 'we have it here', or 'we have it there', as the makers of idols do.

The mystery may be 'incomprehensible' in the sense that it cannot be theoretically mastered by human understanding, but it is decidedly not altogether unintelligible. A mature reflective theist faith which accepts the mysteriousness of its proper object may legitimately seek to satisfy its desire for a limited, yet practically and ethically advantageous, understanding of what it is for reality to be the God-way. That desire, we have suggested, may be satisfied by understanding things to be as euteleology claims they are— namely, that reality is eutelic, that is, inherently directed upon the realization of the supreme good as its *telos*, with the contingent Universe existing just because, in it, that *telos* is (multiply) fulfilled. Worshipping God is then intelligible as, most basically, a practical harmonizing with reality's euteleicity, given acceptance within a specific theist religious tradition of a special revelation to humanity of the nature of the supreme good (on the Christian view we have been using as an example, as *agapē*-love).[23] The God who is worshipped may be described as 'the One Who Is' (or, following Aquinas, *ipsum esse subsistens*): but this 'One', this *ipsum esse*, does not appear *to the understanding* as any identifiable *item* in the understanding's best account of what it is for reality to be such that theism is true. Admittedly, theist

---

[23] If, as we conceded earlier might be feasible (Chapter 3, pp. 84–5), a euteleological metaphysics could provide an ontology of ultimate reality for a *non-theist* religion or worldview, then the adherents of such a religion or worldview might also engage in practices which promote a harmonizing with reality's inherent directedness upon the supreme good. Those adherents would not, of course, think of themselves as 'worshipping God'. And their understanding of the supreme good (though its content may overlap significantly with Abrahamic theist understandings) wouldn't be attributed to special divine revelation. Furthermore, such 'harmonizing with reality' practices in some non-theist religions or 'spiritualities' might be regarded *by (some) theists* as *effectively* worship of the true God—but we won't enter the debate about whether such a claim could be true, and, even if true, able to be asserted by theists without being patronizing. At any event, we think that a euteleological metaphysics of ultimate reality is of considerable interest for proponents of religious pluralism and for the widest form of inter-faith dialogue, in which (for instance) secular humanism and Dawkins-style atheist evolutionary consciousness are included amongst the 'faiths'. But it is beyond our scope to pursue these important matters in this book.

traditions typically do allow that a sense of the presence of this 'One' may be a gift to some, perhaps a good many, believers. Experiences of divine presence vary: some are mystical, some mundane; some are of a personal presence, others of something numinously transcendent, yet others are of a 'nothingness' or even a disintegration of the subject-object relation. None of those kinds of experiences, however, valuable as they may be, are to be treated as able to convey a positive intellectual apprehension of God's reality as it is in itself. Awareness of 'the One', whether mystical or mundane, is rather to be valued by its fruits in upright living. What the ideals of the theist traditions esteem above all in human existence are lives lived in accordance with God's will—that is, on the euteleological understanding of theism we have here been proposing, by being involved in making concrete, in myriad ways, realizations of the ultimate *telos* for the sake of which all that is real exists.

We conclude, then, that prayer to God and worship of God, and of God alone, are wholly well-founded practices on a euteleological understanding of theism—as must be so if this understanding is to be religiously adequate. But the personal God-talk essential to these practices may be understood, not as transparent to the underlying ontology, but as deploying an analogizing cognitive construction of God-as-a-being, apt for enabling right human responses to ultimate divine reality, and itself a gift of divine providence. In this way, the use of personal language to talk to and about God in prayer and worship in ways that align with the truth is quite consistent with a reflective understanding of theism, such as euteleology's, in which God is not a personal being, nor any kind of entity in basic ontology. This reflective understanding of theist ontology and analogizing God-talk may be thought sophisticated—but the religious commitments and practices concerned are not. Those who belong to the Abrahamic faiths use God-talk, so to say, at its face value; our concerns in this chapter, and in this book as a whole, have been with what it's best to say from the perspective of theist faith seeking understanding.

Conclusion

Time to take stock. We've been concerned with *the content* of theism under reflective understanding—what it is that theists are 'metaphysically' committed to affirming about how to understand reality if it is 'the God-way'. A widespread standard answer—certainly, amongst philosophers in the analytic tradition—is that theist faith understands itself as affirming the existence of a supremely powerful and wise, perfectly good, personal being, God, who creates the Universe to fulfil God's purposes in creating. We've highlighted specifically religious grounds for dissatisfaction with this kind of answer, though we acknowledged that many philosophical doubts about its coherence arise as well. We argued (in Chapter 1) that an understanding of the theist object of worship as the personal omniGod may reasonably be thought inadequate on the grounds: (i) that such a God is both insufficiently transcendent and insufficiently immanent; and (ii) that, given the facts about evil and certain reasonable normative views about right relationship, such a God logically cannot be understood as acting so as to be in perfectly good relationship with creaturely persons. (We thus noted our conviction that *a version of* a 'logical' Argument from Evil against the existence of a personal omniGod is still very much in play.) Those grounds, we maintained, are sufficiently weighty to motivate a search for a more religiously adequate understanding of theism's metaphysical commitments.

In Chapter 2 we explored a range of alternatives to the standard personal-omniGod account of theism, and explained our preference for non-personalist accounts over those which retain an understanding of God as a personal being but modify one or more of the 'omni-properties'. In effect, we argued that problems for an adequate account of God's perfect goodness, as well as for God's transcendence and immanence, will remain for a metaphysics that retains God as a supreme personal being, even though that being is not the omniGod. We then proposed, for 'faith seeking understanding', a euteleological understanding of theism. In Chapter 3, we developed our account of euteleological metaphysics. According to euteleology, reality as such and as a whole is essentially *but inherently* directed upon the realization of its overall good, the supreme good. Furthermore, euteleology holds that the contingent Universe exists as it does ultimately just because that *telos* is contingently instantiated within it—in multiple ways, potentially without limit, and not necessarily in some final consummation. We added that it is characteristic of theism to hold that the nature of this supreme good is disclosed to humanity (and we have focused on the example of a Christianity which takes reality's overall *telos* to be the concrete existence of *agapē*-love).

Our detailed exposition of euteleology in Chapter 3 also included a defence of its coherence—and especially of euteleology's ultimate explanation of existence (of 'why there is something rather than nothing') which requires appeal to a higher, transmundane, causal order. In Chapter 4, we believe we've rebutted the objection that any attempt at a theism based on euteleological metaphysics must, in the final analysis, turn out to be a version of 'interesting' atheism. Although euteleology has no place in its basic ontology for God as a personal being, or as 'a' being of any kind, a euteleological theism accepts that personal talk about God can convey truths made true by eutelic reality. The expression of those truths, we argued, deploys, not just analogous predication of personal properties to something which is not a person, but the cognitive construction of God-as-a-thing that treats ultimate divine reality by analogy with the 'thing-property' schema we apply to mundane reality. That account, we argued, is quite consistent with the theological realism which a euteleological theism honours. Realists may not assume, we have argued, that the right realist ontology may simply be 'read off' from truth-claims made using personal God-talk. Our whole project, indeed, has been to draw attention to inadequacies in the standard personalist ontology, and to point towards what we think is a preferable non-personalist alternative; but personal God-talk itself and its potential to convey truth is part-and-parcel of the practice of religion in the Abrahamic traditions and we're not attempting to reform it (indeed, the very idea is quite absurd!). What we have been urging is only that the radically analogical status of God-talk be properly understood by those who are seeking reflective understanding of this practice which all theist believers engage in. We applied this understanding of God-talk as radically analogizing in giving euteleological accounts of divine action, both in creating and within creation, and also of the traditional divine attributes. We believe we have thereby shown how it can be intelligible that claims of the form 'God is F' and 'God φs' could be made true when the basic ontology of ultimate reality has no individual agent or being identifiable as the unique secure referent for 'God'.

In our final chapters (Chapters 5 and 6), we have argued that a euteleological understanding of theism avoids the inadequacies we claimed to find in standard, personalist, accounts, and we have gone on to deal with two main concerns about what may be thought its own inadequacies. In the course of developing our euteleological account in recent years, our experience is that these have been the two most frequently raised concerns.

The first of these concerns is that a euteleological theism may not fare any better (and may possibly fare worse) than standard personal-omniGod theism in addressing the problems of evil. We have argued in Chapter 5 that a euteleological theism may offer *a* religiously viable, though 'non-perfectionist', soteriology that enables theists to deal with the existential problem of evil—namely, the problem of how to maintain hopeful commitment to the pursuit of the good in the face of evils. We briefly outlined a Christian 'power of love' soteriology as an example of what a non-triumphalist soteriology which emphasizes 'realized' eschatology may look like. When it comes to intellectual obstacles posed by evil's existence, we've followed the classical privationist understanding of evil (as the lack of the good that ought to be), and suggested that, for all we know or could know, the 'project' of concretely instantiating the supreme good may inherently make both 'natural' and 'moral' evils statistically inevitable—though every particular evil is, as such, pointless, and never itself necessary for some putative 'higher' good. We concluded that the existence of the evils that actually do obtain may reasonably be held to be logically consistent with reality's being as euteological theism understands it.

The second main concern we considered about the adequacy of a euteleological theism is that it cannot make good sense of worship and prayer, since it is a non-personalist account that also holds that God isn't even a 'thing amongst things', however exalted, at the level of fundamental ontology. In our final chapter (Chapter 6), we believe we have shown that there are broad understandings of both worship and prayer that are consistent with euteleological metaphysics. We have argued, furthermore, that address to God in ritual worship and petitionary prayer fits with our view of personal God-talk as involving radical analogizing (as explained in Chapter 4, and briefly summarized again just above).

Our concern in this book, then, has been with how, reflectively, to understand reality if it is as faith in the Abrahamic theist traditions takes it, in practice, to be. We have not been concerned with making a case that justifies maintaining or adopting theist faith. Thus, we conceded, for example, that the facts about evil may well strike reasonable people as evidence that weighs against accepting the truth of theism on a euteleological, or indeed, any other plausible, reflective understanding of the Abrahamic theist worldview. Persons of theist faith, we think, may be reasonably untroubled by claims that, barring what they take themselves to accept through special divine revelation, the truth of theism would hardly seem indicated by our available evidence. Indeed, contemplating the state of our world, they may feel it's something of a miracle that they find themselves still adhering to the Abrahamic revelation of the goodness of creation and the sovereignty of the good.[1]

Mention of a miracle here cannot, of course, in a euteleological context, refer to any intervention by an external supernatural agent in the ordinary course of nature. But the most basic theist religious sense of miracle does not entail that miracles have to involve such intervention. In that most basic sense, miracles are those things at which one should marvel, as especially showing God's goodness and grace. And, for a euteleological theism, those miraculous things will amount to especially significant realizations of the supreme good or contributions to such realizations. Further discussion would be needed, however, to elaborate and defend this kind of account of miracles as religiously adequate.

Other large topics, too, would need consideration in a full defence of the religious adequacy of a euteleological understanding of theism. Related to the issue of how it understands miracles, there is the question how a euteleological account treats special revelation and divine vocation, God's specific 'calling' to individuals and peoples. There's also the issue of how a euteleological theism can make sense of eternity and the Christian promise of eternal life. Eternity is God's eternity, so eternal life is life 'with God', but euteleology is 'monist' in rejecting a supernatural realm where God dwells as a personal being and in which unending relationship with God might be enjoyed by finite persons who are granted personal immortality. How else, then, might a euteleological theism understand ideas about resurrection and a 'life to come' that transcends death?

We are drawing the present project to a close, and will not attempt to deal here with this question about how a euteleological theism could understand human participation in divine eternity, nor with the other large topics just

---

[1] We make this remark with Hume in mind, of course: at the conclusion of his essay 'Of Miracles', he famously says that 'whoever is moved by *Faith* to assent to [the Christian religion], is conscious of a continued miracle in his own person'; but we certainly don't endorse Hume's description of theist faith as a miracle of irrationality, as 'subvert[ing] all the principles of [the believer's] understanding' (Hume 1975 [1777], 131).

mentioned. We are confident, however, that what we have said here about how a euteleological theism can accommodate religiously viable accounts of the nature of evil, of a 'power of love' soteriology, and of worship and prayer, indicates a general approach which may fruitfully be extended to these other related topics.² More needs to be done, then, but we believe we've done enough in this book to achieve our goal: the metaphysics of euteleology deserves to be treated as a serious contender, philosophically and religiously, as the basis for a reflective understanding of theism without the supposedly perfectly good all-powerful and all-knowing personal supernatural agent on whom all else depends.

---

² Further work of our own on the question of how euteleological theism may understand the Christian promise of eternal life has already seen the light of publication: see Bishop and Perszyk (2022). See, also, Bishop (2017), on the theme of the fear of death and what's involved in overcoming it.

Bibliography

Acton, Lord (John Emerich Edward Dalberg) (1907 [1887]). 'Letter to Bishop Mandell Creighton' (5 April 1887), in Figgis and Laurence (eds.), *Historical Essays and Studies* (pp. 503–5). London: Macmillan.
Adams, Marilyn McCord (1999). *Horrendous Evils and the Goodness of God*. Ithaca, NY: Cornell University Press.
Adams, Marilyn McCord (2013). 'Truth and Reconciliation', in Joshua M. Moritz and Derek R. Nelsen (eds.), *Theologians in Their Own Words* (pp. 15–33). Minneapolis, MN: Augsburg Fortress.
Adams, Marilyn McCord (2016). 'Horrors: To What End?', in Andrei Buckareff and Yujin Nagasawa (eds.), *Alternative Concepts of God: Essays on the Metaphysics of the Divine* (pp. 128–44). Oxford: Oxford University Press.
Adams, Marilyn McCord (2017). 'A Modest Proposal? *Caveat Emptor!* Moral Theory and Problems of Evil', in James P. Sterba (ed.), *Ethics and the Problem of Evil* (pp. 9–26). Bloomington, IN: Indiana University Press.
Aikin, Scott F. (2010). 'The Problem of Worship', *Think* 9.25: 101–13.
Alexander, Samuel (1920). *Space, Time, and Deity*, 2 vols. London: Macmillan & Co.
Alston, William (1981). 'Can We Speak Literally of God?', in Axel D. Steuer and James William McClendon (eds.), *Is God GOD?* (pp. 146–77). Nashville, TN: Abingdon. Reprinted in Alston (1989, 39–63).
Alston, William P. (1985). 'Functionalism and Theological Language', *American Philosophical Quarterly* 22.3: 221–30. Reprinted in Alston (1989, 64–80).
Alston, William P. (1988). 'Divine and Human Action', in Thomas V. Morris (ed.), *Divine and Human Action* (pp. 257–80). Ithaca, NY: Cornell University Press. Reprinted in Alston (1989, 81–102).
Alston William P. (1989). *Divine Nature and Human Language: Essays in Philosophical Theology*. Ithaca, NY: Cornell University Press.
Alston, William P. (1995). 'Realism and the Christian Faith', *International Journal for Philosophy of Religion* 38.3: 37–55.
Anselm. *The Complete Philosophical and Theological Treatises of Anselm of Canterbury*. Translated by Jasper Hopkins and Herbert Richardson. Minneapolis, MN: Arthur J. Banning Press, 2000.
Aquinas, Thomas. *Summa Theologiae*. Translated by the English Dominican Fathers. London: Burns, Oates, and Washburne, 1912–36; New York: Benziger, 1947–8; New York: Christian Classics, 1981 (from *The Collected Works of St. Thomas Aquinas. Electronic Edition*. Charlottesville, VA: InteLex Corporation).
Aquinas, Thomas. *Summa Contra Gentiles, Book 1 (God)*. Translated with Introduction and notes by Anton C. Pegis. Notre Dame, IN: University of Notre Dame Press, 1975.
Aquinas, Thomas. *Summa Contra Gentiles, Book III (Providence)*. Translated with Introduction and notes by Vernon J. Bourke. Notre Dame, IN: University of Notre Dame Press, 1975.

Aristotle. *Nicomachean Ethics*. Translated by W. D. Ross. In *The Basic Works of Aristotle* (pp. 935–1112). Edited with an Introduction by Richard McKeon. New York: Random House, 1941.

Ashworth, E. Jennifer (2017). 'Medieval Theories of Analogy', in Edward N. Zalta (ed.), *The Stanford Encyclopedia of Philosophy* (Fall 2017 Edition). http://plato.stanford.edu/archives/fall2017/entries/analogy-medieval/.

Augustine. *The Works of Saint Augustine: A Translation for the 21st Century*. 4th release; Electronic edition. *On Christian Belief*, Vol. 1/8. New York: New City Press, 2014.

Barrett, Justin L. (2004). *Why Would Anyone Believe in God? Cognitive Science of Religion Series*. Walnut Creek, CA, and Oxford: Altamira Press.

Barrow, John and Tipler, Frank (1986). *The Anthropic Cosmological Principle*. Oxford: Oxford University Press.

Bartlet, J. V. (1980). 'Worship (Christian)', in James Hastings (ed.), *Encyclopedia of Religion and Ethics*, Vol. 12 (pp. 762–76). Edinburgh: T & T Clark.

Basinger, David (2013). 'Introduction to Open Theism', in Jeanine Diller and Asa Kasher (eds.), *Models of God and Alternative Ultimate Realities* (pp. 263–76). Dordrecht: Springer.

Bayne, Tim and Nagasawa, Yujin (2006), 'The Grounds of Worship', *Religious Studies* 42.3: 299–313.

Bishop, John (1998). 'Can There Be Alternative Concepts of God?' *Noûs* 32.2: 174–88.

Bishop, John (2007a). *Believing by Faith: An Essay in the Epistemology and Ethics of Religious Belief*. Oxford: Oxford University Press.

Bishop, John (2007b). 'How a Modest Fideism May Constrain Theistic Commitments: Exploring an Alternative to Classical Theism', *Philosophia* 35.3/4: 387–402. Reprinted in Diller and Kasher (2013), pp. 525–42.

Bishop, John (2009). 'Towards a Religiously Adequate Alternative to OmniGod Theism', *Sophia* 48.4: 419–33.

Bishop, John (2017). 'The Fear of Death', in Yujin Nagasawa and Benjamin Matheson (eds.), *The Palgrave Handbook of the Afterlife* (pp. 333–51). London: Palgrave Macmillan.

Bishop, John (2018a). 'What Theological Explanation Could and Could Not Be', *European Journal for Philosophy of Religion* 10.4: 141–60.

Bishop, John (2018b). 'A "Naturalist" Christian Theism', in Graham Oppy and Nick Trakakis (eds.), *Inter-Christian Philosophical Dialogues*, Vol. 4 (pp. 3–24). London: Routledge.

Bishop, John (2021). 'Evil and Suffering', in Stewart Goetz and Charles Taliaferro (eds.), *The Encyclopedia of Philosophy of Religion*. New York: John Wiley and Sons, Inc. https://doi.org/10.1002/9781119009924.eopr0136

Bishop, John and Perszyk, Ken (2011). 'The Normatively Relativised Logical Argument from Evil', *International Journal for Philosophy of Religion* 70.2: 109–26.

Bishop, John and Perszyk, Ken (2014). 'Divine Action Beyond the Personal OmniGod', in Jonathan Kvanvig (ed.), *Oxford Studies in Philosophy of Religion*, Vol. 5 (pp. 1–21). Oxford: Oxford University Press.

Bishop, John and Perszyk, Ken (2016a). 'Concepts of God and Problems of Evil', in Andrei Buckareff and Yujin Nagasawa (eds.), *Alternative Concepts of God: Essays on the Metaphysics of the Divine* (pp. 106–27). Oxford: Oxford University Press.

Bishop, John and Perszyk, Ken (2016b). 'A Euteleological Conception of Divinity and Divine Agency', in Thomas Schärtl, Christian Tapp, and Veronika Wegener (eds.), *Rethinking the Concept of a Personal God: Classical Theism, Personal Theism, and Alternative Concepts of God* (pp. 211–25). Munster: Aschendorff.

Bishop, John and Perszyk, Ken (2016c). 'God as Person—Religious Psychology and Metaphysical Understanding', in Thomas Schärtl, Christian Tapp, and Veronika Wegener (eds.), *Rethinking the Concept of a Personal God: Classical Theism, Personal Theism, and Alternative Concepts of God* (pp. 227–41). Munster: Aschendorff.

Bishop, John and Perszyk, Ken (2017). 'The Divine Attributes and Non-personal Conceptions of God', *Topoi* 36.4: 609–21.

Bishop, John and Perszyk, Ken (2022). 'A-Personal Concepts of God and the Christian Promise of Eternal Life', in Simon Kittle and Georg Gasser (eds.), *The Divine Nature: Personal and A-Personal Perspectives* (pp. 251–68). London: Routledge.

Bonar, Horatius (1983). *Hymns Ancient and Modern, New Standard*. Norwich: Canterbury Press Norwich.

Brower, Jeffrey E. (2008). 'Making Sense of Divine Simplicity', *Faith and Philosophy* 25.1: 3–30.

Brüntrup, Godehard and Jaskolla, Ludwig (eds.) (2017). *Panpsychism: Contemporary Perspectives*. Oxford: Oxford University Press.

Buckareff, Andrei A. (2022). *Pantheism*. Cambridge: Cambridge University Press.

Buckareff, Andrei and Nagasawa, Yujin (eds.) (2016). *Alternative Concepts of God: Essays on the Metaphysics of the Divine*. Oxford: Oxford University Press.

Bultmann, Rudolf (1961). *Kerygma and Myth: A Theological Debate*. New York: Harper and Row.

Burrell, David (1987). 'Distinguishing God From the World', in B. Davies (ed.), *Language, Meaning and God: Essays in Honour of Herbert McCabe OP* (pp. 75–91). London: Geoffrey Chapman.

Burrell, David (1993). *Freedom and Creation in Three Traditions*. Notre Dame, IN: University of Notre Dame Press.

Cahn, Stephen (2017). 'Why Worship God?' *Think* 16.46: 9–17.

Calton, Patricia Marie (2001). *Hegel's Metaphysics of God. The Ontological Proof as the Development of a Trinitarian Divine Ontology*. Aldershot: Ashgate.

Carnley, Peter (1993). *The Structure of Resurrection Belief*. Oxford: Oxford University Press.

Chalmers, David (2006). 'Strong and Weak Emergence', in Philip Clayton and Paul Davies (eds.), *The Re-emergence of Emergence: The Emergentist Hypothesis from Science to Religion* (pp. 244–56). Oxford: Oxford University Press.

Chisholm, Roderick (1968/9). 'The Defeat of Good and Evil', *Proceedings of the American Philosophical Association* 42: 21–38.

Clarke, Randolph (2003). *Libertarian Accounts of Free Will*. Oxford: Oxford University Press.

Clayton, Philip (2008). 'Open Panentheism and *Creatio ex nihilo*', *Process Studies* 37.1: 166–83.

Clayton, Philip and Peacocke, Arthur (eds.) (2004). *In Whom We Live and Move and Have our Being: Panentheistic Reflections on God's Presence in a Scientific World*. Grand Rapids, MI: Eerdmans.

Cobb, John B. (2003). *The Process Perspective: Frequently Asked Questions about Process Theology*. Edited by Jeanyne B. Slettom. St. Louis, MO: Chalice Press.
Cobb, John B. (2011). *The Process Perspective II*. Edited by Jeanyne B. Slettom. St. Louis, MO: Chalice Press.
Cobb, John B. and Griffin, David Ray (1976). *Process Theology: An Introductory Exposition*. Louisville, KY, and London: Westminster John Knox Press.
Coburn, Robert C. (1963). 'Prof. Malcolm on God', *Australasian Journal of Philosophy* 41.2: 143–62.
Cooper, Rabbi David (1997). *God is a Verb: Kabbalah and the Practice of Mystical Judaism*. New York: Riverhead Books.
Craig, William Lane (2000 [1979]). *The Kalām Cosmological Argument*. Eugene, OR: Wipf & Stock Publishers. Originally published by Macmillan Press.
Craig, William Lane (2017). *God and Abstract Objects: The Coherence of Theism: Aseity*. Dordrecht: Springer.
Cray, Wesley D. (2011). 'Omniscience and Worthiness of Worship', *International Journal for Philosophy of Religion* 70.2: 147–53.
Crisp, Oliver D. and Rea, Michael C. (2009). *Analytic Theology: New Essays in the Philosophy of Theology*. Oxford: Oxford University Press.
Cross, F. L. and Livingstone, E. (eds.) (2005). *Oxford Dictionary of the Christian Church*. Oxford: Oxford University Press.
Cupitt, Don (1980). *Taking Leave of God*. London: SCM Press.
Curley, Edwin (2003). 'The Incoherence of Christian Theism', *Harvard Review of Philosophy* 11: 74–100.
Daly, Mary (1985 [1973]). *Beyond God the Father: Toward a Philosophy of Women's Liberation*. Boston, MA: Beacon Press.
Dauenhauer, Bernard P. (1975). 'Some Aspects of Language and Time in Ritual Worship', *International Journal for Philosophy of Religion* 6.1: 54–62.
Davies, Brian (1987). 'Classical Theism and the Doctrine of Divine Simplicity', in Davies (ed.), *Language, Meaning and God: Essays in Honour of Herbert McCabe* (pp. 51–74). London: Geoffrey Chapman.
Davies, Brian (2000). 'A Modern Defence of Divine Simplicity', in Davies (ed.), *Philosophy of Religion: A Guide and Anthology* (pp. 549–64). Oxford: Oxford University Press.
Davies, Brian (2004). *An Introduction to the Philosophy of Religion*, 3rd ed. Oxford: Oxford University Press.
Davies, Brian (2006). *The Reality of God and the Problem of Evil*. London: Continuum.
Davies, Brian (2010). 'Simplicity', in Charles Taliaferro and Chad Meister (eds.), *The Cambridge Companion to Christian Philosophical Theology* (pp. 31–45). Cambridge: Cambridge University Press.
Davies, Brian (2011). *Thomas Aquinas on God and Evil*. Oxford: Oxford University Press.
Davis, Stephen T. (1983). *Logic and the Nature of God*. Grand Rapids, MI: Eerdmans.
Davis, Stephen T. (2008). 'Is God Timeless, Immutable, Simple and Impassible? Some Comments', in D. Z. Phillips (ed.), *Whose God? Whose Tradition? The Nature of Belief in God* (pp. 161–6). Aldershot: Ashgate.

Davis, Stephen T. (2017). 'Divine Incomprehensibility: Can We Know the Unknowable God?' *Topoi* 36.4: 565–70.
Dawes, Gregory (2009). *Theism and Explanation*. New York: Routledge.
Deng, Natalja (2015). 'Religion for Naturalists', *International Journal for Philosophy of Religion* 78.2: 195–214.
Diller, Jeanine and Kasher, Asa (eds.) (2013). *Models of God and Alternative Ultimate Realities*. Dordrecht: Springer.
Dodd, C. H. (1961 [1935]). *Parables of the Kingdom*. New York: Charles Scribner.
Dostoyevsky, Fyodor (1958 [1880]). *The Brothers Karamazov*. Translated by David Magarshak, in two volumes. Harmondsworth: Penguin Books.
Dougherty, Trent and McBrayer, Justin P. (eds.) (2014). *Skeptical Theism: New Essays*. Oxford: Oxford University Press.
Ellis, Fiona (2014). *God, Value, and Nature*. Oxford: Oxford University Press.
Eshleman, Andrew S. (2005). 'Can an Atheist Believe in God?' *Religious Studies* 41.2: 183–99.
Evans, C. Stephen (1996). 'On Taking God Seriously', in William J. Wainwright (ed.), *God, Philosophy, and Academic Culture* (pp. 59–70). Atlanta, GA: Scholars Press.
Everitt, Nicholas (2004). *The Nonexistence of God*. New York: Routledge.
Fakhry, Majid (2004). *A History of Islamic Philosophy*, 3rd ed. New York: Columbia University Press.
Farris, Stephen (2002). 'The Canticles of Luke's Infancy Narrative: The Appropriation of a Biblical Tradition', in Richard N. Longenecker (ed.), *Into God's Presence: Prayer in the New Testament* (pp. 91–112). Grand Rapids, MI: Eerdmans.
Fergusson, David (2014). *Creation*. Grand Rapids, MI: Eerdmans.
Feser, Edward (2013). 'Craig on Theistic Personalism'. http://edwardfeser.blogspot.com/2013/04/craig-on-theistic-personalism.html. Accessed 5 November 2021.
Fiddes, Paul S. (1992). *The Creative Suffering of God*. Oxford: Clarendon Press.
Fiddes, Paul S. (2017). '"God is love: love is God." A Cutting-edge Issue for the Theology of Love'. https://loveinreligionorg.files.wordpress.com/2017/02/fiddes-god-is-love.pdf.
Flew, Antony and MacIntyre, Alasdair (eds.) (1955). *New Essays in Philosophical Theology*. London: SCM Press.
Flint, Thomas P. and Freddoso, Alfred J. (1983). 'Maximal Power', in Freddoso (ed.), *The Existence and Nature of God* (pp. 81–113). Notre Dame, IN: University of Notre Dame Press.
Forrest, Peter (1996). *God without the Supernatural: A Defense of Scientific Theism*. Ithaca, NY: Cornell University Press.
Forrest, Peter (2007). *Developmental Theism: From Pure Will to Unbounded Love*. Oxford: Clarendon Press.
Gale, Richard M. (1991). *On the Existence and Nature of God*. Cambridge: Cambridge University Press.
Gallie, W. B. (1956). 'Essentially Contested Concepts', *Proceedings of the Aristotelian Society*, New Series, 56: 167–98.
Geach, Peter T. (1956). 'Good and Evil', *Analysis* 17.2: 33–42.
Geach, Peter T. (1977). *Providence and Evil*. Cambridge: Cambridge University Press.

Geering, Lloyd (1994). *Tomorrow's God: How We Create Our Worlds.* Wellington: Bridget Williams Books.
Green, Adam and Stump, Eleonore (eds.) (2015). *Hidden Divinity: New Perspectives.* Cambridge: Cambridge University Press.
Gregory, Brad S. (2008). 'No Room for God? History, Science, Metaphysics, and the Study of Religion', *History and Theory* 47.4: 495–519.
Griffin, David Ray (2000). 'Process Theology and the Christian Good News: A Response to Classical Free Will Theism', in John B. Cobb and Clark H. Pinnock (eds.), *Searching For An Adequate God: A Dialogue Between Process and Free Will Theists* (pp. 1–38). Grand Rapids, MI: Eerdmans.
Griffioen, Amber and Zahedi, Mohammed Sadegh (2019). 'Medieval Christian and Islamic Mysticism and the Problem of "Mystical Ethics"', in Thomas Williams (ed.), *The Cambridge Companion to Medieval Ethics* (pp. 280–305). Cambridge: Cambridge University Press.
Guroian, Vigen (1995). 'Seeing Worship as Ethics: An Orthodox Perspective', *Journal of Religious Ethics* 13.2: 332–59.
Gutiérrez, Gustavo (1971). *Teología de la liberación.* Lima, Peru: CEP. Translated into English as *A Theology of Liberation*, Maryknoll, MD: Orbis Book, 1973. New introduction to the 15th anniversary English edition in 1988.
Hart, David Bentley (2013). *The Experience of God: Being, Consciousness, Bliss.* New Haven, CT: Yale University Press.
Hartshorne, Charles (1984). *Omnipotence and Other Theological Mistakes.* Albany, NY: State University of New York Press.
Hartshorne, Charles and Reece, William L. (eds.) (1953). *Philosophers Speak of God.* Chicago, IL: University of Chicago Press.
Harvey, Thomas (2018). *After Theodicy: A Philosophical Study of the Argument from Evil and its Implications for the Elucidation of Concepts of God*, PhD thesis, University of Auckland.
Hasker, William (2010). 'Objections to Social Trinitarianism', *Religious Studies* 46.4: 421–39.
Hasker, William (2013). *Metaphysics and the Tri-Personal God.* Oxford: Oxford University Press.
Heil, John (2005). 'Real Tables', *The Monist*, 88.4: 493–509.
Heil, John (2019). *Philosophy of Mind: A Contemporary Introduction*, 4th ed. New York: Routledge.
Henderson, Edward H. (1979). 'Theistic Reductionism and the Practice of Worship', *International Journal for Philosophy of Religion* 10.1: 25–40.
Hewitt, Simon (2020). 'Disowning the Mystery: Stump's Non-Apophatic Aquinas', *Medieval Mystical Theology* 29.1: 3–14.
Hewitt, Simon (2021). 'Grammatical Thomism', *Religious Studies* 57.1: 30–48.
Hick, John (1973). *The Philosophy of Religion*, 2nd ed. Englewood Cliffs, NJ: Prentice Hall.
Hick, John (1989). *An Interpretation of Religion: Human Responses to the Transcendent.* London and New Haven, CT: Macmillan Press and Yale University Press.
Hodgson, Peter C. (2005). *Hegel and Christian Theology. A Reading of the Lectures on the Philosophy of Religion.* Oxford: Oxford University Press.

Hoffman, Joshua, and Rosenkrantz, Gary S. (2002). *The Divine Attributes*. Oxford: Blackwell.
Holley, David M. (2002). 'The Role of Anthropomorphism in Hume's Critique of Theism', *International Journal for Philosophy of Religion* 51.2: 83–99.
Howard-Snyder, Daniel and Moser, Paul (eds.) (2002). *Divine Hiddenness: New Essays*. Cambridge: Cambridge University Press.
Hudson, Hud (2009). 'Omnipresence', in Thomas P. Flint and Michael C. Rea (eds.), *The Oxford Handbook of Philosophical Theology* (pp. 199–216). Oxford: Oxford University Press.
Hudson, Hud (2014). *The Fall and Hypertime*. Oxford: Oxford University Press.
Hughes, Christopher (2010). *On a Complex Theory of a Simple God: An Investigation in Aquinas' Philosophical Theology*. Ithaca, NY: Cornell University Press.
Hume, David (1975 [1777]). *Enquiries Concerning Human Understanding and Concerning the Principles of Morals*, edited by L.A. Selby-Bigge, 3rd ed., with text revised and notes by P. H. Nidditch. Oxford: Clarendon Press.
Hume, David (1993 [1779]). *Dialogues Concerning Natural Religion*, in *Principal Writings on Religion*, edited with an introduction and notes by J. C. A. Gaskin. New York: Oxford University Press.
Inman, Ross (2017). 'Omnipresence and the Location of the Immaterial', in Jonathan Kvanvig (ed.), *Oxford Studies in Philosophy of Religion*, Vol. 8 (pp. 168–206). Oxford: Oxford University Press.
Insole, Christopher J. (2006). *The Realist Hope: A Critique of Anti-Realist Approaches in Contemporary Philosophical Theology*. London: Routledge.
James, William (1956). 'The Will to Believe', in *The Will to Believe and Other Essays in Popular Philosophy, and Human Immortality* (pp. 1–31). New York: Dover.
Janzten, Grace (1998). *Becoming Divine: Towards a Feminist Philosophy of Religion*. Manchester: Manchester University Press.
Johnston, Mark (2009). *Saving God: Religion after Idolatry*. Princeton, NJ: Princeton University Press.
Johnston, Mark (2010). *Surviving Death*. Princeton, NJ: Princeton University Press.
Kahane, Guy (2011). 'Should We Want God To Exist?', *Philosophy and Phenomenological Research* 82.3: 674–96.
Kane, Robert (2005). *A Contemporary Introduction to Free Will*. Oxford: Oxford University Press.
Kaufman, Gordon (1981). *The Theological Imagination: Constructing the Concept of God*. Philadelphia, PA: Westminster Press.
Kenny, Anthony (1979). *The God of the Philosophers*. Oxford: Clarendon.
Kittle, Simon and Gasser, Georg (eds.) (2022). *The Divine Nature: Personal and A-Personal Perspectives*. London: Routledge.
Kraut, Richard (2011). *Against Absolute Goodness*. Oxford: Oxford University Press.
Kretzmann, Norman (1966). 'Omniscience and Immutability', *Journal of Philosophy* 63.14: 409–21.
Kretzmann, Norman (1997). *The Metaphysics of Theism: Aquinas's Natural Theology in Summa Contra Gentiles*, Vol. I. Oxford: Clarendon.
Kvanvig, Jonathan L. (2011). *Destiny and Deliberation: Essays in Philosophical Theology*. Oxford: Oxford University Press.

Kvanvig, Jonathan L. (2022). 'Metatheology and the Ontology of Divinity', in Simon Kittle and Georg Gasser (eds.), *The Divine Nature: Personal and A-Personal Perspectives* (pp. 139–57). London: Routledge.

La Croix, Richard R. (1977). 'The Impossibility of Defining "Omnipotence"', *Philosophical Studies* 32.2: 181–90.

Larrimore, Mark (2008). 'Evil as Privation: Seeing Darkness, Hearing Silence', in M. David Eckel and Bradley L. Herling (eds.), *Deliver Us from Evil* (pp. 149–65). New York: Continuum.

Lauer, Quentin (1983). *Hegel's Concept of God*. Albany, NY: SUNY Press.

Le Poidevin, Robin (1996). *Arguing for Atheism: An Introduction to the Philosophy of Religion*. London: Routledge.

Le Poidevin, Robin (2016). 'Playing the God Game: The Perils of Religious Fictionalism', in Andrei Buckareff and Yujin Nagasawa (eds.), *Alternative Concepts of God: Essays on the Metaphysics of the Divine* (pp. 178–91). Oxford: Oxford University Press.

Lebens, Samuel (2021). 'Is God a Person? Maimonides, Crescas, and Beyond', *Religious Studies*, 17 September 2021, 1–27. Published online.

Leech, David and Visala, Aku (2011). 'The Cognitive Science of Religion: Implications for Theism?', *Zygon* 46.1: 47–64.

Leftow, Brian (1998). 'Omnipresence', in *The Routledge Encyclopedia of Philosophy*. London: Routledge. DOI: 10.4324/9780415249126-K060-1.

Leftow, Brian (2009). *Time and Eternity*. Ithaca, NY: Cornell University Press.

Leftow, Brian (2016). 'Naturalistic Pantheism', in Andrei A. Buckareff and Yujin Nagasawa (eds.), *Alternative Concepts of God: Essays on the Metaphysics of the Divine* (pp. 64–87). Oxford: Oxford University Press.

Legenhausen, Gary (1986). 'Is God a Person?', *Religious Studies* 22.3/4: 307–23.

Leidenhag, Joanna (2020). 'Deploying Panpsychism for the Demarcation of Panentheism', in Godehard Brüntrup, Benedikt Paul Göcke, and Ludwig Jaskolla (eds.), *Panentheism and Panpsychism: Philosophy of Religion Meets Philosophy of Mind* (pp. 65–90). Leiden: Brill.

Leslie, John (1979). *Value and Existence*. Totawa, NJ: Rowman & Littlefield.

Leslie, John (1989). *Universes*. London: Routledge.

Leslie, John (2001). *Infinite Minds: A Philosophical Cosmology*. Oxford: Clarendon Press.

Leslie, John (2016). 'A Way of Picturing God', in Andrei A. Buckareff and Yujin Nagasawa (eds.), *Alternative Concepts of God: Essays on the Metaphysics of the Divine* (pp. 50–63). Oxford: Oxford University Press.

Leslie, John (2019). 'What God Might Be', *International Journal for Philosophy of Religion* 85.1: 63–75.

Levine, Michael (1994). *Pantheism: A Non-theistic Concept of Deity*. London: Routledge.

Lewis, David K. (2007). 'Divine Evil', in Louise M. Antony (ed.), *Philosophers without Gods: Meditations on Atheism and the Secular Life* (pp. 231–42). Oxford: Oxford University Press.

Lipton, Peter (2007). 'Science and Religion: The Immersion Solution', in Andrew Moore and Michael Scott (eds.), *Realism and Religion: Philosophical and Theological Perspectives* (pp. 31–46). Aldershot: Ashgate.

Locke, John (1979 [1690]). *An Essay Concerning Human Understanding*. Edited by Peter N. Nidditch. Oxford: Clarendon.
Lodahl, Michael (1992). *The Story of God: Wesleyan Theology and Biblical Narrative*. Kansas City, MO: Beacon Hill Press.
Lodahl, Michael (2014). 'Creatio Ex Amore!', in Thomas Jay Oord (ed.), *Theologies of Creation: Creation Ex Nihilo and Its New Rivals* (pp. 99–107). New York: Routledge.
MacIntyre, Alasdair (1963). 'God and the Theologians', in John A. T. Robinson and David L. Edwards (eds.), *The Honest to God Debate* (pp. 215–31). London: SCM Press.
Mackie, J. L. (1955). 'Evil and Omnipotence', *Mind*, New Series, 64: 200–12.
Mackie, J. L. (1982). *The Miracle of Theism: Arguments For and Against the Existence of God*. New York: Oxford University Press.
Mann, William E. (1983). 'Simplicity and Immutability in God', *International Philosophical Quarterly* 23.3: 267–76.
Martin, Michael (1990). *Atheism: A Philosophical Justification*. Philadelphia, PA: Temple University Press.
Martin, Michael and Monnier, Ricki (eds.) (2003). *The Impossibility of God*. Amherst, NY: Prometheus Books.
Mawson, T. J. (2005). *Belief in God: An Introduction to the Philosophy of Religion*. Oxford: Oxford University Press.
Mawson, T. J. (2013). 'The Case against Atheism', in Stephen Bullivant and Michael Ruse (eds.), *The Oxford Handbook of Atheism* (pp. 22–37). Oxford: Oxford University Press.
Mawson, T. J. (2019). 'Pantheism, Panentheism, Theism'. Presented at the 'Pantheism and Panentheism Project Workshop' in Birmingham, UK, on 29 May.
May, Gerhard (1994). *Creatio Ex Nihilo: The Doctrine of 'Creation out of Nothing' in Early Christian Thought*. Trans. A. S. Worrall. London: T & T Clark. German original published in 1978.
McCabe, Herbert (1987). *God Matters*. London: Geoffrey Chapman.
McCall, Thomas and Rea, Michael C. (eds.) (2009). *Philosophical and Theological Essays on the Trinity*. Oxford: Oxford University Press.
McCauley, Robert N. (2020). 'Recent Trends in the Cognitive Science of Religion: Neuroscience, Religious Experience, and the Confluence of Cognitive and Evolutionary Research', *Zygon* 55.1: 97–124.
McCloskey, H. J. (1964). 'Would Any Being Merit Worship', *Southern Journal of Philosophy* 2.4: 157–64.
McTaggart, J.M.E. (1906). *Some Dogmas of Religion*. London: Edward Arnold. Reprinted New York: Kraus Reprint Co., 1969.
Mesle, C. Robert (1993). *Process Theology: A Basic Introduction*. St. Louis, MO: Chalice Press.
Min, Anselm (1976). 'Hegel's Absolute: Transcendent or Immanent?' *Journal of Religion* 56.1: 61–87.
Moltmann, Jürgen (1974). *The Crucified God: The Cross of Christ as the Foundation and Criticism of Christian Theology*. Translated by R. A. Wilson and J. Bowden: London: SCM Press.

Moore, G. E. (1959 [1903]). *Principia Ethica*. Cambridge: Cambridge University Press.
Moreland, J. P., Meister, Chad, and Sweis, Khaldoun A. (eds.) (2013). *Debating Christian Theism*. Oxford: Oxford University Press.
Morris, Thomas V. (1986). *The Logic of God Incarnate*. Ithaca, NY: Cornell University Press.
Morris, Thomas V. (1987a). *Anselmian Explorations*. Notre Dame, IN: University of Notre Dame Press.
Morris, Thomas V. (1987b). 'Perfect Being Theology', *Nous* 21.1: 19–30.
Morriston, Wes (1984). 'Is Plantinga's God Omnipotent?', *Sophia* 23.3: 45–57.
Morriston, Wes (2000). 'Must the Beginning of the Universe Have a Personal Cause?', *Faith and Philosophy* 17.2: 149–69.
Mulgan, Tim (2015). *Purpose in the Universe: The Moral and Metaphysical Case for Ananthropocentric Purposivism*. Oxford: Oxford University Press.
Mullins, R.T. (2016). 'The Difficulty with Demarcating Panentheism', *Sophia* 55.3: 325-46.
Murray, Michael J. (2008). *Nature Red in Tooth and Claw: Theism and the Problem of Animal Suffering*. Oxford: Oxford University Press.
Murray, Michael J. and Rea, Michael C. (2008). *An Introduction to the Philosophy of Religion*. Cambridge: Cambridge University Press.
Nagasawa, Yujin (2008). 'A New Defence of Anselmian Theism', *Philosophical Quarterly* 58.233: 577–96.
Norenzayan, Ara (2013). *Big Gods: How Religion Transformed Cooperation and Conflict*. Princeton: Princeton University Press.
Oakes, Robert (1977). 'Classical Theism and Pantheism: A Victory for Process Theism?' *Religious Studies* 13.2: 167–73.
O'Connor, Timothy (2008). 'Theism and the Scope of Contingency', in Jonathan L. Kvanvig (ed.), *Oxford Studies in Philosophy of Religion*, Vol. 1 (pp. 134–49). Oxford: Oxford University Press.
O'Connor, Timothy (2012). *Theism and Ultimate Explanation: The Necessary Shape of Contingency*. Oxford: Blackwell.
Oord, Thomas Jay (2010). *The Nature of Love: A Theology*. St. Louis, MO: Chalice Press.
Oord, Thomas Jay (2015). *The Uncontrolling Love of God: An Open and Relational Account of Providence*. Downers Grove, IL: InterVarsity Press.
Oppy, Graham (2004). 'Arguments from Moral Evil', *International Journal for Philosophy of Religion* 56.2/3: 59–87.
Owen, H. P. (1967). 'Theism', in Paul Edwards (ed.), *The Encyclopedia of Philosophy*, Vol. 8 (pp. 97–8). New York: Macmillan and Free Press.
Owen, H. P. (1971). *Concepts of Deity*. London: Macmillan.
Page, Ben (2019). 'Wherein Lies the Debate? Concerning Whether God is a Person', *International Journal for Philosophy of Religion* 85.3: 297–317.
Perry, John (1978). *A Dialogue on Personal Identity and Immortality*. Indianapolis, IN: Hackett Publishing.
Perszyk, Ken (1998). 'Free Will Defence with and without Molinism', *International Journal for Philosophy of Religion* 43.1: 29–64.
Perszyk, Ken (2013). 'Recent Work on Molinism', *Philosophy Compass* 8: DOI: 10.1111/phc3.12057.

Perszyk, Ken (2018a). 'Motivating the Search for Alternatives to Personal OmniGod Theism: The Case from Classical Theism', *European Journal for Philosophy of Religion* 10.4: 97–118.
Perszyk, Ken (2018b). 'Divine Infinity and Personhood', in Benedikt Göcke and Christian Tapp (eds.), *The Infinity of God: New Perspectives in Theology and Philosophy* (pp. 317–40). Notre Dame, IN: University of Notre Dame Press.
Perszyk, Ken (2019). 'Open Theism and the Soteriological Problem of Evil', in Benjamin H. Arbour (ed.), *Philosophical Essays Against Open Theism* (pp. 159–77). New York: Routledge.
Peterson, Michael; Hasker, William; Reichenbach, Bruce; and Basinger, David (2009). *Reason & Religious Belief: An Introduction to the Philosophy of Religion*, 4th ed. Oxford: Oxford University Press.
Pfeifer, Karl (2020). 'Naïve Panentheism', in Godehard Brüntrup, Benedikt Paul Göcke, and Ludwig Jaskolla (eds.), *Panentheism and Panpsychism: Philosophy of Religion Meets Philosophy of Mind* (pp. 123–38). Leiden: Brill.
Philipse, Herman (2012). *God in the Age of Science? A Critique of Religious Reason.* Oxford: Oxford University Press.
Philipse, Herman (2017). 'Swinburne's Apologetic Strategy for Theism Evaluated', *Religious Studies* 53.3: 307–20.
Pike, Nelson (1969). 'Omnipotence and God's Ability to Sin', *American Philosophical Quarterly* 6.3: 208–16.
Pike, Nelson (1970). *God and Timelessness.* New York: Schocken.
Pike, Nelson (1979). 'Plantinga on Free Will and Evil', *Religious Studies* 15.4: 449–73.
Pinnock, Charles, Rice, Richard, Sanders, John, Hasker, William, and Basinger, David (1994). *The Openness of God: A Biblical Challenge to the Traditional Understanding of God.* Downers Grove, IL: InterVarsity Press.
Plantinga, Alvin (1967). *God and Other Minds: A Study of the Rational Justification of Belief in God.* Ithaca, NY: Cornell University Press.
Plantinga, Alvin (1974a) *God, Freedom, and Evil.* Grand Rapids, MI: Eerdmans.
Plantinga, Alvin (1974b). *The Nature of Necessity.* Oxford: Clarendon Press.
Plantinga, Alvin (1980). *Does God Have a Nature?* Aquinas Lecture 44. Milwaukee, WI: Marquette University Press.
Plantinga, Alvin (1984). 'Advice to Christian Philosophers', *Faith and Philosophy* 1.3: 253–71.
Plantinga, Alvin (1985a). 'Reply to Robert M. Adams', in James E. Tomberlin and Peter van Inwagen (eds.), *Profiles: Alvin Plantinga* (pp. 371–82). Dordrecht: D. Reidel.
Plantinga, Alvin (1985b). 'Self-Profile', in James E. Tomberlin and Peter van Inwagen (eds.), *Profiles: Alvin Plantinga* (pp. 3–97) Dordrecht: D. Reidel.
Plantinga, Alvin (1993). *Warrant and Proper Function.* Oxford: Oxford University Press.
Plantinga, Alvin (2000). *Warranted Christian Belief.* Oxford: Oxford University Press.
Plantinga, Alvin (2011). *Where the Conflict Really Lies: Science, Religion, and Naturalism.* New York: Oxford University Press.
Plato. *The Republic.* English translation by Paul Shorey, Loeb Classical Library. Cambridge, MA and London, 1953. First printed 1930.

Plotinus. *The Enneads*. Translated by Stephen Mackenna, 2nd ed., revised by B. S. Page. London: Faber and Faber, 1956.

Pogin, Kathryn (2020). 'God is Not Male', in Michael Peterson and Raymond VanArragon (eds.), *Contemporary Debates in Philosophy of Religion*, 2nd ed. (pp. 302–10). Oxford: Wiley.

Pouivet, Roger (2018). 'Against Theistic Personalism: What Modern Epistemology Does to Classical Theism', *European Journal for Philosophy of Religion* 10.1: 1–19.

Prior, A. N. (1962). 'The Formalities of Omniscience', *Philosophy* 37.140: 114–29.

Pruss, Alexander R. (2008). 'On Two Problems of Divine Simplicity', in Jonathan Kvanvig (ed.), *Oxford Studies in Philosophy of Religion*, Vol. 1 (pp. 150–67). Oxford: Oxford University Press.

Pruss, Alexander R. (2013). 'Omnipresence, Multilocation, the Real Presence and Time Travel', *Journal of Analytic Theology* 1.1: 60–73.

Rachels, James (1971). 'God and Human Attitudes', *Religious Studies* 7.4: 325–37.

Rawls, John. (1999). *A Theory of Justice*, revised ed. Cambridge, MA: Belknap Press of Harvard University Press.

Rea, Michael (2016). 'Gender as a Divine Attribute', *Religious Studies* 52.1: 97–115.

Rea, Michael (2020). 'Is God a Man?', in Michael Peterson and Raymond VanArragon (eds.), *Contemporary Debates in Philosophy of Religion*, 2nd ed. (pp. 293–301). Oxford: Wiley.

Robinson, John A. T. (1963). *Honest to God*. Philadelphia, PA: Westminster John Knox/SCM Press.

Rogers, Katherin (1996). 'The Traditional Doctrine of Divine Simplicity', *Religious Studies* 32.2: 165–86.

Rogers, Katherin (2000). *Perfect Being Theology*. Edinburgh: Edinburgh University Press.

Rogers, Katherin (2020). 'An Anselmian Approach to Divine Simplicity', *Faith and Philosophy* 37.3: 308–22.

Rowe, William (1979). 'The Problem of Evil and Some Varieties of Atheism', *American Philosophical Quarterly* 16.4: 335–41.

Rowe, William (2004). 'Evil is Evidence Against Theistic Belief', in Michael L. Peterson and Raymond J. VanArragon (eds.), *Contemporary Debates in Philosophy of Religion* (pp. 3–13). Oxford: Blackwell.

Schärtl, Thomas (2019). 'The Divine Self-Mediation in the Universe: Euteleology Meets German Idealism', *European Journal for Philosophy of Religion* 11.1: 83–116.

Schärtl, Thomas, Tapp, Christian, and Wegener, Veronika (eds.) (2016). *Rethinking the Concept of a Personal God: Classical Theism, Personal Theism, and Alternative Concepts of God*. Munster: Aschendorff.

Schellenberg, J. L. (1993). *Divine Hiddenness and Human Reason*. Ithaca, NY: Cornell University Press.

Schellenberg, J. L. (2015). *The Hiddenness Argument: Philosophy's Challenge to Belief in God*. Oxford: Oxford University Press.

Schlesinger, George N. (1988). *New Perspectives on Old-Time Religion*. Oxford: Oxford University Press.

Scott, Michael and Malcolm, Finlay (2018). 'Religious Fictionalism', *Philosophy Compass* 13. DOI: 10.1111/phc3.12474.

Sennett, James F. (1999). 'Is There Freedom In Heaven?', *Faith and Philosophy* 16.1: 69–82.

Shortt, Rupert (2016). *God is No Thing: Coherent Christianity*. London: C. Hurst & Co.
Smart, Ninian (1972). *The Concept of Worship*. London: Palgrave Macmillan.
Smith, Quentin (1997). *Ethical and Religious Thought in Analytic Philosophy of Language*. New Haven, CT: Yale University Press.
Sokolowski, Robert (1982). *The God of Faith and Reason: Foundations of Christian Theology*. Notre Dame, IN: University of Notre Dame Press.
Soskice, Janet Martin (2005). 'Philosophical Theology', in Rupert Shortt (ed.), *God's Advocates: Christian Thinkers in Conversation* (pp. 24–42). London: Darton, Longman and Todd.
Speaks, Jeff (2018). *The Greatest Possible Being*. Oxford: Oxford University Press.
Stenmark, Mikael (2013). 'Religious Naturalism and Its Rivals', *Religious Studies* 49.4: 529–50.
Stenmark, Mikael (2015). 'Competing Conceptions of God: The Personal God versus the God Beyond Being', *Religious Studies* 51.2: 205–20.
Sterba, James P. (2019). *Is a Good God Logically Possible?* London: Palgrave Macmillan.
Stump, Eleonore (1979). 'Petitionary Prayer', *American Philosophical Quarterly* 16.2: 81–91.
Stump, Eleonore (2013). 'The Nature of a Simple God', *Proceedings of the American Catholic Philosophical Association* 87: 33–42.
Stump, Eleonore (2016). *The God of the Bible and the God of the Philosophers*. Milwaukee, WI: Marquette University Press.
Swinburne, Richard (1993 [1977]). *The Coherence of Theism*, revised ed. Oxford: Oxford University Press.
Swinburne, Richard (1996). *Is There a God?* Oxford: Oxford University Press.
Tanner, Kathryn (2013). 'Creation *Ex Nihilo* as Mixed Metaphor', *Modern Theology* 29.2: 138–55.
Tertullian. *The Treatise against Hermogenes*. Translated and annotated by J. H. Waszink. Westminster, MD: Newman Press, 1956.
Tillich, Paul (2001 [1957]). *The Dynamics of Faith*, revised ed. New York: HarperCollins.
Thomas, Emily (2016). 'Samuel Alexander's Space-Time God: A Naturalist Rival to Current Emergentist Theologies', in Andrei Buckareff and Yujin Nagasawa (eds.), *Alternative Concepts of God: Essays on the Metaphysics of the Divine* (pp. 255–73). Oxford: Oxford University Press.
Thomson, Judith Jarvis (2008). *Normativity*. Chicago, IL: Open Court.
Thorsteinsson, Runar M. (2010). *Roman Christianity & Roman Stoicism: A Comparative Study of Ancient Morality*. Oxford: Oxford University Press.
Trakakis, Nick (2007). *The God Beyond Belief: In Defence of William Rowe's Evidential Argument from Evil*. Dordrecht: Springer.
Trakakis, N. N. (2018). 'Anti-Theodicy', in Trakakis (ed.), *The Problem of Evil: Eight Views in Dialogue* (pp. 94–122). Oxford: Oxford University Press.
Vallicella, William F. (2016). 'William E. Mann, God, Modality, and Morality', *Faith and Philosophy* 33.3: 374–81.
van Eyghen, H., Peels, R., and van den Brink, G. (2018). 'The Cognitive Science of Religion, Philosophy and Theology: A Survey of the Issues', in *New Developments in the Cognitive Science of Religion, The Rationality of Religious Belief* (pp. 1–14). Cham: Springer Nature.
van der Horst, Pieter W. (1994). 'Silent Prayer in Antiquity', *Numen* 41.1: 1–25.

van Inwagen, Peter (2006). *The Problem of Evil*. Oxford: Oxford University Press.
Viney, Donald (2014). 'Process Theism', in Edward N. Zalta (ed.), *The Stanford Encyclopedia of Philosophy* (Spring 2014 Edition). http://plato.stanford.edu/archives/spr2014/entries/process-theism/.
Wainwright, William J. (2010). 'Omnipotence, Omniscience, and Omnipresence', in Charles Taliaferro and Chad Meister (eds.), *The Cambridge Companion to Christian Philosophical Theology* (pp. 46–65). Cambridge: Cambridge University Press.
Wainwright, William (2017). 'Concepts of God', in Edward N. Zalta (ed.), *The Stanford Encyclopedia of Philosophy* (Spring 2017 Edition), https://plato.stanford.edu/archives/spr2017/entries/concepts-god/.
Welch, Sharon D. (1990). *A Feminist Ethic of Risk*. Minneapolis, MN: Fortress Press.
Wierenga, Edward R. (1989). *The Nature of God: An Inquiry into Divine Attributes*. Ithaca, NY: Cornell University Press.
Wierenga, Edward R. (1997). 'Omnipresence', in Philip Quinn and Charles Taliaferro (eds.), *A Companion to Philosophy of Religion* (pp. 286–90). Oxford: Blackwell.
Wildman, Wesley (2006). 'Ground-of-Being Theologies', in Philip Clayton and Zachary Simpson (eds.), *The Oxford Handbook of Religion and Science* (pp. 612–32). Oxford: Oxford University Press.
Williams, Bernard (1962). 'Aristotle on the Good: A Formal Sketch', *Philosophical Quarterly* 12.49: 289–96.
Williams, Bernard (1973). 'The Makropulos Case: Reflections on the Tedium of Immortality', in *Problems of the Self: Philosophical Papers 1956–1972* (pp. 82–100). Cambridge: Cambridge University Press.
Wolterstorff, Nicholas (1987). *Lament for a Son*. Grand Rapids, MI: Eerdmans.
Wolterstorff, Nicholas (1988). 'Suffering Love', in Thomas V. Morris (ed.), *Philosophy and the Christian Faith* (pp. 196–237). Notre Dame, IN: University of Notre Dame Press.
Wolterstorff, Nicholas (2010). 'God Everlasting', in *Selected Essays*, Vol. 1 (pp. 133–56), edited by Terence Cuneo. Cambridge: Cambridge University Press.
Wolterstorff, Nicholas (2015). *The God We Worship: An Exploration of Liturgical Theology*. Grand Rapids, MI: Eerdmans.
Wolterstorff, Nicholas (2016). 'Knowing God Liturgically', *Journal of Analytic Theology* 4: 1–16.
Wynn, Mark (2013). *Renewing the Senses: A Study of the Philosophy and Theology of the Spiritual Life*. Oxford: Oxford University Press.

Index

For the benefit of digital users, indexed terms that span two pages (e.g., 52–3) may, on occasion, appear on only one of those pages.

abstraction, abstract entities 63, 73–5, 93–4, 120–3
action, divine 100–5, 112–15, 130–1, 173
Adams, Marilyn 9n.2, 19n.21, 30–3, 33n.43, 92–5, 159n.2
  on God's relationship with participants in evils 32–3
after-life 30–1, 33n.43, 136, 182–3
agapē 55–6, 57n.33, 64–5, 67, 111–12, 138–40, 142, 147–8
agent-causation 70–2, 82
Aijaz, Imran 104n.21
Aikin, Scott 159–60
Alexander, Samuel 95n.11
Alston, William 9n.2, 49n.23, 116n.35
alternative concepts of God. *See* concept of God, alternative concepts
analogy
  in address to God 167–70
  in talk of God 17–18, 79, 89, 98–106, 111
  'radical' (*versus* 'mundane') 89, 102–4, 106–8, 111, 121–2, 170
  significance of, for problem of evil 152–4
analytic theology 3–4, 24n.29
ananthropocentric purposivism 63
Anselm
  God, that than which a greater cannot be thought 20–1, 21n.25, 38
Anthropic Principle, Strong 80n.22
anthropomorphism, in concepts of God 22–3, 27–8, 68n.12
anti-theodicy 147n.25
apophaticism 25–6, 51–2, 98–100, 111–12, 122, 175n.19
Aquinas
  all power as God's power 113n.31
  analogous predication 17–18, 101–2, 116n.35
  divine essence, not knowable 175n.19

divine simplicity 21n.25
evil as privation of the good 132n.3
final and efficient causes of existence coinciding 85n.25
God as pure act, Being itself 52–5, 88n.3, 177–8
God, not a person 19n.21
omnipresence 24n.30
Ontological Argument rejected 38n.3
persona, in doctrine of the Trinity 17n.18
Aristotle
  the most final end and the supreme good 65n.6
Argument from Evil. *See* evil, Argument from
aseity, divine 52–3, 63n.3, 123–4
atheism
  accepting euteleological metaphysics 84–5
  atheist naturalism 98, 106–7
  God as 'no-thing' tantamount to 100
  implied by incoherence of ultimate explanations of existence 71n.14
  relative to personal-omniGod conception ('personal-omniGod atheism') 14n.12, 35
  'religious' 38
Augustine 25n.31, 100n.14, 101–2
axiarchism, extreme 72–5, 84–5

Bartlet, J. V. 162n.5
Basinger, David 11, 126n.44
'boot-strapping' objection 75–7
Burrell, David 18n.19, 22n.26, 114n.32

Cahn, Stephen 159–60
causation, varieties of 70–1, 73–4, 77, 79–82
causation, transmundane 76–81, 98, 142
Christology 76–7
classical theism. *See* theism, classical

INDEX

Cobb, John 138n.12, 139n.15
Cognitive Science of Religion (CSR) 106-7
concept/conception distinction 15-16
concept of God
    alternative concepts 11-12, 14-16, 19-20, 35-7, 60, 129
    'constructed', 'projected'. *See* analogy, 'radical' (*versus* 'mundane')
    emergentist conceptions 56, 94-5
    as an immanent universal 94-5
    non-personalist conceptions 47-9, 59, 69, 111-12, 122
    as personal omniGod. *See* personal-omniGod theism
    as religiously adequate. *See* religious adequacy
    as 'role' concept 15, 20-1
    versus conceptions of God 15-16
    See also euteleological theism
Cooper, David 90n.4
Craig, William Lane 70n.13
Cray, Wesley 160n.3
creatio ex amore 126n.44
creation *ex nihilo* 46, 71-2, 75-6, 79, 81, 97-100
cross, of Christ 155-6

Daly, Mary 90n.4
Davies, Brian 18n.19, 19n.21, 22n.26, 23-4, 50n.24
developmental theism 45
divine goodness
    as distinct from moral goodness 33, 159n.2
    on a euteleological, non-personalist, account 117, 130-1, 143-54
    as personal goodness, in the face of evil 26-34, 41-7, 131n.1, 136
    in tension with divine power 27-8, 40
divine hiddenness, argument from 29n.36
divine incomprehensibility 52-3, 79-84, 101-4, 111-12, 174-5, 177-8
divine power. *See* power, divine
Dostoyevsky, Fyodor 32n.42
dualism
    mind/body 71-2, 82
    natural/supernatural 22-4, 48-9, 57, 69, 124-5, 137n.11, 142
    Platonic 74-5, 122-3

Ellis, Fiona 8n.1, 49n.22, 97n.13, 142n.21
emanationism 74-5
emergence, emergentism 56, 94-5, 137-9, 142
epistemology of religious belief 6, 60
eschatology 66-7, 139-40
    'realized' 141n.19, 181
eternal life 143, 182-3
ethical requiredness, abstract 73-5
    See also Leslie, John
ethics
    motivating metaphysics 82-4
    theist 15, 27, 55-6, 64-5, 83-4, 135, 139-40
    of theological non-realism 108
eudaimonia 65n.6
euteleological metaphysics. *See* euteleology
euteleological theism, *passim*, Chapters 4-6
    distinguished from euteleology 6, 85
    place of God in 86, 95-7
    summarized 127, 178
euteleology, *passim*, Chapter 3
    apt for non-theist worldviews 84-5, 177n.23
    definition 2, 66n.9
    outlined 56-8
    summarized 84
evidential ambiguity of theism. *See* theism, evidential ambiguity of
evil, *passim*, Chapter 5
    amount and degree of 151-2
    Argument from, evidential 29n.37, 144-5, 151-2
    Argument from, logical 29-30, 145-6, 151-3
    Argument from, normatively relativized, logical 31-4, 145
    collective, social 135, 148-9
    defeated 30-1, 66-7, 135-6, 141, 154
    for the sake of good 156-7
    horrendous 30-1, 46, 55-6, 118, 151, 155-6
    matter, inherently evil 149n.28
    moral/natural distinction 148, 150
    pointless 154-6
    problem of 118, 130-1
        existential problem 133, 154
        intellectual problem 143-6, 151-2
    privation of the good 54, 131-2, 140-1, 145-6, 151n.30, 156-7
    statistically, not logically, inevitable 149-51

evolutionary psychology of religion.
  See Cognitive Science of Religion
expansive naturalism. *See* naturalism,
  expansive

faith
  crisis of, in face of evil 154–6
  reflective, seeking understanding 2,
    15–16, 35, 51–2, 82–3, 172
Farris, Stephen 165n.12
Fergusson, David 98–9
fictionalism, theological. *See* non-realism,
  theological
Fiddes, Paul 55n.31
Forrest, Peter 45, 114n.33
freedom, divine 112–13, 121, 126n.44
freedom, human
  and divine power 29, 114
  in euteleological theodicy 148–51
  libertarian 41–2, 136n.9
'Free Will Defence' 30–1, 41–3, 150

Geach, Peter 43–4, 62n.2, 159n.2
God
  as agent. *See* action, divine
  alternative concepts of. *See* concept of
    God, alternative concepts
  analogous to a person 88n.3, 102–4,
    116–17, 153–4, 168–9
  a se. *See* aseity, divine
  'Being itself' 52–5, 105n.23, 120–1,
    177–8
  beyond naming 25–6, 104.
    See also apophaticism
  classical attributes of 17–18, 121–3
  concept of. *See* concept of God
  creator *ex nihilo*. *See* creation *ex nihilo*
  'co-sufferer' 45–7
  descriptions of, positive 17–18, 51,
    104–5, 175–6
  entity, only in broadest sense 103–4,
    105n.23, 108, 119–20, 174–5
  First Cause 61, 75–6, 92–3, 123
  'God exists' 90–1, 96–7, 120–1
  'God is Love' 55–7, 94–5
  as a human projection, construction.
    See analogy, 'radical' (versus
    'mundane')
  immanent. *See* immanence, divine
  as necessary 122–4

  not 'a' being, 'no-thing' 90, 95–7, 99–100,
    104–6, 108–9, 119–20, 122, 174–5
  not a proper name 16n.15
  not subject to moral norms 33,
    159n.2, 172
  'omni'-attributes, of 9, 96–7, 115–19
  as a person 8–11, 21–3, 27–9, 49–50
  as personal omniGod. *See*
    personal-omniGod theism
  in personal relationship 27–34, 104–5
  'pure act' 52–4
  in relation to the world 56, 91–2,
    96–100, 125–6
  saviour 47. *See also* soteriology
  simple. *See* simplicity, divine
  that than which a greater cannot be
    thought. *See* Anselm
  transcendent. *See* transcendence, divine
  uniquely worthy of worship 15,
    51–2, 174–8
God-ing 90–1
God-roles, the 15–16
God-talk
  as involving analogy. *See* analogy
  under divine providence 104, 121–2
good, goodness
  absolute goodness 62n.2
  arising from evil. *See* evil, for the
    sake of good
  attributive use of 'good' 62
  existence ethically required 72, 74–5
  Form of 73
  preponderant over evil 42–3, 151–2
  See also divine goodness; supreme
    good, the
Gregory, Brad 24n.28
Guroian, Vigen 165n.11

Hart, David Bentley 18n.19
Hartshorne, Charles 45n.12, 46n.18,
  125n.42
Harvey. Thomas 103n.17
Hasker, William 11, 17n.18, 21n.23
Hegelianism 137
Heil, John 120n.38
Hewitt, Simon 17n.18, 22n.26, 175n.19
Hick, John 49n.23, 135n.7
Hobbes, Thomas 44n.10
hope 139–41
Hume, David 68n.12, 182n.1

ideal elements, in euteleology 122–3
idolatry 15–16, 22–3, 27, 28n.35, 51–2, 159–61, 175–7
immanence, divine 20–6, 96n.12, 100n.14, 130–1
immortality. *See* after-life; eternal life
Incarnation, the, doctrine of 17, 67
incarnations, of the supreme good 67
Insole, Christopher 109n.28
inter-faith dialogue 2, 177n.23

Jantzen, Grace 133n.5
Job 148n.26
Johnston, Mark 16n.15, 28n.35, 53n.28

Kahane, Guy 28n.34
kenosis 44–5, 126n.44
Kraut, Richard 62n.2
Kretzmann, Norman 126n.44
Kvanvig, Jonathan 171n.16

Larrimore, Mark 140n.17
Lebens, Sam 19n.21
Leftow, Brian 18n.20, 88n.3, 132–3, 161–2, 164, 167–71, 175n.20
Legenhausen, Gary 23n.27
Leslie, John 72–5, 77–8, 84–5
liberation theology 135n.8, 139n.14
Locke, John 33n.45
Lodahl, Michael 126n.44
love
  'God is love' 55–6
  power of. *See* power, divine, as power of love
  revealed as reality's ultimate purpose, the supreme good 64–5, 67, 137n.11
  See also *agapē*

Mackie, J. L. 29n.37, 30n.38, 41n.5, 42–3, 42n.7, 74n.17, 132n.4
Mary, *theotokos* 76–7
Mawson, T. J. 11, 125n.43
McCabe, Herbert 18n.19, 22n.26
McCann, Hugh 103n.18
McCloskey, H. J. 160n.3
McTaggart, J. M. E. 160n.3
metaphysics, ethically motivated 82–4
miracles 114, 182
Molinism, middle knowledge 41–3, 47n.19, 136n.9, 156n.32

Mulgan, Tim 63
Mullins, R. T. 125n.43
mystery. *See* divine incomprehensibility
mysticism 26n.32, 120n.37, 177–8

Nagasawa, Yujin 44
natural theology 60, 123, 144n.23
naturalism 8n.1, 47–9
  expansive 49n.22, 142n.21
  naturalist theism 8n.1
  See also atheism, atheist naturalism
necessity, divine, and of ultimate realities 77–8, 94, 122–3
non-realism, theological 37–9, 87–8, 106, 108
Normatively Relativized Logical Argument from Evil. *See* evil, Argument from

O'Connor, Timothy 126n.44
omniGod. *See* personal-omniGod theism
omnibenevolence, divine 9, 117
omnipotence, divine 9, 27–9, 39–44, 117
omnipresence, divine 24n.30, 118
omniscience, divine 9, 117–18, 160n.3
Oord, Thomas Jay 55n.31, 126n.44
open theism 29n.36, 46–7, 126n.44, 136n.9
original depravity 150–1
Owen, H. P. 49n.23, 100n.15

Page, Ben 19n.21, 22n.26, 24n.29
panentheism 46–7, 92n.7, 95n.11, 124–7
panpsychism 68
pantheism 46–7, 91–2, 124–5
person, concept of 17n.18, 33
personal-omniGod theism
  and the classical divine attributes 18–19, 121
  its coherence 12–14
  defined 9
  as a degenerating research programme 14n.11
  its religious adequacy 14–35
  variant versions 13–14
personal relationships
  agapeistic 55–6
  between God and creaturely persons 27–34, 45, 104–5
  See also 'God is love'
Peterson, Michael 11
Pike, Nelson 18n.20, 42n.8

Plantinga, Alvin
  defining omnipotence 40n.4
  divine simplicity 18n.20, 24n.29
  Free Will Defence 29n.37, 41–3
  God as person 8–10, 9n.2, 10n.4, 96n.12
  naturalism 8n.1, 115n.34
Plato 73
post-mortem existence. *See* after-life
Pouivet, Roger 18n.19
'power corrupts' 27
power, divine
  guaranteeing defeat of evil 136
  operating within the natural
    Universe 112–15, 126, 137–8
  as power of love 45–6, 138–43, 151–2,
    155–7
  as unlimited power of a personal
    agent 27–9, 39–44
powers, natural 113–14
pragmatism, in approach to theist
  metaphysics 82–4
prayer
  aligning with divine will 173
  petitionary 29n.36, 166–70, 173–4
  as related to worship 158–9
privatio boni. *See* evil, privation of the good
problem of evil. *See* evil, problem of
process theism 45, 125, 138n.12, 139n.15
purpose
  essentially mind-dependent 68
  inherent (without a 'purposing'
    agent) 67–9
  overall (of reality) 57, 61–4, 92–4
purposivism 63

Rachels, James 159–60
Rea, Michael 10n.3, 24n.29
realism
  axiological 62, 93–4
  theological 38–9, 87–8, 106–10, 176–7
reality, as such and as a whole
  divine, but not identical with God 90–2
  having inherent purpose 57, 62, 67–9,
    77–8, 122–3
  'more than' the Universe 77–8
Reichenbach, Bruce 11
religious adequacy
  of a conception of God (in general) 15,
    35, 160–1
  of personal-omniGod theism 14–35, 129

  of euteleological theism, *passim*,
    Chapters 5 and 6
religious experience 25–6, 177–8
religious pluralism 177n.23
Resurrection, the 141
revelation, special 63–5, 82–3, 101, 104–5,
  115, 151–2
Rogers, Katherin 19n.21, 21n.25
Rowe, William 29n.37

salvation 133–4
  See also soteriology
Schellenberg, J. L. 29n.36
Schlesinger, George 44n.11
self-centredness
  root of moral evil 150–1
  transformation away from 133–5
simplicity, divine 17–18, 18n.20, 21–6, 53–4,
  101n.16, 103n.17, 121–2
skeptical theism 29n.37
Schärtl-Trendel, Thomas 50n.24, 56, 137n.11
Sokolowski, Robert 23n.27
Soskice, Janet 100n.14
soteriology 132–8
  non-triumphalist 137–41, 143
  triumphalist 136
Speaks, Jeff 21n.24
Stenmark, Mikael 96n.12
Sterba, James 29n.37
Stump, Eleonore 21n.25, 29n.36, 88n.3
suffering
  by non-human animals 31n.40
  See also evil
supreme good, the
  divine, but not identical with God 92–4
  as the divine 'character' 93–4
  as the good for reality 57, 62–5, 122–3
  manifest in the Universe 66–7, 94–5,
    112–13, 137–8, 141
  See also love, revealed as supreme good;
    telos (end, purpose)
Swinburne, Richard 9n.2, 10n.4, 12n.7,
  18n.19, 49n.23, 103n.18

Tanner, Kathryn 24n.28
teleology 62–3, 68, 75–6
  ultimate. *See* euteleology
telos (end, purpose)
  of reality/the Universe as a
    whole 62–4, 92–4

telos (end, purpose) (*cont.*)
  realized in the Universe 66–7, 94–5, 112–13, 118, 133–4, 137, 147–8, 177–8
  See also euteleology; supreme good, the
theism
  classical 17–20, 91n.6, 109n.27
    as 'non-personalist' 50–5
    distinguished from theistic personalism 18n.19
    See also evil, privation of the good
  evidential ambiguity of 144–5
  naturalist 47–9, 138–9, 142
  ontology of 60. *See also* personal-omniGod theism; euteleology
  personalist 18–20, 21n.25, 39–47
  standard account, in analytic philosophy 8–9
  term for Abrahamic traditions 1n.1
  See also euteleological theism; personal-omniGod theism
theistic personalism 18n.19, 50n.24
theodicy 146–54
theological explanation 69, 71–2, 74–5, 92–3, 97–100
  contrasted with scientific explanation 14n.11, 81–2, 113
Thorsteinsson, Runar 165n.10
Tillich, Paul 15–16
transcendence, divine 20–6, 96–7, 96n.12, 109
translation
  of God-talk into euteleological terms, not needed 110–11
transmundane causation. *See* causation, transmundane
Trinity, the
  doctrine of 11n.5, 17, 55–6
  social doctrine of 21
triumphalism. *See* soteriology, triumphalist
truth-makers
  for theological claims 108, 110–12, 168–70

  not in general identifiable with meanings 120n.38

universalism 33n.43, 136n.9, 143
Universe, the
  'does what it's for' 66, 69–71
  efficient cause of 57, 70–1, 75–6, 79
  existing as brute fact 75–6, 98
  final cause of 57, 70
  final and efficient causes coinciding 84–5, 92–3
  as multiverse 61–2, 94–5, 135, 140n.16
  'purposive' 61–2
  ultimate explanation for existence of 57, 69–75, 92–3, 97–100

Vallicella, William 19n.21
van der Horst, Pieter 167n.14
van Inwagen, Peter 96n.12, 131n.2
via negativa. *See* apophaticism

Wainwright, William 49n.23
Welch, Sharon 90n.4, 139n.14
Wildman, Wesley 105n.23
will, divine, direct and permissive 153–4
Wolterstorff, Nicholas 19n.21, 46n.15, 163–4, 164n.9, 166–7
worship
  broader and narrower senses 162–5, 174
  ethics of 159–60, 172
  euteleological account of 170–4
  images, used in 176n.21
  involves address 165–8
  its object, God 174–8
  its object, personal 161–2, 166–7, 170–1
  as right relation to ultimate reality 172–3
  ritual, cultic 164–6
  theist understanding of 15
Wynn, Mark 100n.14

Zimmerman, Dean 110n.29